AF477976

THE EUROPEANISATION OF THE WESTERN BALKANS

Manchester University Press

 SERIES EDITORS: Thomas Christiansen and Emil Kirchner

FLORIAN TRAUNER

THE EUROPEANISATION OF THE WESTERN BALKANS

EU justice and home affairs in Croatia and Macedonia

MANCHESTER UNIVERSITY PRESS
Manchester and New York

*distributed in the United States exclusively
by Palgrave Macmillan*

Published by Manchester University Press
Oxford Road, Manchester M13 9NR, UK
and Room 400, 175 Fifth Avenue, New York, NY 10010, USA
www.manchesteruniversitypress.co.uk

Distributed in the United States exclusively by
Palgrave Macmillan, 175 Fifth Avenue, New York,
NY 10010, USA

Distributed in Canada exclusively by
UBC Press, University of British Columbia, 2029 West Mall,
Vancouver, BC, Canada V6T 1Z2

British Library Cataloguing-in-Publication Data
A catalogue record for this book is available from the British Library

Library of Congress Cataloging-in-Publication Data applied for

ISBN   978 0 7190 8345 7 hardback

First published 2011

Typeset in Minion with Lithos
by Action Publishing Technology Ltd, Gloucester
Printed in Great Britain
by CPI Antony Rowe Ltd, Chippenham, Wiltshire

Contents

CARDS	Community Assistance for Reconstruction, Development and Stabilisation
CEECs	Central and Eastern European Countries
CFSP	Common Foreign and Security Policy
COWEB	Council Working Group on the Western Balkans
DCAF	Geneva Centre for the Democratic Control of Armed Forces
DG	Directorate-General
EAR	European Agency for Reconstruction
EC	European Community
ECJHAT	European Commission Justice and Home Affairs Team
ENP	European Neighbourhood Policy
ESDP	European Security and Defence Policy
EU	European Union
EUPAT	European Union Police Advisory Team
FRONTEX	European Agency for the Management of Operational Co-operation at the External Borders
FYROM	The Former Yugoslav Republic of Macedonia
HDZ	Croatian Democratic Union
HRK	Croatian Kuna
IBM	Integrated border management
ICG	International Crisis Group
ICMPD	International Centre for Migration Policy Development
ICTY	International Criminal Tribunal for the former Yugoslavia
IFOR	Implementation Force
IOM	International Organisation for Migration
IPA	Instrument for Pre-Accession Assistance
JHA	Justice and home affairs
KFOR	Kosovo Force
MARRI	Migration, Asylum, Refugees Regional Initiative
NATO	North Atlantic Treaty Organization
NBMCC	National Border Management Coordination Centre
NGO	Non-Governmental Organisation
NLA	National Liberation Army

OSCCP	South-Eastern Europe Cross-border Cooperation Programme
OSCE	Organization for Security and Cooperation in Europe
PHARE	Poland and Hungary: Aid for Restructuring of the Economies
RCC	Regional Cooperation Council
RRM	Rapid Reaction Mechanisms
SAA	Stabilisation and Association Agreement
SAP	Stabilisation and Association Process
SCIFA	Strategic Committee for Immigration, Frontiers and Asylum
SDP	Social Democratic Party
SECI	Southeast European Cooperative Initiative
SEECP	South-East European Cooperation Process
SEEPAG	Southeast European Prosecutors Advisory Group
SFOR	Stabilisation Force
SIS	Schengen Information System
SP	Stability Pact for South-Eastern Europe
TAIEX	Technical Assistance Information Exchange Office
THAP	Temporary Humanitarian Assisted Persons
TIP-Report	Trafficking in Persons-Report
TREVI	Terrorisme, Radicalisme, Extrémisme et Violence Internationale
UN	United Nations
UNHCR	United Nations High Commissioner for Refugees
UNMIBH	United Nations Mission in Bosnia and Herzegovina
UNMIK	United Nations Interim Administration Mission in Kosovo
UNPREDEP	United Nations Preventive Deployment Force
UNPROFOR	United Nations Protection Force
VMRO-DPMNE	Internal Macedonian Revolutionary Organisation – Democratic Party for Macedonian National Unity

*P*REFACE

This book, which is interested in the scope and nature of the EU's external influence on domestic policy-making in South-Eastern Europe, is the result of a long-lasting and fruitful journey in which I benefited greatly from the support and advice of colleagues and friends. I would like to express my sincere gratitude to the publishers at Manchester University Press and the editors of MUP's series 'Europe in Change', Thomas Christiansen and Emil Kirchner. Financial support was provided by the project 'EU Consent: Wider Europe, Deeper Integration?', which was financed by the sixth Framework Programme of the European Commission. I am particularly grateful to Gunilla Herolf, Attila Ágh, Gianni Bonvicini, Michele Comelli, Wolfgang Wessels and Funda Tekin for their support in the EU-Consent project and for their constant efforts to promote young researchers in European research communities.

The present book is based on my PhD research, which I conducted in the framework of the postgraduate course 'European Integration 2004–2007' at the Institute for Advanced Studies (IHS) and defended at the University of Vienna. I am very grateful to my supervisors Paul Luif from the Austrian Institute for International Affairs (OIIP) and Dieter Segert from the University of Vienna for their valuable advice and assistance. For their support at the IHS, I would like to thank Gerda Falkner, Oliver Treib, Sylvia Kritzinger, Irena Michalowitz and Andreas Wimmel as well as my colleagues Heidrun Maurer, Juan Casado Asensio, Zoe Lefkofridi, Patrick Müller, Reinhard Slepcevic, Florian Feldbauer, Eric Miklin, Nicole Alecu de Flers, Erik Tajalli, Lisa Hunt and Andreas Obermaier. Valuable comments came from the IHS visiting professors, in particular from Jörg Monar, Fritz W. Scharpf, Katharina Holzinger, Klaus H. Goetz and Frank Schimmelfennig, as well as from my present colleagues at the Austrian Academy of Sciences, Institute for European Integration Research (EIF). Special thanks to Lindsay Hughes, who did a great job in language editing.

I also benefited very much from the stimulating feedback and constructive criticism of colleagues I met at conferences and summer schools when I was presenting parts of this work. Many of them have become my friends in the meantime. Finally I would like to express a big thank you to my family, in particular to Franz and Elisabeth Trauner, and my friends for their positive thinking and untiring encouragement. This book is dedicated to my wife Adeline and our son Leopold, whose love and support mean everything to me.

PART I

The analytical framework

1

Introduction and research interest

> The choice for us in this case is very clear: either we export stability to the Balkans, or the Balkans export instability to us. (EU Commissioner for External Relations Chris Patten, 2002)

How strong is the EU's leverage in South-Eastern Europe?

The way the EU tackles intrinsically internal policy problems such as irregular migration and organised crime has changed profoundly. Policy-makers have increasingly emphasised the external (extra-European) origin and dimension of these threats and have urged that they be tackled at their origin. As a result, the distinction between the allegedly inward-looking policy realm of justice and home affairs and foreign policy has gradually blurred. This trend was boosted by the unique events of 11 September 2001 and the terrorist attacks in Madrid and London. Third countries that were perceived as a source of such internal security threats were increasingly confronted with EU policies that made institutional affiliation or/and financial support conditional on cooperation on these issues (see, among others, Bigo, 2001, Lavenex, 2004, Monar, 2004a, Mitsilegas, 2007, Rees, 2008, Kurowska and Pawlak, 2009, Balzacq, 2009, Wolff et al., 2009).

This development was of particular significance for the neighbourhood of the EU. When in May 1999 the EU launched the Stabilisation and Association Process (SAP) providing the Western Balkan states with the status of potential candidate countries for EU membership,[1] it defined cooperation in justice and home affairs as a priority area. The region has been plagued with war legacies and a political climate in which organised crime, corruption, irregular migration and trafficking in human beings could flourish. Tackling these security challenges has become a major concern for the EU, also with a view to realise the area of freedom, security and justice (AFSJ) within the EU.

These policies stand in the centre of this analysis, which is concerned with the ways and the extent to which the EU has managed to shape domestic policy-making in justice and home affairs in the Western Balkans. The research puzzle that this book seeks to explain is derived from the very nature of the EU's involvement in South-Eastern Europe. The extensive EU action in the policy field of justice and home affairs in the Western Balkans is to a great extent 'self-interested'. The EU's underlying assumption is that if the EU makes the Western Balkan states strengthen their border control and law enforcement capacities (thus, adhering to the justice and home affairs' *acquis* while coming closer to the EU), these states will be increasingly capable of coping with soft-security problems themselves. Consequently, these (possibly future) internal problems would be kept outside the common EU territory and the potential source of internal social tension and xenophobic political propaganda would be reduced significantly in the domestic political arena (see also Pastore, 2001: 16f).

However, due to a certain enlargement fatigue, the discussions on the EU's integration capacity – and several other factors – it is unclear when or even whether these aspiring candidate countries will actually make it into the EU. Since it is known from previous enlargements that third countries cannot be expected to implement the *acquis communautaire* unless the Union provides clear and tangible incentives to do so, the question remains: With only a loose prospect of membership, how strong is the EU's leverage in the Western Balkans? Does the EU successfully transfer its rules and institutions to the Western Balkans and if so, what are the factors that affect the countries' choice for rule adoption?

By elaborating on the Europeanisation of the Western Balkans in a systematic, theory-oriented and comparative way, the book provides the reader with insights into the dynamics underlying the EU pre-accession strategy for South-Eastern Europe and presents the different routes of influence that the EU has established in the sensitive policy domain of justice and home affairs. The study pursues the double goal of intersecting the research on the use of conditionality from previous enlargement rounds with the current enlargement strategy for South-Eastern Europe and offering a comprehensive analysis of the EU's avenues of external leverage in justice and home affairs in the Western Balkans. The comparisons across enlargement rounds identify the differences in the Europeanisation processes of candidate countries, a subject hitherto neglected in the literature (for this claim, see Sedelmeier, 2006: 20).

Overall the book builds upon and aims at contributing to three areas of the EU foreign policy research:

1) The EU's potential to invoke compliance, adaptation and transformation processes in candidate (see, among others, Pridham and Ágh, 2001, Dimitrova, 2004a, Kelley, 2004, Grabbe, 2005, Schimmelfennig and Sedelmeier, 2005a, Vachudova, 2005, Sedelmeier, 2005, Batory, 2008) and other third countries (Lavenex, 2004, 2008, Weber et al., 2007, Schimmelfennig, 2009)

2) The external dimension of EU justice and home affairs as an increasingly important area of EU foreign policy-making that alters the EU's

interactions with the outside world and provides a new impetus for EU Common Foreign and Security Policy (Bigo, 2001, Lavenex and Uçarer, 2002, Tonra and Christiansen, 2004, Lavenex, 2004, Monar, 2004a, Mitsilegas, 2007, Kirchner and Sperling, 2007, Rees, 2008, Balzacq, 2009, Wolff et al., 2009)

3) The EU–Western Balkans relations and the implications of the EU's policies of stabilisation, partnership and integration on the region's instability and transformation challenges (van Meurs, 2003, Batt, 2004b, Pippan, 2004, Massari, 2005, Blockmans and Lazowski, 2006, Blockmans, 2007, DeBardeleben, 2008, Noutcheva, 2009)

The Europeanisation of the Western Balkans

The book's approach to studying the EU's routes of influence is to adapt the literature on Europeanisation and external governance to the particular circumstances of the Western Balkans' EU integration process. Scholars within the Europeanisation research field have tried to shed light on the EU's impact on policies and institutions, typically, of member states (for some recent overviews, see Graziano and Vink, 2007; Goetz and Meyer-Sahling, 2008, Ladrech, 2009).

An early definition was provided by Ladrech (1994: 69) referring to Europeanisation as 'a process reorienting the direction and shape of politics to the degree that EC political and economic dynamics become part of the organisational logic of national politics and policy making'. Drawing on this definition, Radaelli (2000: 4) refines the notion of Europeanisation processes and broadens them to 'domestic discourse, identities, political structures, and public policies'. In this way, Europeanisation is perceived as a permanent two-level interaction in which member states are both contributors to and products of European integration. The question then arises as to whether a concept that is explicitly geared at analysing the impact of European integration at the national level of member states can really be extended to non-member states.

Although not uncontested (on Europeanisation and concept stretching see Radaelli, 2000), a consensus has emerged that this extension is possible, provided that the research is focused on 'a process of change in national institutions and practices that can be attributed to European integration' (Hix and Goetz, 2000: 27). The decisive distinction lies in the question of how these changes can be ascribed to the European integration process. Most studies on Europeanisation *within* Europe perceive these processes as a result of an incongruence or 'misfit' (Börzel, 1999) between the European level and the national level.[2] In contrast to this dynamic, the external dimension of Europeanisation occurs in a rather diverse manner, thus changing the very nature of these processes (Lavenex and Uçarer, 2004, Schimmelfennig, 2009).

Such external effects of EU policies may be the result of an intentional action by the EU or the unintended consequence of another intentional action. The transfer or diffusion of EU policies may even occur without direct EU involvement if a third country government decides – for one reason or another – to alter its domestic policies according to EU rules. Alternatively, diffusion can also be actively stimulated by EU actors when the export of EU policies seems to enhance the capacity to solve common problems at home. In this respect, Lavenex and Uçarer (2004: 422f) argue that the ways and possibilities for EU influence on third countries depend on several factors, i.e. on the geographic proximity and institutional affiliation between the EU and the country concerned, the degree of (perceived) 'fit' and 'misfit' between EU policies and domestic arrangements in the third countries and the (strategic) interplay of domestic political actors in the target country. To put it simply, countries that have strong institutional and geographic links to the EU and that aspire towards EU membership are more easily obliged to comply with EU-defined preferences and rules than are countries with loose association ties. In other words, the EU's strongest impact can be expected to occur in a candidate state, a status all Western Balkan states are striving for.

Europeanisation in candidate countries

Europeanisation processes within a state seeking accession to the EU occur in a different manner than those occurring in EU member states (Dimitrova, 2004a, Kelley, 2004, Schimmelfennig and Sedelmeier, 2005a, Sedelmeier, 2006, Grabbe, 2006). Whereas these processes are understood within the EU member states as two-level interactions with member states being both contributors and products of European integration, they are characterised in applicant countries by an absence of the bottom-up dimension, namely of effecting Europeanisation; these states are only ascribed the role of a consumer (Papadimitriou, 2003: 12). The applicant is exposed to the EU in an asymmetric relationship, which gives the EU more coercive influence in domestic policy-making processes. Even though the candidate state is excluded from EU policy-making from the inside, it has a stronger incentive to implement EU policies than existing member states because it wants to gain accession.

As shown in scholarly work on the Eastern enlargement, the 'enlargement governance' (Dimitrova, 2004a) or 'governance by conditionality' (Schimmelfennig and Sedelmeier, 2004) occurs in a rather distinct manner, as the EU can use an additional and powerful instrument that is absent in other settings: 'the conditionality for membership gives the EU significant leverage in transferring to the applicant countries its principles, norms, and rules, as well as in shaping their institutional and administrative structures' (Grabbe, 2002: 93). While the notion of governance frequently refers to softer modes of cooperation (Eising and Kohler-Koch, 1999), the enlargement governance involves many facets of 'old governance' including the highly asymmetric relationship between the EU and the candidate countries, the top-down communication structures, the non-negotiable nature of the EU rules to be transferred and the dominant participation of bureaucratic actors (Schimmelfennig and Sedelmeier, 2004: 674f).

The EU accession process may even push the applicant country towards greater coherence than that observed in the existing member states. Grabbe (2003: 306f) points to three reasons for this hypothesis examined in the Eastern enlargement. First, she mentions the speed of adjustment required. Applicant countries are expected to adjust their institutions and policies prior to EU membership. Therefore, the accession process forces the applicant country's institutions and structures to adapt much faster and more thoroughly than the rule implementation of the old member states. Second, she points to the Central and Eastern European countries' openness to EU influence deriving from the post-communist transformation. And last but not least, there has been the non-negotiable character of the EU's rules in applicant countries. The Central and Eastern European countries have not been given any possibilities for opt-outs from parts of the agenda, such as e.g. those obtained by the United Kingdom regarding the Schengen rules.

Grabbe set out a typology of five conditionality instruments with which the EU managed to change governance patterns in Central and Eastern Europe (Grabbe, 2003: 312f). The 'mechanisms of Europeanisation' referred, first, to 'models: provisions of legislative and institutional templates' corresponding with the legal downloading of the *acquis communautaire* and the harmonisation with EU regulations; second, to 'money: aid and technical assistance' that had 'an important role in reinforcing the transfer of EU models' (ibid: 314); third, to 'benchmarking and monitoring', meaning to rank candidates, benchmark in particular policy areas and to provide examples that the applicant seeks to emulate; fourth, to 'advice and twinning' which involved the direct secondment of civil servants from EU member states to work as advisers in domestic institution-building programmes; and finally, to 'gate-keeping: accession to negotiations and further stages in the accession process', which was 'the EU's most powerful conditionality tool' and related to 'access to different stages in the accession process, particularly achieving candidate status and starting negotiations' (ibid: 316). Although these five Europeanisation mechanisms were powerful instruments for the EU, they did not automatically result in strong external influence. Scholars have conceived different models of EU external governance to theorise about the conditions under which EU rule transfer to applicant states is the most effective.

Theories of external governance

The literature so far distinguishes between two principal explanations for why candidate countries adjust to the EU. A first set of studies suggests a strong focus on rational cost–benefit calculations and on actors in pursuit of maximising their own power and welfare (e.g. Schimmelfennig and Sedelmeier, 2004, Pridham, 2005, Vachudova, 2005). According to the external incentives model, the most crucial mechanism employed by the EU to make candidate countries accept its rules is the use of conditionality, meaning that the EU sets its rules as conditions that the applicant country has to fulfil in order to receive rewards (Schimmelfennig et al., 2003: 496f). The strongest rewards relate to the progressive improvement of institutional ties with the EU, with the ultimate goal of full membership. Balancing EU, domestic and international pressures, the target government weighs the external incentives against domestic interests. The successful adoption of EU rules depends on whether the rational actors involved perceive the external EU rewards to be higher than the costs of domestic adaptation (Schimmelfennig and Sedelmeier, 2004: 663-67).

The most prominent alternative explanation to this argument derives from constructivist thinking (e.g. Checkel, 2001, Kelley, 2004, Schimmelfennig and Sedelmeier, 2004: 667f). Constructivists argue that the EU might apply strategies other than conditionality to affect domestic change. Candidate countries would accept the EU's influence due to socialisation and persuasion processes in which domestic actors internalise identities, values and norms. For intrinsic reasons, political actors choose in a given situation what they consider good and appropriate. The EU's impact is therefore expected to stem from a 'logic of appropriateness' rather than from a 'logic of consequences' (March and Olsen, 1998). Accordingly, the core assumption is that domestic actors will only adhere to a given EU rule if they are persuaded of its appropriateness. The process of a candidate country's government adopting EU rules is therefore characterised by 'arguing about the legitimacy of rules and the appropriateness of behaviour (rather than bargaining about conditions and rewards), persuasion (rather than coercion), and "complex" learning (rather than behavioural adaptation)' (Schimmelfennig and Sedelmeier, 2004: 667).

The conditionality hypothesis and the Western Balkans

Research on the Eastern enlargement made a strong argument for the rational institutionalist argument. Pre-accession alignment was mainly driven by the EU's strategy of rule transfer based on conditionality rather than by persuasion and social learning (see Kelley, 2004, Schimmelfennig and Sedelmeier, 2005a, Vachudova, 2005). Regarding *acquis* conditionality, Frank Schimmelfennig and Ulrich Sedelmeier (2004: 671) argue that 'the external incentives model [...] appears highly successful in explaining rule transfer' in the case of the Central and Eastern European countries. The process of exporting EU rules to the candidate countries remained patchy or slow until the EU offered a credible prospect of EU membership and a credible link between membership and rule adoption. The membership incentive proved sufficiently strong to overcome domestic resistance even in issue areas of high political sensitivity (see e.g. Kelley, 2004).

Since the 2004 'big bang' enlargement towards Central and Eastern Europe, however, the EU's enlargement policy has lost its central position as an external policy strategy of the EU vis-à-vis neighbouring countries. The Eastern and Southern European neighbours are subsumed under the cooperation framework of the European Neighbourhood Policy (ENP) that, despite including many features of the EU's enlargement policy (Kelley, 2006), explicitly bypasses the issue of membership.[3]

Contrary to these neighbouring states, the Western Balkan states still have the prospect of eventually joining the EU; however, they are also confronted with a different EU enlargement context. The key to successful rule adoption in the Eastern enlargement was to make sure that EU membership conditionality was credible and that incumbent governments did not consider the domestic adaptation costs as a potential threat to their power. As Ulrich Sedelmeier noted, 'credibility has two sides. The candidates have to be certain that they will receive the promised rewards after meeting the EU's demands. Yet they also have to believe that they will only receive the reward if they indeed fully meet the requirements' (Sedelmeier, 2006: 12). The credibility of EU conditionality has become a major difference to previous enlargements. The Western Balkan states (and Turkey) are less certain when or even if they will receive the ultimate reward of EU accession.

Since the 2004 enlargement, discussions on the EU's 'integration capacity' and efforts to bring the reform of the current treaty framework to an end have dominated the agenda in Brussels. The failed European Constitution and Ireland's initial rejection of the Lisbon Treaty have increased the level of uncertainty for the Western Balkans as to whether they are indeed among the EU's next member states. In some member states political parties have taken the political stance that, with the Eastern enlargement successfully accomplished, future enlargements must be subject to a national referendum. The uncertainty for would-be members has increased.

Against this background, some scholars assumed that the changed circumstances of the Western Balkans' EU integration and the questionable credibility of the membership perspective would affect how the candidate countries weighed the costs of non-adaptation (Lavenex and Uçarer, 2004: 432–33). Othon Anastasakis and Dimitar Bechev stated that the EU's regional strategy would suffer from a 'commitment deficit' resulting in, among other things, a decrease in 'the chances of success for domestic reforms' (Anastasakis and Bechev, 2003: 15–16). The question therefore remains: has the altered enlargement context influenced the candidate countries' calculations of non-adaptation costs and reduced the EU's capacity to transfer its rules to South-Eastern Europe? How strong is the EU's external influence in the present enlargement towards South-Eastern Europe?

The analytical framework

The fact that the EU has become an actor in the field of internal security is, on its own, an astonishing development (Mitsilegas et al., 2003). Bearing in mind that the control of state borders, civil liberties, residence and citizenship, and law and order are closely interlinked with the sovereignty of a nation state, member states were initially hesitant to transfer competences in the field of justice and home affairs to the supranational level (see Lavenex and Wallace, 2005). At the beginning of EU cooperation in the area of justice and home affairs the objectives in the domain were primarily to provide 'compensatory measures' for the competition of the single market project and to deal with the emergence and/or increase of trans-national threats such as terrorism and organised crime (ibid: 459–63).[4] The path towards deeper integration in the field of justice and home affairs was paved by the Treaty of Amsterdam, which first introduced the objective of establishing a European area of freedom, security and justice. EU action in this field was no longer seen as complementary to the functioning of the single European market, but as a means to realise the ambitious project of an area of freedom, security and justice. On the basis of the Amsterdam Treaty, the EU's cooperation in justice and home affairs took on an entirely new quality and developed a substantial growth dynamic (see e.g. Lavenex and Wallace, 2005, Monar, 2006).

The Treaty of Amsterdam was also a landmark with regard to EU external action in the field of justice and home affairs (JHA). The EU member states agreed to transfer several treaty-making powers for external aspects in the JHA field to the EU level both to the Community first and the intergovernmental third pillars (Monar, 2004a). Moreover, they made a far-reaching decision with regard to the then candidate countries of Central and Eastern Europe. Due to security concerns in the Central and Eastern European countries, the EU-15 had agreed to include the Schengen regulations and rules – 'an uncatalogued miscellany of decisions and agreed working practices, a sort of disjointed incrementalism par excellence' (Lavenex and Wallace, 2005: 465) – in the EU's *acquis communautaire* which was to be incorporated into the legal order of the countries seeking accession. Article 8 of the Schengen Protocol annexed to the Amsterdam Treaty states that the 'Schengen *acquis* and further measures taken by the institutions within its scope [...] must be accepted in full by all States candidates for admission'. Opt-outs like those of the United Kingdom and Ireland were thus no longer permissible for new member states.

The process of adopting the EU justice and home affairs and Schengen *acquis* was one of the biggest challenges for the Central and Eastern European countries in the context of the Eastern enlargement (see in particular the work of Grabbe, 2000, 2002, 2005, 2006, Borissova, 2003). These states were seen as potential 'buffer states' (Borissova, 2003: 106) and were expected to play a crucial role in preventing illegal migration and organised crime from farther east. Scholars invented different terms for describing this process, such as 'enlarging Fortress Europe' (Phuong, 2003) or 'extending the sharp edges of Europe' (Grabbe, 2000). In her research, Heather Grabbe (2000) proposed the expressions 'border policies' and *acquis frontalier* for the concrete EU policies to be transposed and implemented by the candidate countries in Central and Eastern Europe and identified two sources of motivation behind the accession conditions on EU borders. The first was to bring the applicant border policies progressively in line with the Schengen *acquis* and the second to address pressing EU concerns about threats perceived by the existing member states. 'The most evident and pervasive of these concerns [was] the potential for illegal immigration by east Europeans or third-countries nationals travelling through the applicant countries' (Grabbe, 2000: 9).

This analysis elaborates on the process of transferring these border policies to the current aspiring candidates of South-Eastern Europe. Out of the broad justice and home affairs *acquis*, the focus is placed on border management and the Western Balkans' preparations for the implementation of the Schengen *acquis*. The policies discussed in this analysis constitute a central area of cooperation and an important pre-requisite for the eventual integration of the Western Balkan countries into the EU. Following the 1995 Dayton Peace Accords, the countries emerging from the former Yugoslavia had to demarcate roughly 5,000km of newly created borders among themselves. These borders were frequently ill-demarcated, poorly protected and characterised by a lack of regional structures and networks to tackle common cross-border problems. Organised crime networks managed to revitalise the traditional Balkan smuggling route as a transit route for illegal immigrants and all kinds of goods on their way into the EU (Schelter, 2003: 7, Hills, 2004a: 12). The EU therefore placed a particularly strong emphasis on reshaping the weak institutional arrangements of border policing as well as on sealing the porous borders between South-Eastern European states.

EU rule transfer in the field of justice and home affairs is examined in the cases of Croatia and Macedonia, two countries subsumed under the Stabilisation and Association Process. These countries are significant cases because the policy field has been politically relevant in both cases. Croatia is a strategically important border country for the EU, so the EU has been particularly interested in making Croatia strengthen its border control system. Due to Croatia's geopolitical position and the sheer length and composition of the borders, the country has been exposed to flows of illegal migrants and organised transfers of larger groups across its state borders. Most illegal migrants and asylum seekers view Croatia as a transit country on their route to the EU, not as a final destination. The reform of Macedonia's border security system was considered particularly urgent and thus highly relevant in the wake of the 2001 near-civil war, when Albanian insurgents from the National Liberation Army managed to cross the border into Macedonia without any difficulty. Therefore, the improvement of border security was seen as an important measure in securing the overall stability in the country.

Moreover the two countries provide a good basis for similarities but also differences in the candidate countries' politics of adjusting to the EU. Croatia and Macedonia are advanced in their EU integration process in comparison to other states in the region, yet they differ in some important aspects. Both of them concluded a Stabilisation and Association Agreement in 2001 (Macedonia in April, Croatia in October) and were the first countries to shift their status from potential candidates to real candidates (Croatia in June 2004 and Macedonia in December 2005). However, in spite of these relatively simultaneous steps, their current status differs considerably. Whereas Croatia was allowed to enter accession talks with the EU in October 2005, Macedonia's EU integration has slowed significantly. Since 2005, the opening of accession negotiations has been delayed several times, leaving Macedonia further behind and possibly more doubtful about its chances of accession. As a result, it is interesting to compare the situation in these two countries and the stance the EU takes towards them. The empirical findings will reveal to what extent the rapprochement process contains common patterns and at the same time attune to the individual circumstances of the countries concerned.

Methodology
The study systematically analyses relevant textual material of EU, Croatian and Macedonian state institutions, and of relevant secondary literature and media reports. One of the challenges is determining how to distinguish the EU's impact from other potential factors of influence. The Western Balkan states are strongly institutionalised in terms of international actors, as many European and international actors are present in their efforts to deal with the various challenges and problems of the region. An adequate understanding of the topic therefore requires attention to the other international organisations, processes and bilateral co-operations even if, in view of the overarching research interest, the EU is the major frame of reference for this project.

The methodology applied to filter out the Union's impact from other potential factors of influence has been 'a process-tracing analysis that seeks to reconstruct the policy-making process in sufficient detail to establish the causal importance of IO influence' (Schimmelfennig, 2002: 23). The process-tracing method helps trace the process in a theoretically informed way (Checkel, 2005: 5) and establish the causal chains and mechanisms between the independent variable(s) and the dependent variable (Bennet and George, 2005: 206). For the present study, this involves establishing the causal mechanisms leading to EU rule adoption in justice and home affairs in Croatia and Macedonia and opening up the 'black box' of political processes (Schimmelfennig, 2006: 265) that may result in adjustment to the EU. It needs mentioning that the EU's policy might exert an impact on the Western

Balkans even without the direct involvement of EU institutions. For instance, the Stability Pact for South-Eastern Europe, which evolved into the Regional Cooperation Council in 2008, set its priorities in line with the EU integration process, thus contributing to the export of EU rules without being an EU institution.

In addition, the project draws on forty-five semi-structured interviews conducted in Brussels, Zagreb, Skopje and Vienna between 2006 and 2009. The first round of interviews was made in Brussels in February 2006 and included expert interviews with officials from the European Commission, the Council of the EU and the two permanent missions of Croatia and Macedonia to the EU. In April and May 2006, the major round of interviews was made in Skopje and Zagreb with Macedonian and Croatian officials from the governments, parliaments and ministries of the interior and foreign affairs and EU delegations. Other interviews were made in the course of 2006 with officials of the International Organisation for Migration (IOM), the Vienna-based International Centre for Migration Policy Development (ICMPD) and the Stability Pact for South-Eastern Europe. Ten further interviews were conducted in Brussels in March and September 2009. To ensure the anonymity of the interviewees, the book uses interview codes when referring to the data provided by the interviews.

The structure of the analysis

The book is organised in four parts with nine chapters in total.

Following the introductory chapter, Part II presents the EU policies and strategies for the South-Eastern European countries. In Chapter 2, I elaborate on the border policies which the EU seeks to transfer to aspiring candidate countries in South-Eastern Europe. Drawing from the experiences of the Central and Eastern European countries in the context of the Eastern enlargement, the EU/Schengen requirements for the national border security system of a state seeking accession to the EU are presented. The chapter's main emphasis, however, is placed on the question of how the EU has adapted the accession requirements on borders to the specific situation of the Western Balkan states. Chapter 3 turns attention to the concrete strategies and instruments with which the EU seeks to encourage the Western Balkans to deepen their reform efforts in the area of justice and home affairs. The first part of this chapter introduces the set-up and specific features of the EU's pre-accession strategy, the Stabilisation and Association Process. The second part elaborates on the most prominent European supplement to the Stabilisation and Association Process for bringing these states closer to the Euro-Atlantic, the Stability Pact for South-Eastern Europe. In addition to the routes of influence the EU employs within these two initiatives, the third part also presents the Ohrid Border Process as a joint effort of the EU, NATO, OSCE and the Stability Pact to improve border security in the Balkans.

Part III sheds light on the receiving end of the EU's engagement.

In Chapter 4 and 5, the EU's influence on the domestic political processes and structures is investigated in Croatia and Macedonia. Both chapters proceed by first evaluating the Europeanisation of the border security policies of these two countries and then by tracing back the underlying dynamics of the interactions. Chapter 6 provides for a cross-discussion of the findings including their embedment into the broader regional framework. Whereas the first part assesses the possibilities and limitations of EU influence in the context of the current pre-accession framework, the second part elaborates on how the EU has sought to counterbalance its possible weaknesses. The chapter also considers how the findings on the EU's external governance approach in the Western Balkans are relevant for the wider European region.

Part IV (Chapter 7) recapitulates the study's most important findings and discusses its broader implications.

Notes

1   The Western Balkans include Albania, Bosnia and Herzegovina, Croatia, Macedonia, Montenegro, Serbia and Kosovo.
2   If a certain level of misfit exists between a European norm or law and national policies and structures, the national level will be pressured for adaptation. In comparison, if the European demands and the national conditions are compatible, the pressure for adaptation will be low and the implementation will be carried out easily. In other words, the degree of adaptational pressure is determined by the 'goodness of fit' (Cowles et al., 2001) between the European and the national level.
3   The question with regard to these neighbouring states was therefore how effective the EU's strategy of rule transfer based on conditionality would be if the major incentive, i.e. the prospect of membership, were absent. 'Without the membership prospective, the ENP countries may not be motivated to undertake domestic reforms' (Kelley, 2006: 36, see also Schimmelfennig and Sedelmeier, 2002, Weber et al., 2007). These relatively gloomy expectations on the EU's potential of external influence on ENP participating states have not been entirely realised. Scholars showed, however, that the EU eventually made a shift towards softer forms of EU external governance vis-à-vis these neighbouring countries. In particular Sandra Lavenex and her collaborators proposed looking at the role of transgovernmental networks or network governance in replacing more hierarchical modes of policy transfer (Lavenex, 2008, Lavenex and Wichmann, 2009).
4   These objectives were pursued in intergovernmental cooperation forms outside the EC framework, most notably in the TREVI and Schengen cooperation. The Maastricht Treaty first added an intergovernmental justice and home affairs pillar to the EU's treaty architecture and asked 'to develop close cooperation on justice and home affairs' (Title 1, Art. b TEU-Maastricht).

PART II

EU policies and strategies for South-Eastern Europe

2

EU policies for Balkan borders

External borders delimit the territory over which a state is authorised to exercise its sovereignty and present the point where each individual seeking entry to the country must prove his or her admissibility. The policies of external border control are sovereignty-sensitive aspects of a nation state's broader efforts to provide security for the people. It is therefore not surprising that the policies related to the management of the external borders of the European Union have been of high concern for the member states ever since the idea of a European area without internal frontiers was born (House of Lords, 2003, Hobbing, 2005, Berg and Ehin, 2006).

Likewise, it is not surprising that the improvement of candidate countries' external border controls was an important component of previous enlargements. In the context of the Eastern enlargement, the responsibility of controlling the eastern border of the European Union, hitherto mainly fulfilled by Germany and Austria, was delegated to the Central and Eastern European countries (CEECs). Since their accession to the EU, the new member states have assumed a central role in protecting the external borders of the European area of freedom, security and justice, in particular with regard to its surveillance of irregular immigration and organised crime.

By looking on the experiences of the CEECs in the Eastern enlargement, this chapter elaborates on the EU/Schengen requirements to be met by a state seeking accession to the EU. The emphasis is placed on the question of how the EU has adapted the accession requirements on borders to the specific situation of the Western Balkan states.

The Schengen *acquis*

The Schengen *acquis* has been the core source for EU-relevant border management.

The name Schengen refers to the small village in Luxembourg in which five EC member states (Belgium, Luxembourg, the Netherlands, Germany and France) signed an agreement in 1985 that aimed at realising the principle of free movement of persons among the signatory states. This intergovernmental approach was launched outside the EC framework but was closely linked to the single market project of the European Community. To achieve the objective of creating a single market based on the free movement of goods, capitals, services and persons, it was deemed necessary to abolish internal border controls and barriers. The Schengen cooperation was seen as a laboratory of those member states willing to proceed in the establishment of all legal and technical measures necessary to realise the principle of the free movement of persons.

The history and structure of the Schengen system

Five years after the adoption of the Schengen Agreement, the participating states signed the 'Convention Implementing the Schengen Agreement of 14 June 1990 between the Governments of the States of the Benelux Economic Union, the Federal Republic of Germany and the French Republic on the gradual abolition of checks at their common borders'. This document, referred to as the Schengen Convention, presented a core agreement of the Schengen system because it spelled out the conditions under which the free movement of persons was to be established.

The Schengen participating states based the principle of free movement on three pillars: first, the Schengen area should present a common territory without internal border controls alongside a common external border policy; second, the entry at one Schengen border constitutes admission into the whole Schengen area; and third, if permission is given to enter the common territory, the person is entitled to move freely within the whole Schengen territory for a period up to three months out of every six months (Apap et al., 2004: 5).

Political actors quickly linked the downgrading of internal frontier controls to the necessity of strengthening the external border control policies. Based on the understanding that 'if we diminish internal border controls then we must harmonise and strengthen the control at the external borders of the European Community to guarantee a sufficient level of control of who and what can legitimately enter the space of free movement' (Huysmans, 2000: 759), they agreed on a range of 'compensatory measures' to safeguard the upholding of internal security in the Schengen area. These compensatory measures of the Schengen Convention included the harmonisation of external border checks, the establishment of a common visa regime, the definition of which state would be responsible for an asylum seeker's application, improved coordination between the police, customs and judiciary, and several other measures (e.g. carrier sanctions) to respond to cross-border activities such as irregular immigration. Many of the measures adopted as Schengen compensatory measures laid the basis for EU cooperation in the JHA field. The Schengen system was therefore the 'most important laboratory' for the development of the EU as an actor in the field of internal security (Monar, 2001a: 750–52).

The major themes of the Schengen Convention were as follows:

Harmonisation of external border checks: The Schengen Convention contains a basic but far-reaching condition that obliges contracting parties to refrain from checking individuals who cross their internal borders (Article 2). In turn, all persons passing the external borders shall be checked in a similar way through commonly defined criteria for entry. The Schengen Convention defines basic rules concerning the conditions for legitimately crossing the external borders (Articles 3 to 8). The validity of passports, visas and residence permits for third country nationals shall always be verified. Article 6 suggests that all border checks shall be carried out (a) systematically at authorised crossing points only; (b) in an equal fashion all along the external borders; and (c) by taking into account the interest of all Schengen participating states.

A common visa policy: A common policy on the meaning and the issuance of visas has a prominent role in the Schengen Convention. The stipulations on a common visa policy concern only short-stay visas of three-month duration. Long-stay visas remain within the competence of each member state and are issued according to national jurisdictions only (Article 18).

Carrier sanctions: The Schengen Convention demands responsibility from (private and public) carriers by land or by sea. If a state refuses entry to an alien, the carrier has to assume the responsibility for the rejected person. As a result, carriers are obliged to ensure that their customers are in possession of all travel documents required for entry into the Schengen area.

Responsibility for processing applications for asylum: All Schengen signatory states confirm their obligations under the Geneva Convention relating to the Status of Refugees of 28 July 1957, and as amended by the New York Protocol of 31 January 1967. Although all refugees are given the right to apply for asylum, stipulations are made to clarify which state is in charge of dealing with an asylum seeker's application (the regulations are almost identical to the 1990 Dublin Convention on Asylum which later became an EC Regulation). As a consequence, only one country is responsible for deciding whether to grant asylum. This is usually the first country that the applicant enters or the country that has issued his or her visa. The asylum seeker's application is decided in line with the respective national asylum regulations, but has to be accepted by all signatory states (exception to this rule may be made on grounds of family reunification or for cultural reasons). If the application is refused, the examining state is assigned the task to readmit the person in his or her country of origin.

Police cooperation and border police cooperation: The enhancement of police and border police cooperation is outlined in a specific title in the Schengen Convention (Title III: Police and Security). The stipulations concern mainly the regulation of cross-border pursuit and surveillance, the control of the external borders and the exchange of liaison officers. Cross-border surveillance and pursuit requires the approval of a previously submitted request. In urgent cases, however, no such approval is needed if two conditions are met: 1) the local authorities are promptly notified during the act of surveillance that the national border has been crossed; and 2) a request for assistance is sent immediately.

Policies on criminal law: Concerning the policies on criminal law, a major objective is to enhance mutual legal assistance in criminal matters. Stipulations under this heading are considered complementary to already existing conventions in the field, but cover other fields of cooperation that go beyond these conventions.[1] Additionally, the signatory states agree to apply the principle 'ne bis in idem' meaning not to judge a criminal twice (in different countries) for the same offence. Provisions on extradition and on the transfer of the enforcement of criminal judgments, as well as the harmonisation of narcotic drugs, firearms and ammunition laws complement the policies under the heading 'criminal law'.

The Schengen Information System (SIS): The Schengen Information System is an instrument for national authorities to alert each other regarding persons and property. Its purpose, as defined, is to 'to maintain public policy and public security, including national security, in the territories of the contracting parties' (Article 69). Concretely, member states store data in the SIS on people to be refused admission (immigration offenders or security risks); on people wanted for arrest; on people to be placed under surveillance or subject to specific checks; and lost or stolen property (vehicles, works of art, identity documents etc.). It thus covers the gathering, analysis and exchange of information on immigration, asylum and visa matters as well as police and justice cooperation.

Although the Schengen Convention introduces a border-free zone among the signatory states, it provides these states with possibilities to temporarily cancel the principle of free movement of persons. If a state considers its national security at stake – in so-called 'states of emergency' or 'exceptionalism' (Apap et al., 2004: 5) – it may reintroduce border controls or may refuse the access of a third-country national to its territory, regardless of whether this person has a valid short-stay visa (Article 96 of the Schengen Convention).[2]

The practical implementation of the Schengen Convention was conferred to the Schengen Executive Committee, a special organ set up by Title VII of the Schengen Convention. Each state was represented in the committee by a national representative (usually a minister assisted by national experts) and the decisions were taken by unanimous vote. The Schengen Executive Committee realised the principle of free movement in Europe through a series of decisions from 1993 onwards. In March 1995, the Schengen system became operational.

By that time, the Schengen founding states had already accepted other EU member states to join their intergovernmental cooperation (Portugal and Spain). Since then, most EU member states have joined the Schengen area, with the notable exception of the United Kingdom and Ireland. When the Schengen *acquis* became part of the EU's legal framework (see next section), these two countries opted out and refrained from participating in it. However, they agreed to sign special provisions allowing them to participate in certain Schengen provisions.[3] Although a signatory of the Schengen Convention, Denmark applies special rules regarding the Schengen *acquis* and the measures building on it.[4] The Schengen cooperation is not confined to EU member states but encompasses also neighbouring non-EU member states, the so-called Schengen Associates (Wichmann, 2006). Norway and Iceland signed special association agreements in 1999 and have participated in the Schengen cooperation since March 2001. Switzerland, another non-EU member state, fully implemented a similar agreement in March 2009.

Integrating the Schengen acquis into the European Union
The Schengen system was established as an intergovernmental cooperation forum with no or only little involvement of the Community institutions. This institutional setup changed with the signing of the Treaty of Amsterdam, which integrated the Schengen *acquis* into the legal framework of the EU.

When the Treaty of Amsterdam was signed in October 1997, the member states had not yet clarified the defining elements of the Schengen *acquis*. This was a rather surprising fact given that 'the member governments had [thus] signed, and ratified, a treaty without having agreed the text of one of its most sovereignty-sensitive subordinate documents' (Lavenex and Wallace, 2005: 465). The Council first had to determine which Schengen provisions needed to be allocated to the EC Treaty or EU Treaty. The task would involve a relatively complicated legal procedure as certain Schengen regulations were redundant or had been overtaken by EC law (such as most of the firearms provisions) and other conventions (Peers, 2006: 46).[5] The Schengen regulations that related to free movement of persons were inserted into the Community pillar and followed the Community method.[6] The Schengen provisions that dealt with police and judicial cooperation in criminal matters were placed in Title VI of the EU Treaty, where all decisions were based on the intergovernmental method.

When the task was accomplished, the Council published a 580-page document named 'The Schengen *acquis* integrated in the European Union' (1999b) which outlined the elements of the Schengen *acquis* (it is important to note that some parts of the *acquis* were not published because the Schengen executive committee decided to keep them secret).[7] In legal terms, the Schengen *acquis* contains some special features that distinguish it from other parts of the *acquis communautaire*. The Schengen *acquis* includes provisions that cannot be referred to as EU law, even though they are supposed to create a political commitment for the participating states. These non-binding provisions of the Schengen *acquis*, called the Schengen Standards, define norms and best standards, e.g. with regard to the organisation of border police services and border control practices in the Schengen area. These non-binding provisions, outlined in the Schengen Catalogue of Recommendations and Best Practices, were drafted in view of the Eastern enlargement and should provide the candidate countries with a clear idea how to implement the Schengen *acquis* (Council of the European Union, 2002a: 9).

The evolving nature of the Schengen regime
The Schengen cooperation has not been a static system, but is a regime 'still in the making' (Apap et al., 2004: 6). The Amsterdam Treaty's introduction of qualified majority voting in some JHA issue areas, together with the launch of the European area of freedom, security and justice as a major political project, evoked a strong growth of the JHA *acquis*. This development was reinforced by the terrorist attacks of 9/11 and the Madrid and London terrorist bombings. In the aftermath of these events, the EU adopted a wide range of anti-terrorism measures, including the European arrest warrant and enhanced tasks and resources for Europol (Dittrich, 2005). Some measures adopted in response to the changing threat scenario have fallen within the direct realm of the Schengen cooperation, including the establishment of an 'integrated management' of EU external borders, the development of a second generation of the Schengen Information System (SIS II), the incorporation of biometrics in travel and identification documents, improved custom controls, and more (Apap et al., 2004: 6).

The creation of strong and effective external border controls has become a particularly important objective, since the 'better management of the Union's external borders' was believed by the heads of state and government to 'help in the fight against terrorism, illegal immigration networks and the traffic in human beings' (European Council, 2001). The problem was that the existing rules and practices at the external border did not meet expectations. When the Schengen system went operational, it quickly turned out that they were 'insufficient for ensuring coherent border management' (Hobbing, 2005: 12).

While the objective of improving border management at the external border was shared among the EU capitals, the concrete way forward was subject to controversy. The member states had different points of view as to whether the cooperation should lead to more harmonised legislation and centralised structures, or rather place an emphasis on decentralised cooperation and the improvement of operational links between law enforcement agencies. The views diverged in particular with regard to the most contentious question: whether the EU cooperation in border management should result in the creation of a European Corps of Border Guards. The proposal to eventually install a European border guard was first made in a communication by the European Commission (Commission of the European Communities, 2002b).[8]

These ideas were too far-reaching for some member states, which rejected the view that an integrated border management strategy should ultimately result in a centralised Corps of European Border Guards. They maintained that the European border guards, should such a corps be created, must not replace but rather support the various national border police forces (Monar, 2004b: 125). According to this model, the European border guards should be more like network of national units that only become operational in risk areas. Oscillating between these models, the JHA Council opted for a compromise and agreed on the creation of an External Border Practitioners Unit as steering body of the SCIFA+ Committee. Furthermore, some Ad-Hoc Centres should provide for better cooperation on external border controls (Council of the European Union, 2002b).

Under this framework of cooperation, the EU member states launched a remarkable list of activities and projects aimed at improving EU external border control.[9] As argued by Jörg Monar, the framework quickly revealed some deficiencies, however: first, the EU's funding for the projects was bound to rather restrictive conditions and cumbersome procedures; second, the level of commitment differed widely among member states and within cooperation projects; third, the projects were carried out on an ad-hoc basis, therefore lacking a strategic plan or effective coordination; and finally, the lack of a proper legal framework for seconding border guards to other member states frequently turned them to mere observers without any executive power (Monar, 2005: 159).

The 2004 multi-annual The Hague Programme sought to move beyond the fragmented framework of cooperation and called for the establishment of a 'European Agency for the Management of Operational Co-operation at the External Borders of the Member States of the European Union' (Frontex) (Council of the European Union, 2004c). The agency, legally created in October 2004 and seated in Warsaw, was designed as a community body having legal personality as well as operational and budgetary autonomy. Its purpose is 'to facilitate the application of existing and future Community measures relating to the management of the external borders by ensuring the coordination of Member States' action in the implementation of those measures' (Council of the European Union, 2004b: 2).

Frontex was tasked to improve operational cooperation at the external borders of the EU and provide added value to the national border control systems of the member states yet it has no direct operational competences. In concrete terms, the agency carries out collective action, develops risk analysis, diffuses best practices, advances the development of common rules and curricula for training border guards, and supports member states in organis-ing return operations. So, despite the lack of operational competences, Frontex obtained sufficient power to 'put its own stamp on the sector' (Hobbing, 2005: 19).

Other efforts to establish integrated border management at the EU level concerned the consolidation of the legal framework and the improvement of burden-sharing mechanisms among member states. A new Schengen Border Code outlining norms that are mostly technical in nature entered into force in 2006 (Council of the European Union, 2006g). The Schengen Border Code provided 'a much needed common framework of reference for authorities and agencies dealing with EU border management' (Balzacq, 2008: 33). The two major burden-sharing mechanisms agreed upon at EU level were the so-called Schengen Facility established to support the Central and Eastern European countries in their process of implementing the Schengen *acquis* and the External Border Fund, which sought to enhance the financial solidarity within the existing member states. The latter instrument has been funded with €1,820 million for the period 2007–2013.

In 2008, the Commission published a communication on how border management should look in the future (Commission of the European Communities, 2008c). The Commission's agenda is ambitious and controversial and is centred around the creation of a new entry/exit system that would register the movement of specific categories of third country nationals at the EU's external borders. Furthermore, with the use of biometric technology as well as an electronic travel authorisation system, the traveller's identity (both citizens of the EU and third country nationals) would be automatically verified. The Commission's new border package would transform the way border checks are made in the EU, and yet the focus on new security tools and techniques prompted scholars to ask whether the EU is taking another step toward a 'cyber-fortress Europe' (Guild et al., 2008).

The Schengen system as part of the accession criteria for candidate countries

With the entering into force of the Treaty of Amsterdam, the Schengen system became part of the accession criteria for candidate countries. The implementation of the Schengen and justice and home affairs *acquis* was a particular challenge in the context of the Eastern enlargement. The domain was a quickly evolving area of EU policy-making and the candidate countries of Central and Eastern Europe started relatively late with their adjustment process (Monar, 2001b: 6). Because the EU specified the precise JHA regulations to be implemented by the candidates as late as in 1999, the adaptation process in this policy domain started half a decade later than in the internal market *acquis*.

Moreover, the European area of freedom, security and justice was driven by a 'security rationale' making it a very sensitive policy domain in the context of enlargement (ibid). Several 'old' member states voiced concerns that the Eastern enlargement in general and the Schengen enlargement to the East in particular would undermine the existing EU internal security standards. Efforts to create mutual trust between the candidate countries and the EU-15 were hence a central element of the process of transferring the JHA *acquis* (Mitsilegas, 2007: 461). The EU member states set the benchmarks in domain high for the candidate countries in Central and Eastern Europe, at times even higher than for old member states (ibid).

The body of laws and practice to be implemented upon accession was sizeable and complex and involved substantial financial and administrative efforts by the Central and Eastern European countries. The conditions set by the EU in the field included some general and broad requirements such as the ratification of international treaties, the improvement of the rule of law, the strengthening and better functioning of the administrative and judicial institutions and data protection. In addition, the candidates were encouraged to meet a range of more specific conditions including the establishment of equitable asylum procedures and laws, the incorporation of the EU's visa regime and admission system, the strengthening of enforcement and deportation procedures, the introduction of penalties for illegal immigration, the signing of readmission agreements and the improvement of the control and surveillance of borders (Grabbe, 2005: 126f). The EU sustained the efforts of the applicants with financial and technical assistance, both in the framework of the EU's PHARE programme and through bilateral channels (for detailed analyses, see House of Lords, 2000, Monar, 2001b, Grabbe, 2002, 2006, Borissova, 2003).

When on 1 May 2004 the eight Central and Eastern European countries plus Malta and Cyprus joined the EU, they had already implemented a substantial part of the Schengen *acquis* on visa regimes and border controls. Still, the border controls between the old and new member states remained in place. It is a particular feature of the Schengen *acquis* to be implemented in a two-stage procedure. A candidate country has to accept substantial parts of the Schengen *acquis* at the latest by the time of its accession to the EU. The border controls between the new and the old member states, however, will not be removed on the day of accession but when the Schengen participating states agree that adequate controls at the new external borders are in place.[10]

To support the progress of new member states in meeting the requirements of the Schengen *acquis*, the EU set into being the instrument of the Schengen Facility defined 'as a temporary instrument to help beneficiary member states between the date of accession and the end of 2006 to finance actions at the new external borders of the Union for the implementation of the Schengen acquis and external border control' (Treaty of Accession, 2003: Art. 35, par. 1). The financial support under this programme covered investment in construction, renovation or upgrading of border crossing infrastructure, investments in operating equipment (e.g. SIS hardware and software), training of border guards and costs for logistics and operations.

Table 2.1   Breakdown of available funding under the Schengen Facility (€ million)

	Estonia	Latvia	Lithuania	Hungary	Poland	Slovenia	Slovakia	Total
2004	25.35	26.24	49.58	54.58	103.35	39.46	17.64	316.23
2005	25.48	26.37	67.95	54.86	103.85	39.64	17.72	335.91
2006	26.17	27.08	34.11	56.34	106.66	40.72	18.2	309.3
Total SF/ country	77.01	79.7	151.6	165.7	313.87	119.8	53.58	961.45

Note: The Czech Republic was not a beneficiary of the Schengen Facility, as the programme only targeted countries at the EU's new external borders.
Source: European Commission, DG Justice, Freedom and Security.

The progress of the Central and Eastern European countries towards establishing a Schengen border was closely supervised by the old member states. The ministers of justice and home affairs of the old member states were not inclined to make compromises in safeguarding internal security for the sake of political integration, hence pushing the new member states to intensify their efforts to establish sufficient controls of land and air borders between themselves and the neighbouring non-EU-states. In this process, a technical question turned out to be almost as tricky as the political concerns of EU ministers of justice and home affairs (Bertozzi, 2008: 20). The second generation of the Schengen Information System could not come on stream as foreseen in April 2007, thus threatening to delay the Schengen Eastern enlargement. For the new member states, it was politically unacceptable that their accession to the Schengen area would be delayed due to a technical problem. The solution that was put forward by the Portuguese delegation was to install a new system called SISone4ALL which would make the fullest use of the existing system for a transitional period of time. Through this, the delays in the timeframe scheduled for the lifting of the internal borders could be minimised (ibid).

On 8 November 2007, the EU ministers of justice and home affairs cleared the way for lifting the internal border controls to the new member states. The final endorsement was given by the European Council on 14 December 2007 who welcomed 'the enlargement of the Schengen area and the abolition of controls at the internal borders of the member states participating in the SISone4ALL project, as from 21 December 2007 for land and sea borders, and by 30 March 2008 for air borders, thus extending the effective free movement of persons' (European Council, 2007: 3). The transitional period, i.e. the period after the new member states' accession to the EU but prior to their full implementation of the Schengen *acquis*, came to an end. The new member states of Central and Eastern Europe, with the exception of Cyprus, Bulgaria and Romania, joined the Schengen zone, transforming it to one of the world's biggest passport-free zones.

The EU's border security policies for the Western Balkans

In the context of the Western Balkans countries' EU integration, the creation of Schengen-style border management has been defined as a long-term objective only. Given the Western Balkans' comparatively low level of European integration and institutional stability, the EU has sought to adapt its border policies to the specific circumstances of their EU rapprochement process. It encouraged these states to implement the EU's integrated border management (IBM) strategy for the Western Balkans, which included not only border control but also trade facilitation and cross-border cooperation.

The EU's integrated border management for the Western Balkans

The EU's integrated border management for the Western Balkans is defined as the 'coordination and cooperation among all the relevant authorities and agencies involved in border control, trade facilitation and border region cooperation to establish effective, efficient and integrated border management systems, in order to ensure the common goal of *open, but controlled and secured borders*' (IBM Guidelines, 2004: 14, emphasis added).

The overall objective is therefore the establishment of a border policy that fulfils two functions. Legitimate cross-border activities such as tourism, trade and trans-border cooperation should be facilitated and/or actively promoted ('open' borders), whereas all illegal cross-border movements such as human and drug smuggling or trafficking should be controlled in the most effective way possible ('controlled and secured borders'). By embarking on this strategy, the EU has established different expectations as to what purpose borders should serve in the region: 'when it comes to trans-border crimes, illegal migration and other cross-border problems, the EU favours *hard* borders with a high degree of hard security and control mechanisms involved. When regional trans-border co-operation is the topic, *soft* borders that should be easy to cross and trans-border activities are emphasised' (Luif and Riegler, 2006: 10).

The EU's border management strategy is presented as a depoliticised and technical concept, against the background that border-related issues are of a politically sensitive nature in South-Eastern Europe. As noted by Svetlozar Andreev, 'here borders still matter' (2004: 382). Compared to other European regions, the borders in South-Eastern Europe are hard and exclusionary rather than soft and inclusionary (ibid). The political salience of border-related issues is increased by the fact that minority populations frequently live in border regions. The rights of minority groups in border regions, for example the Albanian rights in Macedonia and Serbia, have been a source of controversies, making in particular the issue of border delineation a politicised one. There are several border delineation issues in the region that have been difficult to settle due to sovereignty and territorial concerns of the states involved. 'Delineation between Serbia and Kosovo, for example, would symbolise the final break-up of the old Balkans system, while in other cases – notably Macedonia – it might destroy any lingering illusion of a homogenous, centralised, or ethnically-mixed nation state' (Hills, 2004a: 13). In view of this context, the EU has chosen a rather technical approach in its efforts to improve border security in the region, underemphasising questions of border delineation and demarcation.

The EU's IBM concept integrates the three components of border control, trade facilitation and border region cooperation. The Western Balkan countries have been encouraged to develop a comprehensive and 'integrated' approach toward tackling the problems of trade, traffic, insecurity and smuggling across borders. The terms 'cooperation' and 'coordination' are therefore in the centre of the strategy, although they surprisingly lack a precise definition (ibid: 32). The numerous authorities and agencies involved in the management of the external borders are asked to strengthen their cooperation links (in particular those related to border control, migration and customs) and work together on common problems, rather than working separately or even at cross-purposes. Emphasis is placed on going beyond the individual state level as well as improving trans-national and regional cooperation in the management of common borders. For example, the authorities of the Western Balkan states were expected to develop common cross-border programmes that target border regions on both sides of the border, and to sign bilateral agreements on border related issues. The IBM Guidelines identify three levels of cooperation:

1. Intra-service cooperation: Improving the efficiency of processes, information and resources within each agency responsible for specific tasks as well as the central ministries responsible for these services;

2. Inter-agency cooperation: The various agencies and administrative branches should enhance their cooperation links e.g. through coordinated processing at border crossings and the green/blue border; through the development of information technology systems that cover border security, national police and customs information; and through the enhancement of cooperation among the various agencies with regard to risk analysis. According to an EU official, the best way to achieve the goal is to bring the different actors *physically* together in terms of a common location (interview EU9, 3 May 2006, Skopje). The EU has therefore placed an emphasis on the establishment of National Coordination Centres of Border Management. The centres should bring the different actors together in a single room where they are more or less obliged to communicate and coordinate.

3. International cooperation: The regional and international cooperation should be progressively improved by establishing the necessary communication and coordination channels and procedures on local, bilateral and multilateral levels. It was recommended to conclude bilateral agreements to regulate the cooperation between the border police services, customs, phytosanitary and veterinary inspection services (IBM Guidelines, 2004: 16–19, see also Hills, 2004a, Hobbing, 2005).

Another EU priority has been the demilitarisation of the South-Eastern European borders. The EU encouraged these states to withdraw all military from border controls and to shift the chain of command from the ministry of defence to the ministry of the interior, where non-military border guarding structures shall be established. By gradually handing over the duty of border guarding from the military to specialised civil authorities, the EU believed that professionalism in guarding the region's borders would improve.

The IBM Guidelines provided the Western Balkan states with a template for how to implement the concept domestically. As a first step, the present situation should be evaluated against pre-defined benchmarks. Second, the respective country should draft an individual 'integrated border management strategy' and a corresponding action plan, clarifying several points: how to enhance intra- and inter-institutional as well as international cooperation; the duties and responsibilities of each administrative branch; how to improve implementation capabilities and capacities; and the timetables for the implementation of the overall concept.[11] If the concept is successfully realised, the Western Balkans will be ready to prepare a Schengen-style border management, which is the next step in the process toward meeting EU standards in the field.

The objective of promoting 'open borders' in terms of active trans-border cooperation has been primarily pursued under the EU's Regional Policy, which has extended its activities to South-Eastern Europe.[12] The EU's efforts resulted in the definition and the funding of several Euroregions including the Drina-Sava-Majevica Euroregion (Bosnia and Herzegovina-Hungary-Croatia), Prespa-Ohrid Euroregion (Greece-Macedonia-Albania), the Nis-Skopje-Sofia Eurobalkans region (Bulgaria-Macedonia-Serbia, known also as Euroregion Eurobalkans) and the Balasica Euroregion (Bulgaria-Greece-Macedonia). These programmes have built upon the experience in Eastern enlargement; however, similar efforts in Central and Eastern Europe did not evoke the desired efforts, with economic disparities staying the same or becoming even wider across border regions (Baldwin-Edwards, 2006: 3).

What is more, the EU's efforts to enhance cross-border cooperation in the area of the former Yugoslavia might prove to be more difficult than they were in Central and Eastern Europe. 'The European Union should be much more aware of the fact that in the break-up of Yugoslavia the political and military attacks often started in border regions. They were often attacked more than once and ethnically cleansed in counter-attacks. They are still high on the security agenda; as a result, they are often sparsely populated' (Luif and Riegler, 2006: 10). The development of dynamic trans-border regions in South-Eastern Europe is therefore a difficult task that cannot be expected to be achieved within a short-time period.

The problem of definitions related to border management

The EU's IBM concept for the Western Balkans has brought together different policy fields,[13] strategic interests, perceptions and objectives and encouraged a substantial number of agencies, administrations and authorities to establish coordination and communication links with one another. Therefore, the EU's border policies for the Western Balkans might be best understood as a 'composite policy' defined by Ulrich Sedelmeier (2002) as a policy that 'draws its substance from distinctive policy decisions across a range of policy areas'. The nature of such a policy is that it is shaped by different groups of policy-makers who bring in different policy paradigms defined as 'sets of ideas that respectively underpin policy in specific areas' (ibid; see also Eiki Berg and Piret Ehin (2006) who use this concept to analyse the EU's overall border regime).

The broad definition of the EU's integrated border management concept has brought up some challenges in the Western Balkans. According to several interviewees, it has been problematic that the EU has sought to adapt its border management concept to the Western Balkans rather than simply use the definition of border management that it has developed for within the EU. The EU's internal IBM concept focuses on combining trade facilitation with border security (Hobbing, 2005). By contrast, the EU's IBM concept for the Western Balkans was not restricted to these policy fields but subsumed all EU activities relating in any way to the term 'border' under one heading.

A reason for this broad, all-encompassing focus was related to the Eastern enlargement. In the context of the Central and Eastern European countries' accession to the EU, the European Commission was able to gain profound knowledge of how to transfer the *acquis* on external border controls to candidate countries. When the attention gradually shifted to South-Eastern Europe, the Commission became more and more ambitious and the expectations changed. As an EU official noted, the Western Balkan countries were not only expected to upgrade their border security systems but to incorporate the 'fairly academic concept of integrated border management right from the very start' (interview EU9, 3 May 2006, Skopje).

The broad definition became a source of confusion among the actors on the ground. An official of the consortium implementing the CARDS regional IBM project stated that 'among the biggest challenges in the Western Balkans are the different definitions of the term "integrated border management"'. She posed the question, in reference to the IBM model, 'are you referring to border control in the sense of border security or the concept of integrated border management?' (interview IO7, 11 December 2006, Vienna).

In daily practice, the policy actors referred more to their sectoral policy paradigms than to the EU's IBM concept as a common overarching policy paradigm. In interviews, EU experts in justice and home affairs advanced the view that the IBM concept did not prompt them to harmonise their activities with officials of, say, cross-border cooperation programmes. An EU expert on border security in Skopje framed the issue in the following way:

> Cross-border cooperation has mainly to do with the communities living in the border region: trade facilitation, cultural exchange, these kinds of things. That is one aspect of border management and that is why we call it management rather than control – to leave out the bad guys and to encourage the good ones. That is a delicate balance indeed. But that is not what we are dealing with here. [...] The two aspects, cross-border cooperation and integrated border management, do not live in the same basket. In my business, very much is addressed to the exchange of liaison officers, to the flow of information, etc. – that is how we are doing it. (Interview EU9, 3 May 2006, Skopje)

In January 2007, the EU reacted to the unclear definition by publishing an upgraded version of the IBM Guidelines for the Western Balkans. The document explicitly sought to 'respond to one of the main challenges encountered during the implementation process: the different interpretations and definitions of IBM used by various international and national stakeholders, leading (in some cases) to confusion and inconsistencies in approach, as well as to contradictory messages' (IBM Guidelines, 2007: 13). Accordingly, the field 'cross-border cooperation' was omitted from the definition of the IBM concept for the Western Balkans, bringing it closer to the EU's internal model of border management.[14]

Concluding remarks

This chapter has assessed the requirements that a state seeking to join the EU has to fulfil in the field of border security and has elaborated on how the EU has adjusted these requirements to the particular circumstances of the Western Balkan states.

The Schengen *acquis* presents the core source for EU-relevant border management. Since the Treaty of Amsterdam, all candidate countries for EU accession have been obliged to implement it in full. A particular feature of the EU's Schengen regime is its two-stage implementation procedure, which implies that the Central and Eastern European countries were accepted to the Schengen zone not at the time of their EU accession, but rather once the old EU member states were convinced that their level of compliance with this complex and comprehensive body of legislation was sufficient.

Since the creation of a Schengen-like border management system has been unrealistic for the Western Balkan states in the near future, the EU has sought to adapt its border security policies to the regional setting. These states were encouraged to implement the EU's integrated border management strategy for the Western Balkans, which, besides border control, encompassed trade facilitation and border region cooperation. The overall aim was to facilitate legitimate cross-border activities such as tourism, trade and transborder cooperation and to close the borders for criminal activities ('open but controlled and secure borders'). The key components of the EU's IBM concept were the request to improve the intra-service, inter-agency and international cooperation in border management and to transfer the operational responsibility for border policing from the army to the police. In practice, the concept's broad definition, which departed from the EU's internal definition of IBM, has been a source of confusion for EU actors on the ground as well as for Balkan stakeholders.

Notes

1   Examples are the European Convention on Mutual Assistance in Criminal Matters of 20 April 1959 and the Chapter of the Benelux Treaty concerning Extradition and Mutual Assistance in Criminal Matters of 27 June 1962, as amended by the protocol of 11 May 1974.
2   The clause has gained importance as 'there seems to have emerged a sort of permanent state of emergency in the European Union after the events of 11 September 2001 in the United States and 11 March 2004 in Madrid' (Apap et al., 2004: 6).
3   The two states take part in police and judicial cooperation in criminal matters, the fight against drugs and the Schengen Information System but refrained from participating in the common border controls and EU visa arrangements (Peers, 2006: 59–60).
4   According to the Protocol integrating the Schengen *acquis* in the European Union, Denmark is exempted from almost all Title IV measures. In practice, however, the country has consistently opted in to the measures adopted under this title (Peers, 2006: 59–60).
5   An example was the Schengen asylum provisions which were replaced by the Dublin Convention (ibid).
6   The legal basis was laid out in Title IV of the EC Treaty (Visas, Asylum, Immigration and other policies related to Free Movement of Persons).
7   This document consisted of (1) the agreement between the governments of the states of the Benelux economic union, the Federal Republic of Germany and the French Republic on the gradual abolition of checks at their common borders; (2) the Convention implementing the Schengen Agreement of 14 June 1985 between the governments of the States of the Benelux economic union, the Federal Republic of Germany and the French Republic on the gradual abolition of checks at their common borders; (3) different agreements with countries acceding the Schengen group (Italy, Spain and Portugal, Greece, Austria, Denmark, Finland and Sweden and Norway and Iceland); and (4) all decisions taken by the Schengen Executive Committee and the central group (to which the Executive Committee had delegated some decision-making competences). Since the entry into force of the Treaty of Amsterdam, the Council of Ministers has taken over the responsibilities of the Executive Committee (Council of the European Union, 1999b)
8   The European Commission suggested action in five areas in order to establish an EU integrated border management: (1) a common corpus of legislation; (2) common mechanisms for coordination and cooperation; (3) common risks analyses; (4) harmonised staffing and equipment; and finally (5) financial burden-sharing between EU member states, which would then all add up to the creation of a European corps of border guards (Commission of the European Communities, 2002b).
9   Shortly after its official creation in autumn 2002, the External Border Practitioners Unit initiated some joint operations and pilot projects at the EU's external borders, the most well-known of which was Operation Ulysses from January to May 2003. Under Spanish leadership, the operation pursued the objective of strengthening or

developing new forms of cooperation among EU member states in the fight against human trafficking at the EU's sea borders. Other operations included the Western Balkan states. Operation Immpact, for instance, provided border guards of Serbia and Montenegro with specialist immigration training and advice (see Monar, 2005: 157).

10   This decision is a politically sensitive one, as efficient border controls are widely regarded as a key to safeguard the internal security of the European area of freedom, security and justice. In view of the sensitivity of the issue, it can take a while for the Council to agree in a unanimous vote on the accession of new members to the Schengen area. Italy, for instance, had to wait seven years (from 1990 to 1997) before it was allowed to enter, regardless of the fact that Italy was a founding member of the European Economic Community.

11   The Western Balkan states were expected to draft a national version of the document which would include the following aspects: (1) the country's border management situation, technical infrastructure and ongoing border related programmes; (2) the identification of priorities, programmes and indicators of achievement; (3) strategies to facilitate coordination and cooperation at national level and with neighbouring countries; (4) a baseline against which progress or a lack of progress can be determined; information on the financial and human resources available and indications of the recourses required to implement the new IBM approach; and (5) the preparation of a feasible and integrated action plan that will ensure implementation of the strategy (IBM Guidelines, 2004: 41f).

12   Established in 1975, the EU's Regional Policy has aimed at promoting socio-economic development in border regions and intensifying cross-border relations and contacts.

13   The concept included issue areas such as trade facilitation, phytosanitary and veterinary inspections, the control of goods and people, border and transport infrastructure, and border region development.

14   In the 2007 IBM Guidelines for the Western Balkans, the EU officially defines integrated border management as the 'coordination and cooperation among all the relevant authorities and agencies involved in border security and trade facilitation in order to establish effective, efficient and integrated border management systems in order to reach the common goal of open, but controlled and secure borders' (IBM Guidelines, 2007: 13).

3

The Europeanisation strategies for the Western Balkans

This chapter deconstructs the ways in which the EU has used its most powerful foreign policy tool, i.e. the incentive of membership, to influence domestic policy-making in justice and home affairs in the Western Balkan states. The analysis proceeds by elaborating on the Stability Pact for South Eastern Europe, an EU-led initiative of different international actors and organisations to develop a long-term conflict prevention strategy after the 1999 Kosovo war, and the Ohrid Border Process which has brought together four international organisations and the Western Balkan states to engage in the joint project of improving border security and management in South-Eastern Europe.

The Stabilisation and Association Process: analysing the JHA dimension

The EU's Stabilisation and Association Process (SAP) for the Western Balkans is the overall Europeanisation instrument for the region. Launched in the aftermath of the 1999 Kosovo war 'the SAP is an ambitious strategy that helps the region to secure political and economic stabilisation and to develop a closer association with the EU, opening a road towards EU membership once the relevant conditions have been met' (Commission of the European Communities, 2001d: 2).

The prospect of the Western Balkan states joining the EU was first expressed at the European Council in Santa Maria De Feira in 2000. The conclusions stated that all of the countries in the region were 'potential candidates for EU membership' (European Council, 2000: Point 67). This statement marked a clear shift from the EU's previous Regional Approach, adopted 29 April 1997, which only offered unilateral trade preferences and financial incentives in exchange for the countries' commitment to meet the conditions set by the EU. The Regional Approach hence already applied the principle of conditionality and sought to bring the states closer to the EU (Altmann, 1998, Blockmans, 2006: 320–24), yet bypassed the issue of membership.

After first being announced, the prospect for membership was reiterated several times, notably at the European Council of Thessaloniki of June 2003, which was largely dedicated to EU–Western Balkans relations (European Council, 2003). Even though the countries concerned hoped for a more precise time frame for accession on that occasion, the Thessaloniki Council Conclusions remained silent on the issue and the countries remained 'potential' rather than 'real' candidates. However, the Council endorsed the so-called 'Thessaloniki Agenda for the Western Balkans: moving towards European integration' which enriched the SAP process and bolstered it by methods based on the experiences of the Eastern enlargement. The chief of these was the introduction of European Partnerships, modelled on the Accession Partnership employed in Central and Eastern Europe. Other means to 'enrich' the Stabilisation and Association Process were the promotion of political dialogue and cooperation in the area of CFSP, the strengthening of parliamentary cooperation, more financial means for institution building and the opening of Community programmes (Council of the European Union, 2003d).

EU mechanisms for exerting influence domestically

Conditionality, or as the Council understands it 'the cement of the Stabilisation and Association process' (Council of the European Union, 2001c: Point III), pervades the EU's strategy for the region and has to be viewed as its decisive cornerstone. In its pre-accession strategy for the Western Balkans, the EU has refined the conditionality approach as applied in the Eastern enlargement. An unusually broad range of political and economic conditions are linked to the coveted perspective of EU member-ship. In addition to the 1993 Copenhagen Criteria, the aspiring candidate countries are also expected to meet country-specific conditions stemming from different peace agreements (e.g. UN Resolution 1244 and the Dayton, Ohrid and Belgrade agreements) and to promote regional cooperation and reconciliation. If the EU chooses, it can also invoke programme conditional-ity and project level conditionality, threatening to freeze financial means if the country concerned fails to meet the objectives set by the EU:

> Failure to comply with this level of conditionality [i.e. programme and project conditionality] may result in the delay, suspension or cancellation of the planned or committed assistance without the possibility of reallocating the funds to another sector. (Commission of the European Communities, 2001a: 25)

What follows are the five conditionality instruments, as defined by Heather Grabbe (2003: 321f) for the Eastern enlargement, adjusted to the Western Balkan setting.

Models: provisions of legislative and institutional templates
Under the 1993 Copenhagen criteria, membership requires that a candidate be capable of fulfilling the obligations of membership, which entail the implementation of the entire EU *acquis* as it evolves. Domestic regulations and standards are to be harmonised with EU rules and the entire EU *acquis* is to be integrated into the legal order of the candidate country.

Given the medium- to long-term perspective of EU membership, the EU has not perceived the legal downloading of the *acquis* as a top priority for all countries. Rather it sought to adapt its policy templates to the circumstances of the region and set priority objectives in terms of cooperation. As regards justice and home affairs, the European Commission has defined four priorities. The first was the fight against organised crime, with a particular focus on fighting all forms of trafficking, especially of human beings, drugs and arms, as well as the smuggling of goods. In the same priority the strengthening of public order and police were subsumed. The reform of the judicial system was the strategy's second key objective, bearing in mind that the states' court systems were frequently overwhelmed by an immense backlog of cases, which led to corruption, public mistrust of the system and unacceptable delays. Third, the Western Balkan states were expected to re-organise their external border control systems in line with the EU's integrated border management concept for the region (see previous chapter). Finally, the priorities were complemented with the title 'migration and asylum' in which the strengthening, or in certain cases, the creation of responsible state institutions and the alignment with European and international standards have dominated the agenda (see Commission of the European Communities, 2001b).

In doing so, two strategies – a regional one and a country-by-country one – are to complement each other. The regional strategy aims at improving regional co-operation through the establishment of contractual relationships in the policy fields of border management, visa policy, migration issues and organised crime. The specific JHA priorities for each of the Western Balkan countries are outlined in the justice, freedom and security chapter of the European or Accession Partnerships.[1] These Partnerships are tailored to each country's particular situation, distinguishing between priorities for short-term action (12 to 24 months) and those for the medium term (3 to 4 years). The Partnerships are politically salient documents, as they provide guidance for the EU's financial assistance. In response to the European or Accession Partnership, the target countries are expected to develop plans with time-tables and details on when and how they intend to implement the Partnership priorities, and to outline the human and financial resources needed to do so. Although justice and home affairs is defined in each of these countries as a key area of cooperation, the individual priority areas of action depend on the domestic conditions in justice and home affairs. In Croatia, for instance, the EU and their Croatian counterparts have begun focusing relatively early on the transposition of the EU *acquis*, whereas the EU's main objective in

Albania is to enhance the capacities of law enforcement institutions on a much more basic level.

The Council of the EU can provide further guidance in the EU–Western Balkans JHA ministerial meeting, usually conducted once a year, and through initiatives of the rotating presidencies. In November 2002, the EU invited the Western Balkans to a conference on organised crime in South-Eastern Europe. The London Statement set out a 'joint commitment' to defeating organised crime in South-Eastern Europe and committed the Western Balkans to individually submit records of achievements (London Statement, 2002). The focus on organised crime was further strengthened at the EU–Western Balkan summit in Thessaloniki in June 2003. Under the heading 'Fighting Organised Crime: Co-operation in Other Justice and Home Affairs Matters', the Thessaloniki Agenda emphasised the growing importance of JHA matters in EU–Western Balkans relations. The document 'urged the countries of the region to define and implement further specific action-oriented measures to be pursued in the immediate future' (Council of the European Union, 2003d). These action-oriented measures were presented by each Western Balkan state at subsequent JHA ministerial meetings, the first of which was held in November 2003.

Under the Austrian presidency in 2006, the Council adopted an 'Action Oriented Paper on Improving Co-operation, on Organised crime, Corruption, Illegal Immigration and Counter-terrorism, between the EU, Western Balkans and relevant ENP countries' (Council of the European Union, 2006b). The document contained unusually precise instructions, including a timeframe by which each recommended action should be implemented. In total, seven priorities were outlined for the coming years, ranging from improving regional cooperation between law enforcement, prosecutors and the judiciary over fighting corruption more efficiently, to more effective donor coordination (ibid).[2]

Money: aid and technical assistance
Financial assistance is offered within the framework of the Instrument for Pre-Accession Assistance (IPA). IPA was established in 2006 to streamline the EU's financial efforts and to achieve a higher impact with the resources available (Council of the European Union, 2006d). Funded with €11.5 billion between 2007 and 2013 (including pre-accession support for Turkey), IPA consists of five components: transition assistance and institution building; cross-border cooperation; regional development; human resources development; and rural development. Of the €840 million earmarked in 2008 for the IPA component transition assistance and institution building, 33 per cent was designed to 'enhance governance, encourage administrative and judicial reform, strengthen the rule of law, support the fight against corruption and organised crime, promote human rights, protect minorities and develop civil society' (Commission of the European Communities, 2008f: 6).

Whereas potential candidates receive funding only under the first two components, candidate countries have access to all components. The extended support should help them in their preparations to fulfil the accession criteria and to build up the proper administrative and judicial capacity for implementing the *acquis*. Furthermore, candidate countries are to be prepared to manage EU funds after their accession. IPA is based on multi-annual planning cycles outlined by the Commission in the so-called Multi-Annual Indicative Financial Framework (MIFF). This document delineates the forthcoming financial support for a period of three years and breaks down the IPA envelope by country and component (Commission of the European Communities, 2006a).

In the last financial perspective (2000–2006), the EU offered €4.6 billion of pre-accession funding within the framework of the Community Assistance for Reconstruction, Development and Stabilisation (CARDS) (Council of the European Union, 2000). In contrast to its predecessor, CARDS also targeted some specifically Western Balkan problems stemming from the conflicts of the 1990s, such as the return of refugees and internally displaced people. In practical terms, CARDS assistance was managed by the Commission, both by its headquarters in Brussels and by its delegations in the Balkans. While the Brussels-based Commission worked out the CARDS strategy papers, the delegations on the ground were given the task of managing the individual project level (in conjunction with national authorities).[3]

The priority of justice and home affairs in the Stabilisation and Association Process was reflected in the allocations under the CARDS programme – roughly €1 in €6 has been devoted to this heading. In Albania, for instance, about 40 per cent of the CARDS funding between 2000 and 2006 targeted reform priorities in JHA, turning the field into the most prominent area of cooperation (Commission of the European Communities, 2007a: 8).

In line with the set-up of the SAP, the CARDS programme has been based upon a regional strategy and country specific strategies. The regional component has accounted for around 10 per cent of the total CARDS programme. The largest amount of money for regional programmes for the period 2002-2004 (some €117 million of the total of €197 million) was allocated to the field of integrated border management (Commission of the European Communities, 2001d: 18). National CARDS programmes, on which the bulk of financial resources were spent, have been based on country strategy papers and multi-annual indicative programmes for each of the five countries. In relation to justice and home affairs, assistance has been typically granted for projects such as infrastructure support, improvement for asylum procedures, institution and capacity building including the training of staff, judges and lawyers, improvement of reception conditions for asylum seekers, and upgrading national legislative standards in line with the European and international asylum *acquis* (see UNHCR, 2003: 160f).

Table 3.1 EU justice and home affairs in the CARDS programme: total allocation for 2005–2006 and allocation for justice and home affairs

	Total allocation (million €)	JHA allocation (million €)	Percentage of total allocation dedicated to JHA (%)
Albania	89.7	27	30.10
Bosnia and Herzegovina	100.4	25	24.90
Macedonia	85	17	20.00
Serbia	349.5	26.6	7.61
Montenegro	46.5	3	6.45
Kosovo under UNSC 1244	143.5	11.6	8.08
Regional	90	5	5.56
Sum	904.6	115.2	12.73

Notes: (1) Croatia is not listed because it was eligible for pre-accession funding other than CARDS after it began accession talks with the EU in October 2005. It could, however, still take part in the CARDS regional activities for 2005 and 2006.
(2) In the CARDS programme the allocation for Serbia and Montenegro, a total € 16 million, is included under that allotted to the former 'State Union', out of which € 1.8 million was for JHA.
Sources: European Commission, DG Enlargement, CARDS financial statistics and own calculations.

Benchmarking and monitoring
In its annual Progress Reports, the European Commission regularly assesses the performance of the Western Balkan states. First introduced in April 2002, these annual reports carefully list achievements, enervations and tasks, and monitor the implementation of the short- and medium-term priorities that are set out in the European or Accession Partnerships. Each country report contains a chapter on cooperation in justice and home affairs, in which the Commission assesses the progress of the target country in coming closer to the EU's JHA priorities as defined. In addition, the Commission writes an annual report on all SAP participating states. A particular and highly important aspect of monitoring is the European Commission's opinion on a country's application for membership (also known as the *avis*). So far, the Commission has expressed its opinion in two cases, namely concerning Croatia (Commission of the European Communities, 2004c) and Macedonia (Commission of the European Communities, 2005b). These reports are very powerful because they form the basis on which the Council decides whether to grant an applicant country with candidate status.

The instrument of benchmarking becomes important after a Western Balkan country has shifted its status from a potential to a real candidate country, and thus is able to start accession talks with the EU. When the EU member states decide, upon a Commission recommendation, whether to open a chapter of the *acquis* for negotiations, they may include benchmarks to be met by the candidate country before the concrete negotiations can be opened. Benchmarking is a new tool of the sixth enlargement round, and its purpose is to 'improve the quality of negotiations, by providing incentives for the candidate country to *undertake* necessary *reforms at an early stage*' (Commission of the European Communities, 2006c: 6, emphasis added).

Obviously, this visible and rigorous approach has been adopted to avoid any suspension of necessary reforms, similar to what the EU experienced in the late stages of Bulgaria's and Romania's accession negotiations. So far, this mechanism only concerns Croatia, for which some screening reports, including the one on 'justice, freedom and security', have led to the stipulation of benchmarks to be attained before negotiations on the respective chapters could begin.

Advice and twinning

Twinning aims at helping the respective countries bring their administrative and democratic institutions in line with European standards. The twinning programme was invented for the Eastern enlargement round and has since been extended to the Western Balkans (Tulmets, 2005). It typically involves the secondment of civil servants from EU member states to work as advisers to beneficiary institutions for a period of at least twelve months. During this period, the advisers help work on institution building programmes. In relation to justice and home affairs, the first twinning programme in the region was the project 'Integrated Border Management: Border Police', implemented in Croatia with Slovenian and German twinning partners between 2002 and 2004. By 2003, around a dozen twinning programmes were running or in preparation in only two of the SAP countries, namely Croatia and Albania. The 2003 Thessaloniki Agenda stated that this situation was insufficient and that the twinning programme had to be enlarged in order to include all the states (Council of the European Union, 2003a).

Additionally, SAP countries became eligible for technical assistance from the Technical Assistance Information Exchange Office (TAIEX). TAIEX was originally set up as part of the pre-accession strategy for the Eastern enlargement to provide technical assistance to candidate countries in bringing their systems in line with Community legislation. The TAIEX programme was designed to react to emerging problems, e.g. an increase in human trafficking, at short notice. As regards JHA, the programme has covered several issue areas such as financial crime, corruption, trafficking and money-laundering measures. The overall objectives of the network activities through the TAIEX programme were to upgrade the standards of policing in the region, to strengthen the regional aspects of policing in the fight against organised crime, to improve management of the borders and to reform the judiciary (Montanaro-Jankovski, 2005: 21).

Gate-keeping: accession to negotiations and further stages in the accession process
The most powerful mechanism to induce changes is 'gate-keeping', that is to allow (or not) a country to proceed on the step-by-step road towards EU membership.

The Stabilisation and Association Process is in each case a bilateral affair between the EU and the applicant country. The EU takes the initiative in the sense that it first has to judge whether the country in question is ready to proceed. The phased strategy ranges from the establishment of a Consultative Taskforce and a Feasibility Study on a Stabilisation and Association Agreement (SAA), to the beginning, conclusion and finally the ratification of this agreement. The Stabilisation and Association Agreements are at the centrepiece of the Stabilisation and Association Process and establish a formal contractual relationship with the Union over the transitional period considered necessary to adopt core EU standards and rules (Pippan, 2004: 233–38). The EU attaches high salience to Stabilisation and Association Agreements and sees them as a chief means to ensure (top-down) reforms:

> The Stabilisation and Association Agreements, then, are posited on respect for the conditionality of the Stabilisation and Association Process agreed by the Council. But they also bring with them a dynamic means of operationalising that conditionality and give the EU the leverage necessary to get the country to adopt genuine reforms with a view to achieving the immediate objectives of the agreements. The mechanisms of the Agreements themselves will enable the EU to prioritise reforms, shape them according to models, to address and solve problems, and to monitor implementation. (Council of the European Union, 2001a)

Each Stabilisation and Association Agreement includes a specific title on justice and home affairs that provides for intense cooperation on issues such as reinforcing the rule of law, migration and asylum, money laundering and illicit drugs. A salient aspect of the title is dedicated to the field of 'prevention and control of illegal immigration', whereby the contracting parties agree to readmit any of their own nationals illegally residing in the other parties' territories. In addition, the EU reserves the right of the 'Stabilisation and Association Council [to recommend] additional subjects for cooperation under this Article' (see for instance Art. 77 of Croatia's SAA).

The proper implementation of the SAA opens the way for the next step in the rapprochement process, namely the application for membership. Following the application, and based on the Commission's opinion (*avis*), the EU may decide to grant the applicant country real 'candidate status'. This approval is an important political sign and implies, in practical terms, that the now-to-be applicant country can use EU assistance 'in all areas relevant to the ability of the country to assume the obligation of membership, such as the preparation for the implementation of the structural funds' (Commission of the European Communities, 2005c: 11). The candidate status is a necessary, but insufficient pre-condition for opening the concrete accession negotiations – the next step on the road to the EU.

Before the negotiations for EU accession can start, the applicant country is supposed to reach a sufficient degree of general compliance with the Copenhagen Criteria and full cooperation with the International Criminal Tribunal for the former Yugoslavia (ICTY). Unless the Commission is satisfied with the country's performance in complying with these conditions, the European Council will not agree to open the negotiations.

Table 3.2 State of relations between the Western Balkan states and the EU (as of January 2010)

	Stabilisation and Association Agreement		Application for membership	Candidate country	Accession negotiations
	Date of Signature	*Entered into force*			
Albania	June 2006	April 2009	April 2009	–	–
Bosnia-Herzegovina	June 2008	–	–	–	–
Croatia	October 2001	February 2005	February 2003	June 2004	October 2005
Kosovo	–	–	–	–	–
Macedonia	April 2001	April 2004	March 2004	December 2005	–
Montenegro	October 2007	–	December 2008	–	–
Serbia	April 2008	–	December 2009	–	–

Source: European Commission, DG for Enlargement.

The legal affiliation of the target third countries with the EU differs therefore in the various stages of the Stabilisation and Association Process:

1. Treaty-based institutional affiliation
The signing of the Stabilisation and Association Agreements is a treaty-based procedure that opens the way to a relatively close institutional affiliation. In the wake of such an agreement, several institutions and sub-institutions are installed. The most visible one is the Stabilisation and Association Council, where ministers of the EU meet their SAP counterparts. Although this meeting has high symbolic significance (namely, to belong to the 'European family of nation states'), the content is 'precooked and rather low in substance' (interview EU7, 10 February 2006, Brussels). The SAA Council usually takes place in side-talks at a Foreign Affairs Council and lasts for around two hours. The real work takes place at the various Stabilisation and Association Committees (high official level) and at several Sub-Committees (technical level) installed hierarchically below the former. In these forums, ordered according to policy areas, officials from the Commission meet their counterparts from the Western Balkans and examine the progress made in

implementing the EU's pre-accession strategy. According to a Commission official, the dynamic of these meetings is comparable to a school class with the 'pupil' presenting the 'homework' conducted at home and the Commission officials in the role of 'teachers', judging the quality of the measures taken (interview EU3, 6 February 2006, Brussels). The last institution installed in the wake of the Stabilisation and Association Agreement is the Joint Parliamentary Committee, involving EU and Western Balkan members of parliament.

2. Institutionalised dialogues

One level below in terms of institutional affiliation are the so-called Institutionalised Dialogues. They are non-treaty based and relevant for the countries that have not yet signed a Stabilisation and Association Agreement. They have slightly different names, such as EU–Albania Consultative Task Force (CTF), EU/Bosnia and Herzegovina Consultative Task Force, or Enhanced Permanent Dialogue (EPD) with Serbia and Montenegro. However, they are all essentially the same thing, namely a non-treaty based institutional framework to monitor reform and to affiliate them with the EU. The meetings are co-chaired by the Council Presidency/Commission and the respective minister of foreign affairs of the Western Balkan state and usually take place every 2 or 3 months.

3. Ad-hoc meetings

The weakest form of institutional affiliations is ad-hoc meetings. They take place on an ad-hoc basis when the Commission wants to get closer information on, say, the asylum sector and travels into one of the countries.

4. The special form: the EU–Western Balkan Forum

A special form of institutional affiliation is the EU–Western Balkan Forum, which was established after the 2003 EU–Western Balkans summit in Thessaloniki (European Council, 2003). Its creation was one of the main political messages of the summit to dispel the doubts of the Western Balkan countries about whether the EU was serious about their prospective joining of the Union. The forum is to meet annually on the level of foreign and JHA ministers and should facilitate high-level political exchange between the EU and the SAP countries.[4]

In brief, the entire Stabilisation and Association process with its manifold rapprochement steps is therefore quite tedious – one scholar called it the 'rocky road to Europe' (Pippan, 2004). Therefore, as one observer noted, it is very important for the EU 'to keep up the momentum' (interview EU3, 6 February 2006, Brussels). This exhortation refers to the need to provide the right incentives at the right time to prevent doubts concerning the EU's sincerity about the regions' integration. Rewards in terms of advancing on the step-by-step process can be given to one country but may be seen as a signal to all SAP countries. For instance, when Croatia was granted the status of a candidate, the EU intended to give a positive sign and incentive to all the other countries in the region as well (ibid).

The strengthening of operational links in justice and home affairs

A particular feature of EU justice and home affairs cooperation is the importance of operational cooperation between national law enforcement bodies, often in conjunction with specialised agencies and bodies.[5] Scholars called this phenomenon 'intense transgovernmentalism' (Wallace, 2000, Lavenex and Wallace, 2005, Lavenex, 2009). This term is used to grasp the operational cooperation networks below the level of heads of state and government (such as ministerial officials or members of police forces), which have a certain degree of autonomy and involve only marginally the supranational EU institutions.

The EU has increasingly opened these network activities for outside countries, including for the Western Balkans countries. Contrary to the ENP participating states, where the extension of the EU transgovernmental networks was seen as a 'vehicle for policy transfer through "softer means"' (Lavenex and Wichmann, 2009: 83), the establishment of operational cooperation between the EU and the Western Balkans was framed as an integral requirement of the Stabilisation and Association Process and as a precondition to prepare for membership, a point which is well reflected in the EU's external JHA strategy of December 2005:

> The prospect of enlargement is an effective way to align with EU standards in justice and home affairs in candidate countries and those with a European perspective, both through the adoption and implementation of the acquis and through improvements in operational contacts and co-operation. (Council of the European Union, 2005d: 6)

Concretely, the EU sought on the one hand to foster the operational cooperation and networking *between* the EU and Western Balkans, and on the other hand to create regional cooperation structures and networks *within* the region.

As regards the first objective, the EU's specialised agencies were of particular relevance. Europol has developed a Western Balkans strategy and negotiated cooperation agreements that regulate the reception and transmission of Europol information and the conclusion of confidentiality agreements. Through exchanging information and data between Europol and these countries, the EU hoped to improve their understanding of regional organised crime networks and to increase their means of fighting against them (Delevic, 2007: 87). Europol signed a strategic cooperation agreement with Albania, Bosnia and Herzegovina, Macedonia, Montenegro and Serbia and an operational agreement with Croatia (Council of the European Union, 2008c: 8).[6] Europol, together with the EU's border management agency Frontex, has also conducted risk assessments and determined the risk routes where joint investigation teams should operate (Council of the European Union, 2006b: 10).

The information channels were further strengthened when member states' liaison officers were asked to provide information for Europol's threat assessments on organised crime in the Balkans. This network of immigration officers, which the EU started to build up in 2001 (as the first such network worldwide), was supposed to establish closer contacts with the authorities of the region 'with a view to contributing to the prevention and combating of illegal immigration, the return of illegal immigrants and the management of legal migration' (Council of the European Union, 2004a). In 2003 the Council suggested broadening the agenda of the liaison officers to cover all areas of organised crime (Council of the European Union, 2003b: 5).

The second objective pursued by the EU was the strengthening of operational cooperation links in the region. The absence of regional structures and networks to tackle common cross-border problems was regarded as a key problem in the JHA policy field. Some observers have also witnessed a lack of will to cooperate. According to an international official who has worked for many years in the region,

> one of the most important things that is creating a lot of problems is cross-border cooperation. It may even concern just basic things: sharing information, consultancy, telling the other side if you heard that on that particular green border area, there will be thirty Chinese people trying to cross. 'We are trying to stop them on our side, but in case they get through, you should stop them on your side.' Things like that. The typical situation in the Western Balkans is that even the wrong information is given on purpose. There is a tendency to somehow not cooperate on purpose. (Interview IO6, 29 November 2006, Vienna)

Against this background, the EU has actively promoted the strengthening and/or creation of regional cooperation networks among these states. In effect, the EU sought to reproduce its internal mode of cooperation in justice and home affairs in the regional setting of the Western Balkans. A case in point has been the Southeast European Cooperative Initiative (SECI) Regional Centre for Combating Trans-border Crime, an operative collaboration between customs and police authorities in the region. Seated in Bucharest, the SECI Centre should help to fight trans-border crime in the region and is, according to Hubert Pirker (2006), the former chairman of the Stability Pact's Initiative against Organised Crime, an attempt to set-up a 'Europol for South-Eastern Europe'. SECI is an operational organisation that seeks to facilitate the exchange of information between law enforcement agencies in and beyond the region. Similar to Europol, it issues analysis and reports and coordinates regional operations within the frames of seven specialised Task Forces that address matters of drugs and human trafficking, stolen vehicles, smuggling and customs fraud, financial and computer crime, terrorism and container security. The EU ministers of justice and home affairs tasked Europol to cooperate with the SECI Centre (Council of the European Union, 2006f). The centre is assisted in operational matters by a network of prosecutors, called the Southeast European Prosecutors Advisory Group (SEEPAG), who seek to facilitate judicial cooperation and the exchange of information in trans-border crime investigations. SEEPAG has a rotating chairmanship and consists of twelve participating countries in the region.

Another EU-guided initiative concerned the promotion of transgovernamental police cooperation similar to the EU-internal model. In the project 'Police Cooperation Convention for South East Europe', implemented in the first six months of 2006, the participating states Albania, Bosnia and Herzegovina, Macedonia, Moldova, Montenegro, Romania and Serbia adopted a multilateral convention for the improvement of police collaboration in the region. The official aim was to 'adopt the Schengen standards in South East Europe through the conclusion of a multilateral convention' (Council of the European Union, 2006e). The convention governs the exchange of information, introduces new forms of cross-border cooperation such as cross-border pursuit, and clarifies a range of further measures such as the exchange of DNA data or the establishment of joint investigation teams.

The Stabilisation and Association Process has been closely linked to another EU-led initiative that aimed at deepening regional cooperation in South-Eastern Europe: The Stability Pact for South-Eastern Europe. In February 2008, the Stability Pact officially ceased to exist and was transformed into the Regional Cooperation Council (RCC), intended to be a truly regionally owned and led framework to support Euro-Atlantic integration.

The Stability Pact for South-Eastern Europe

The launch of the Stability Pact for South-Eastern Europe was linked to the Kosovo crisis of 1998/99, which prompted the EU to rethink its strategy for the area of former Yugoslavia. The objective was to develop a novel, proactive and forward-looking conflict prevention strategy for the region (Friis and Murphy, 2000, Elbasani, 2008: 7–8).

Although initiated by the EU within its Common Foreign and Security Policy in 1999, the Stability Pact was not directly an EU instrument but rather a framework agreement to develop a shared strategy for all international actors in South-Eastern Europe. The Stability Pact was hence not another international organisation, but served as 'a platform for international cooperation and [included] a political commitment by the participating partners to engage in a process of promoting stability and growth in South Eastern Europe' (Pippan, 2004: 227). More than 40 participating countries and organisations signed the founding document and committed themselves to supporting the countries of South-Eastern Europe 'in their efforts to foster peace, democracy, respect for human rights and economic prosperity in order to achieve stability in the region' (Stability Pact, 1999).

The Pact relied on the Special Coordinator, Erhard Busek, a former Austrian politician, and his team of around 30 specialists, who were funded by the EU and situated in Brussels alongside the European Parliament. Appointed by the EU in 2001, Erhard Busek was the second Special Coordinator and successor of Bodo Hombach, a German diplomat. Erhard Busek held the position from the beginning of 2002 until the closure of the Stability Pact in 2008. Organisationally, the Stability Pact was comprised of a Regional Table, the most important political instrument, and chaired by the Special Coordinator and three Working Tables, hierarchically underneath the Regional Table. It was in charge of reaching an agreement on the overall direction of the Pact and officially took place once a year (although it was often held twice a year). The three Working Tables covered specific themes:

- Working Table I: Democratisation and human rights;
- Working Table II: Economic reconstruction, cooperation and development;
- Working Table III: Security issues (with two sub-tables: security and defence, and justice and home affairs).

In articulating its approach, the Stability Pact had explicitly chosen the opposite of the top-down method of the Stabilisation and Association Process:

> A special feature is that at Regional and Working Tables, representatives of South-Eastern European Countries are, for the first time, on an equal footing with those of international organisations and financial institutions in advising on the future of their region and in setting priorities concerning the content of all three working areas. (Stability Pact for South-Eastern Europe, 2008)

Since its initiation, the Pact could refer to certain achievements, particularly in the area of regional cooperation. The Pact had the chance to reinforce intra-regional trade, did much to promote infrastructure development and was able to revitalise the South-East European Cooperation Process (SEECP). Additionally, it was able to secure funding for projects worth €5.4 billion at two regional conferences.

The high expectations of the Stability Pact at its launch were not entirely fulfilled, however. An employee of the special coordinator's team described the dilemma between inflated expectations and its capabilities as follows:

> Mr. Blair was calling the Stability Pact a 'new Marshall plan for the reconstruction of the region'. The countries were exactly expecting this; they were hoping for quick solutions to all of their problems. But the Stability Pact is not another financial institution, but can be mainly considered as a political instrument for lobbying in favour of the region. The aim has always been to bring together all the possible investors and the countries of the region and furthermore, to help the countries to come closer to the European Union. But this takes time. (Interview SP3, 21 March 2004, Brussels)

The unfulfilled expectations contributed to the some early disappoint-ment and criticism. Over time, however, the Stability Pact managed to lower the high expectations according to the actual capabilities and to develop itself into a regionally owned forum. This development was facilitated by several factors, including in particular the strong leadership of the Special Coordinator Erhard Busek and an improved political and socio-economic situation in the Balkans. Several observers noted that the Stability Pact's role in promoting regional cooperation and stabilisation was significant. 'Regional stabilisation has certainly been achieved to the extent to which the SP was able to support it, and the concept of regional cooperation is now firmly embedded in the region at all levels of government and society' (Delevic, 2007: 20).

Justice and home affairs in the Stability Pact

Justice and home affairs has held an essential place in the Stability Pact for South-Eastern Europe and its successor organisation, the Regional Cooperation Council. The SP's sub-table on justice and home affairs was split into five main areas of action: 1) organised crime; 2) anti-corruption; 3) the Migration, Asylum, Refugees Regional Initiative (MARRI); 4) police coopera-tion; 5) mine action. Additionally, there was the issue of border security and management, which lay across these sub-tables and constituted an extra field.

The most visible result of the work of the Stability Pact in the JHA field was the launch of regional initiatives, some of which have continued to be active beyond the end of the Stability Pact. The Stability Pact Regional Anti-Corruption Initiative, then renamed Regional Anticorruption Initiative (RAI), has focused on high-level corruption and giving incentives for imple-menting international anti-corruption standards (Stability Pact, 2008: 19). The Stability Pact Initiative against Organised Crime (SPOC) sought to strengthen regional capacities to fight cross-border organised crime. To permanently provide legal assistance to the SECI Centre in Bucharest, the SPOC secretariat was integrated into the legal department of SECI in January 2008. Other initiatives included the Police Forum Initiative (PFI), which has been a framework for cooperation between interior ministries, police services and international partners in South-Eastern Europe, and the Regional Mine Action Group, which promoted a coordinated approach to mine action. The latter task force was closed in 2004.

The Migration, Asylum, Refugees Regional Initiative (MARRI) was given the task of developing a more comprehensive approach to the related issues of migration, asylum and refugee return in the region. MARRI was actually used as the first initiative that should realise the frequently cited 'regional ownership'. In July 2004, the main office of MARRI was transferred to Skopje as a part of the South-East European Cooperation Process (SEECP). For international actors, 'MARRI is [therefore] kind of a test case on how this works out for all the other initiatives, how it goes, in which directions does it develop, and so on' (interview SP1, 7 February 2006, Brussels). The idea was for the countries to prove their capability to cooperate on their own, to define their own priorities and to contribute to the stabilisation and improvement of the situation in the participating states.

Intersecting the justice and home affairs sub-table, the improvement of border security management became a priority issue following a significant increase of irregular transit migration through the region in 2000. The June 2001 Working Table III meeting in Zagreb cleared the way for the Stability Pact to be involved in this issue area:

> The challenges confronting the five states involved in the Stabilisation and Association Process in, at one and the same time, reforming their border control systems and combating growing trans-frontier crime, are enormous. They can not be met without sustained long-term effort by the international community to assist in adapting the systems to common standards, notably on the basis of EU and Schengen norms, and with heavy financial and infrastructure support. Obviously, such assistance is also in the self-interest of the international community at large, as weak borders control in the region gives space for organised crime and illegal migration, affecting European and other Western countries as a whole. (Stability Pact for South-Eastern Europe, 2001: 4)

In line with its mandate, the Stability Pact concentrated on the regional aspects of improving external border control systems. In pursuit of this objective, the Pact cooperated closely with the intergovernmental Budapest Process.[7] In 2000, the two institutions agreed to transfer some of the responsibilities of the Budapest Process to the Stability Pact. The conclusions of the Working Table III meeting in Sofia officially announced the objective to further integrate the 'Budapest process in the work of the Stability Pact' (quoted in ICMPD, 2000: 16). As a result, the Working Group on South East Europe of the Budapest Process was transformed into the Border Guard Task Force for South East Europe, hosted within the structures of the Stability Pact.[8] The Task Force's activities included a gap analysis on national and regional management and development of border control, a seminar for senior border guard officials on EU visa and readmission standards, a study visit to Austria aimed at becoming more familiar with the Schengen *acquis*, and a quick impact regional meeting on the border guarding reform process, based on the EU's integrated border management concept. Its funding was mainly provided by the Norwegian government (ICMPD, 2005: 1).

The efforts of the Task Force were no longer continued following a restructuring of Working Table III. Most of the tasks were transferred to the Ohrid Border Process (see below) and some were also assumed by the Migration, Asylum, Refugees Regional Initiative of the Stability Pact.

Transforming the Stability Pact into the Regional Cooperation Council

At the Regional Table staged in Belgrade in May 2006, a far-reaching decision was taken with regard to the future of the Pact: the Stability Pact for South-

Eastern Europe should be phased out in its current form and be transformed into a Regional Cooperation Council with the South-Eastern European countries gradually taking over ownership of the entire cooperation processes.

The task of the RCC was defined as the 'the facilitation of regional co-operation and support for European and Euro-Atlantic integration, while ensuring continued involvement of the donor community, thus preserving the legacy of the Pact' (Stability Pact for South-Eastern Europe, 2006). Additionally, the conclusion stated that the Council should closely work with the South-East European Cooperation Process (SEECP), the second major framework of sub-regional cooperation.[9] The idea behind the transformation was, according to the Stability Pact's Special Coordinator Erhard Busek, to 'set the stage for a new era of co-operation in South Eastern Europe, one of real regional ownership' (Busek, 2007).

In the Regional Cooperation Council, the South-Eastern European countries are themselves in charge of setting the agenda and providing money and personnel. Out of the €3 million budget, the EU finances a third, equally shared with the SEECP participating states and the rest of the donors of the Stability Pact. The South-East European Cooperation Process partly owns the RCC and shares its seat and administrational structure in Sarajevo. In addition to the twenty-five employees in the RCC secretariat in Sarajevo, seven liaison officers are posted in the former seat of the Stability Pact in Brussels (the premises have been kept to maintain close contacts with the EU institutions). The Secretary General of the RCC chairs the meetings of SEECP and the RCC and officially represents both of them at international forums.

At the Zagreb summit of May 2007, the head of states and governments of the SEECP countries agreed to appoint the Croat Hido Biscevic, State Secretary at the Ministry of Foreign Affairs and European Integration of Croatia, to be the first Sectary General of the RCC (Biscevic, 2008). In one of his first statements as Secretary General, Hido Biscevic advanced the view that 'enhanced regional ownership and continued international support in the transition phase' were the pre-conditions for the success of the Regional Cooperation Council (Biscevic, 2008).

The countries of the region identified six priority cooperation areas for the RCC and its secretariat: (1) economic and social development; (2) infrastructure and energy; (3) justice and home affairs; (4) security cooperation; (5) building human capital; and (6) parliamentary cooperation (as an overarching theme). At the final meeting of the Stability Pact Regional Table in Sofia on 27 February 2008, the participating states signed a joint declaration on the establishment of the Regional Cooperation Council, which was the formal handover from the Stability Pact to the RCC.

The inauguration of the Regional Cooperation Council was overshadowed by political controversies on how to deal with Kosovo's bid for independence. Instead of dealing with issues of regional cooperation, the dominant topic at the Sofia summit was Serbia's warning to all the other participating states that they should not recognise the independence of Kosovo. While emphasising that Belgrade had 'no intention of obstructing the important work' of the Regional Cooperation Council, the Serbian Foreign Minister Vuk Jeremic stressed that the 'minimum requirement' for Serbia's involvement was that 'the procedural status quo be maintained' (quoted in Setimes, 2008a). In Stability Pact meetings, Kosovo was represented by personnel of the UN Interim Administration Mission in Kosovo (UNMIK).

In addition to the disputed status of Kosovo, the dependence on external financing and a lack of own resources may jeopardise the independence and the functioning of the Regional Cooperation Council. However, there is also reason for optimism, as regional cooperation has steadily improved since the 1999 Kosovo war. According to one of the final statements of the Stability Pact (2008: 4), 'the message that "regional cooperation pays" – politically, economically and socially – is now understood and appreciated by all'.

The Ohrid Border Process: streamlining international efforts

The EU's efforts to improve border security in the Western Balkans were embedded in a broader regional initiative, which came to be known as the Ohrid Border Process. The initiative was the attempt of NATO, the Organization for Security and Cooperation in Europe (OSCE), the EU and the Stability Pact to coordinate their activities and to commit the Western Balkans to modernising their external border security regimes.

The beginnings of the Ohrid Process on Border Security and Management, the official name, can be traced back to a NATO initiative launched in early 2002, which aimed at improving security in the Macedonia–Kosovo–Albania border triangle. The concrete process was initiated one year later at the regional conference on border security and management on 22–23 May 2003, when representatives of NATO, the OSCE, the EU and the Stability Pact met with specialists from the Western Balkan countries in the Macedonian town of Ohrid. The process was based upon the implementation of concrete measures outlined in two founding documents, the Common Platform and the Way Forward Document, both of which were signed at the Ohrid conference.

The Common Platform Document served as a memorandum of understanding between the four partner organisations. They agreed to pursue three political objectives: first, to establish open but controlled and secure borders in accordance with the European Union's border management model for the region; second, to promote further stabilisation by strengthening the rule of law, institutional capacity and regional cooperation; and third, to take advantage of advice and support on military issues regarding border security and smuggling interdiction in some parts of the region (particularly the areas where NATO troops had been dispatched) within the overall framework of the security sector reform (Common Platform, 2003: 1–2). The Western Balkans' border policing was to be re-structured based on the principles of democratic control, efficiency and proper implementation.

The Way Forward Document, in turn, went into more detail about the concrete measures to which these countries were expected to subscribe. The EU's border model was accepted by all actors involved as the overarching long-term objective.

> On the basis of the European border model, the Western Balkan countries undertake the commitment to develop an Integrated Border Security approach, which covers all aspects of border policy and aims at promoting internal security, combating illegal immigration, preventing the trafficking of human beings and economic exploitation of migrants. (Way Forward Document, 2003: 2)

In a first step, the countries were urged to develop initial regional cooperation instruments and to adhere to pre-defined country-specific objectives. The objectives differed depending on the domestic conditions of the country concerned but referred basically to three major tasks: the demilitarisation of the borders and the handing over of border control to a civilian chain of command; the development and implementation of integrated border management strategies and supplementary action plans; and the improvement of cross-border cooperation. Concerning the time-schedule, the document defined that 2006 would represent the end of the transitional period during which the counties were to implement the short- and medium-term commitments (ibid).

In terms of its setup, the Ohrid Border Process was constructed as a clear top-down process in which the international organisations sought to 'download' pre-defined policies on the partner countries. The founding document outlined these basic principles by stating that 'the four Partner Organisations [...] have agreed upon common political goals, objectives, principles and instruments to which they propose that the Western Balkan countries subscribe at the Ohrid Conference' (Common Platform, 2003: 1). They emphasised, however, that the Western Balkan states were previously consulted and that their remarks were taken into account. A European official involved in the Ohrid Border Process described the beginning of the process as follows:

> The way it [the Ohrid Border Process] was presented to the countries, they actually had not much choice. If you have to reach standards that are EU and Schengen standards, there is no real debate. If they want to be part of the area, then they have to comply with the standards. What they argue about, is the pace we ask them to keep, and of course financial difficulties they might face and they think we are not supporting enough. (Interview SP2, 7 February 2006, Brussels)

The four partner organisations: EU, NATO, OSCE and Stability Pact
In the context of the Ohrid Border Process, the four partner organisations aimed at complementing one another: with NATO as the chief means to strengthen border control and interdict smuggling in the crisis areas where NATO forces were dispatched; with the EU as the leading actor to develop integrated border management systems in each country; with the OSCE as a 'civilian actor' with a main focus on training and know-how transfer; and with the Stability Pact as a promoter of regional aspects of border management and as a provider of a common roof for the activities of the four partner organisations.

The European Union
The EU's main instrument remained the Stabilisation and Association Process, particularly its integrated border management strategy (see Chapter 2). In the 2003 Way Forward Document, the EU also agreed to provide support within the European Security and Defence Policy, notably with the EU military operation Concordia in Macedonia and the EU police mission in Bosnia and Herzegovina. In the day-to-day application, however, these military and police operations have not reported any of their activities and, as one observer has noted, can therefore be considered only an indirect contribution to the Ohrid Border Process (interview SP2, 7 February 2006, Brussels).

The North Atlantic Treaty Organization
NATO has been strongly engaged in all security-related developments in the region since December 1995, when the NATO-led Implementation Force (IFOR) was dispatched to maintain security and implement the military aspects of the Dayton Peace Accords. The organisation has also dealt with issues of border security or border protection in cases where they have posed a challenge from an overall security point of view.

In the context of the Ohrid Border Process, the representatives of NATO focused their support on 'the parts of the region where for exceptional reasons and on a temporary basis military units are involved in border control and smuggling interdiction activities during a transitional period' (Common Platform, 2003: 4). This applied for Bosnia and Herzegovina, where the NATO-led Stabilisation Force (SFOR), following the IFOR in December 1996, sought to assist the country in reforming its fragmented police forces and policing structures. However, neither the police reform nor the establishment of the State Border Service, which in 2000 became Bosnia and Herzegovina's first state-level police force, were among SFOR's central tasks. In terms of civilian activities, the NATO-led operation focused on minority returns, the support of mine action programmes, the return of displaced persons and the collections of small arms and light weapons.

The major NATO activities and operations in relation to border control and smuggling interdiction took place in Kosovo, where the NATO-led international Kosovo Force (KFOR) had been dispatched following the NATO air campaign against Yugoslavia to halt ethnic cleansing in Kosovo in 1999. KFOR also sought to improve the cooperation and coordination between local units involved in border security along the international borders of Albania and Kosovo. For this task, local border units were urged to sign the Temporary Operating Procedures Agreement (TOPA) that should prevent all incidents along the border by clarifying what to do in certain situations (Sotnichenko, 2003: 1). The main stipulations of these agreements have referred to confidence-building measures such as coordination exchange, communication and information exchange.

NATO also agreed to provide the relevant authorities with advice on the military aspects of reforming and restructuring border security. In Macedonia, NATO forces were dispatched in the wake of the 2001 inter-ethnic conflict to disarm the insurgents of the National Liberation Army and contribute to the return of security in the crisis areas (Operations Essential Harvest and Amber Fox). During the time of their dispatch (2001–2003), NATO assisted the Macedonian authorities in the reform of their security sector and liaised with KFOR on border security issues.

NATO's engagement in border protection shows that military involvement can be legitimate, provided that certain criteria are met. Within the context of the Ohrid Border Process, the EU and NATO established a common working group charged to define a common approach on border security when military is involved. Nevertheless, as Alice Hills points out, 'while officials from the two organisations may be in agreement, those from the region often take a harsher view of what is seen as evidence of double standards on the part of the EU, which tolerates NATO's involvement but insists that involving indigenous military forces in guarding is unacceptable' (Hills, 2004a: 40).

The Organization for Security and Cooperation in Europe
The Common Platform Document suggested that the OSCE, with its comprehensive concept of security and its experience in the field, should contribute to the Ohrid Border Process by focusing on the civilian aspects of border security and management: (1) advisory activities and training for the border police, (2) assistance with and facilitation of institution-building; and (3) promotion of regional cooperation, particularly cross-border bilateral cooperation (Common Platform, 2003: 4–5).

In response to the document, the OSCE developed the South-Eastern Europe Crossborder Cooperation Programme (OSCCP), which provided objectives and principles for the organisation's activities in this area. The programme was implemented in a series of eleven three-day regional seminars that covered issues such as inter-agency cooperation, cross-border crime and illegal migration, technical requirements and the surveillance of blue borders. The objective was, according to the OSCE's programme manager Anton Petrenko, to 'enable border officials to learn from each other's national experiences and to adopt cross-border cooperation agreements in such areas as the exchange of operational data and the establishment of border police liaison officers with neighbouring countries' (Petrenko, 2006: 10).

Completed in 2005, the programme was widely regarded as a success. According to a survey assessing the activities' impact, most respondents of the Western Balkans stated that the seminars had enhanced their professional knowledge, supported their networking activities and restored mutual confidence. The survey, however, also revealed what might be improved in future activities: a stronger consideration of the countries' specific circumstances and resources, more input on the experiences of (advanced) countries in the region, stronger efforts to avoid duplications between the international partners and, probably most importantly, the attempt to entrust more ownership of the process to the countries themselves (for the results, see Petrenko, 2006: 11).

In addition to the OSCE's involvement in the framework of the South-Eastern Europe Cross-border Cooperation Programme, the organisation's missions in the region played an additional role in assisting the Western Balkans' reform efforts. A geographical focus was placed on the border triangle of Macedonia–Kosovo–Albania. The respective OSCE missions concentrated on some salient aspects of the countries' domestic reform process in border security and management. In Albania, the OSCE mission focused on enhancing the operational capability and effectiveness of the Albanian border and migration police in dealing with cross-border and organised crime. The OSCE spill-over monitor mission in Skopje set priorities for the border demilitarisation process and the establishment of the country's civilian border police. And the OSCE mission in Kosovo, where border security had been the exclusive responsibility of the UN mission in Kosovo and the KFOR, had been primarily concerned with training Kosovo police service cadets.

The Stability Pact for South-Eastern Europe
The Stability Pact's contribution to the Ohrid Border Process has been to act as a secretary or a kind of 'clearinghouse for receiving and disseminating relevant information' (interview SP2, 7 February 2006, Brussels). The resources of the SP were quite limited, however, bearing in mind that only 1–2 persons were entrusted to support the process. In addition, the Pact's other initiatives, such as the Police Forum or the Migration, Asylum, Refugees Regional Initiative were to assist the Western Balkans in their effort to meet the SAP obligations and foster bilateral and regional cooperation in the broader spectrum.

Other contributions: The Geneva Centre for the Democratic Control of Armed Forces

The Geneva Centre for the Democratic Control of Armed Forces (DCAF), a Geneva-based international foundation with 46 member states, was officially associated with the Ohrid Border Process. According to an official involved, this meant that it attended the meetings but did not have access to all the documents circulated among the partner organisations (interview SP2, 7 February 2006, Brussels).

The DCAF has established close cooperation links with the Western Balkan states to assist them in the creation of efficient border security systems. To this end, the centre has provided assistance 'that is as comprehensive as possible, ranging from national capacity-building through to the development of regional cooperation mechanisms' (DCAF, 2007). From 2001–2007, the DCAF Border Security Programme was funded with an annual budget of 1.3 million Swiss francs and offered various activities including a series of workshops entitled 'Lessons learned from the establishment of Border Security Systems'. The seminars brought together specialists from South-Eastern Europe, the EU and Switzerland and dealt with the lessons learnt when states were developing their own border security systems. Through this, the 'strategic needs [are addressed] in the process of creating new, civilian controlled and efficient border security systems built on European standards. They [i.e. the workshops] led to each country drafting a strategy paper and implementation plans for the creation of a civilian-led border police' (Way Forward Document, 2003: 18). The DCAF encompassed through its efforts the entire Western Balkan region, yet Croatia and Macedonia took a special position due to their status as candidate countries for EU membership. They not only benefited from the workshops but were 'able to assist their neighbours through the sharing of their own national experiences' as well (DCAF, 2007: 1).

In interviews, it was emphasised that DCAF was an important player in the Western Balkans regarding the field of border security. The centre had sufficient financial resources to implement its strategic objectives and had access to the highest-ranking political actors. The centre considered its activities to be an effort to bring the Western Balkan states closer to European standards, and hence to support the EU's efforts within the Stabilisation and Association Process. Still, according to a consortium partner implementing the EU's regional IBM project, 'DCAF due to its organisational structure and mandate is using different definitions and concepts. The countries receive a lot of assistance from different organisations and donors; not all of them are necessarily in line with EU standards. Here, there are sometimes conflicting messages sent to the Western Balkans and this can be perceived as problematic' (interview IO7, 11 December 2006, Vienna).

Assessing the Ohrid Border Process

According to officials involved, the Ohrid Border Process was clearly added value. The cooperation on the formal and informal levels was described as successful. In the day-to-day application, the four partner organisations agreed upon a certain level of role sharing. The EU provided for the general guidelines and the political framework, whereas the OSCE and NATO were more involved in concrete actions through their field missions. The Stability Pact's main task was to offer a common framework that the other organisations could refer to. The Western Balkans, in turn, installed a network of national contact points made up of heads or deputy heads of their national border police authorities; comparable contact points were established in the four partner organisations as well. The contact persons were invited to report on their progress or persisting challenges at review meetings, several of which were held (Belgrade in November 2003, Tirana in October 2004, Sarajevo in November 2005, and Podgorica in November 2006). In 2006 the four partner institutions officially assessed the Ohrid Border Process by sending a questionnaire to all countries involved. While the assessment was undertaken, European officials were already aware of the signs that 'the Ohrid Border Process has not achieved all its goals and this can be a reason to maintain the process, maybe with more powers, maybe with less' (interview SP2, 7 February 2006, Brussels).

In January 2007, the Stability Pact's director of Working Table III Pieter Verbeek presented the findings of the assessment report to the EU's Council Working Group on the Western Balkans (Stability Pact for South-Eastern Europe, 2007). Concerning the first objective – the demilitarisation of the borders – the official considered the results as 'fairly satisfying' (ibid: 1). Macedonia completed its process of transfer in August 2006. In Serbia, full completion was scheduled for the first half of 2007 and in Albania, arguably the country with the weakest border control system, the process was in motion with a mid-term goal to complete civilian control of the borders. In Croatia, the military was never dispatched to the borders so the border demilitarisation process was of no relevance for the country. Concerning the second objective, the drafting of an IBM strategy and an action plan, all countries had already achieved good progress by January 2007. All six countries had adopted a national IBM strategy, although only four of the six had established a corresponding action plan. In addition, all countries but Montenegro had created inter-agency working groups to monitor the implementation of the IBM strategy (ibid: 2). Concerning the third objective of the Ohrid Border Process, the enhancement of cross-border cooperation, the assessment was likely the most difficult to make. The Stability Pact had assessed cross-border cooperation through two measures: the signing of formal agreements with neighbouring countries and practical cooperation on the ground (such as the exchange of information, joint patrols and the exchange of liaison officers). Some countries had signed agreements with some or all neighbours but some had not signed any. Furthermore, the value of these agreements was difficult to assess (ibid: 2). Their content varied from one document to another, and some documents were more comprehensive than others. All countries had initiated practical cross-border cooperation – but again, some were at a more advanced level and some were only at the initial stage.

In view of these results, the Ohrid Border Process was prolonged for one more year to finalise the implementation of the reform commitments. Another result of the assessment report was to produce more tailor-made projects and activities for the countries. These were presented in a Roadmap for 2007 which also encouraged the Western Balkan countries to step up their efforts in the following areas; (1) cross-border cooperation and implementation of the signed international agreements; (2) enhancing the 'integrated approach' with respect to the four central authorities involved in border management (border police, customs, veterinary and phyto-sanitary); (3) risk analysis and threat assessment; and (4) enhanced cooperation with neighbouring EU member states to avoid isolation and to make use of best practices (Stability Pact for South-Eastern Europe, 2007: 3).

A shortcoming of the Ohrid Border Process was the rather superficial coordination among NATO, the OSCE, the EU and the Stability Pact. With the exception of the OSCE, the initiative did not make the four partner institutions change their own policies of border security, but only served as an umbrella into which every organisation brought its own policies. None of them looked into the other organisations' programmes of action in detail. Due to this understanding, the coordination among the four organisations remained in certain aspects on a rather 'superficial level' in the sense that none of them guaranteed the others a full inside account of the results of their activities (interview SP2, 7 February 2006, Brussels).

An issue not mentioned in the official documents but that always existed somehow in the background was the delimitation of the borders. In the context of the Ohrid Border Process, the open demarcation issues of the region were completely factored out, which some actors considered a shortcoming because 'one could say it is a bit strange that we do not deal with that issue when we have the perfect framework to deal with' (interview SP2, 7 February 2006, Brussels). However, the inclusion of open border demarcation issues might have politicised the Ohrid Border Process and thus prevented it from delivering the desired results, particularly with regard to border demilitarisation in the Balkan region.

Concluding remarks

This chapter has assessed the strategies with which the EU has sought to evoke EU rule adoption in justice and home affairs in the Western Balkan states.

The EU has used the lever derived from the prospect of membership to develop a range of conditionality instruments aimed at encouraging these states to initiate reforms and adaptation in domestic justice and home affairs. These conditionality instruments are comparable to the ones used in the Eastern enlargement, yet the Stabilisation and Association Process contains some distinctive features (e.g. more comprehensive conditionality requirements) and new instruments, particularly the instrument of benchmarking, which should provide an incentive to launch reforms at an early stage of accession negotiations.

The Stability Pact for South-Eastern Europe constituted the most prominent European supplement for integrating these states in the Euro-Atlantic structures and institutions. Contrary to the SAP, which was constructed as a clear top-down process, the Stability Pact placed an emphasis on enabling the states of the region to participate on an equal footing. In line with its broader understanding, the Stability Pact promoted regional co-operation in dealing with JHA issues, particularly in fighting organised crime and corruption and in migration issues. In February 2008, the Stability Pact was transformed into a Regional Cooperation Forum, which was set up as a truly regionally owned and led cooperation framework.

A third framework within which the issue of border security in the Balkans was addressed was Ohrid Border Process, which served as a framework for NATO, the OSCE, the EU and the Stability Pact to streamline their activities, and to encourage the Western Balkan countries to develop border management systems that are in line with European standards. Despite some shortcomings, the Ohrid Border Process was an innovative and rather successful initiative and one of the few attempts to bring together different international and Western Balkan states to engage in a joint project aimed at tackling a particular source of instability in the Balkans.

Notes

1 Once the target country managed to shift its status from a potential to a real candidate country, the European Partnership was renamed the Accession Partnership.

2 The instrument of the Action-Oriented Paper seems to falls short of meeting with the high expectations voiced at its launch. The problems partly stem from the way it was brought into existence. Instead of using the working group framework of the Council, the paper was developed in the 'group of friends of the presidency', meaning that not all member states were present, but only those interested in the subject. By avoiding the formalities of the working groups/working parties framework of the Council, the paper could be speedily adopted in only four months (Luif and Riegler, 2006: 15). A side effect of this procedure was that the member states that were not involved in the drafting of the document did not perceive the implementation of the paper as a priority. According to the first Progress Report on the state of the implementation, published in November 2006, only 13 member states and Europol contributed to the report (Council of the European Union, 2006h). In the second report, published in May 2008, 16 member states, and some EU bodies reported on the state of the implementation. This report mirrored a growing frustration among the participating states

by stating that the low turnout 'limits substantially the scope and hinders seriously the value of the exercise' (Council of the European Union, 2008c: 25).

3   An exception constituted Serbia, Montenegro, Kosovo and Macedonia between 2000 and 2008, where the EU's pre-accession programmes were run by the European Agency for Reconstruction (EAR) seated in Thessaloniki.

4   The political relevance of the EU–Western Balkan Forum was questioned, however. The Stability Pact for South-Eastern Europe considered that the forum has 'not lived up to expectations [...] [and should] be reinvigorated and filled with more substance of relevance for the region' (Stability Pact for South-Eastern Europe, 2005: 11).

5   The EU's specialised bodies and agencies like the European Police Office (Europol), the European Agency for the Management of Operational Cooperation at the External Borders (Frontex) and the European Judicial Cooperation Unit (Eurojust) have substantial coordination powers, yet no European agency has the authority to apply coercive measures. Europol and Eurojust, however, have eventually gained some operational powers and may participate in joint investigation teams with the consent of the member state concerned.

6   The strategic agreements regulate the exchange of operational and technical information but exclude the exchange of personal data.

7   The Budapest Process was launched in 1991 with the main aim to better control irregular migration from and through Central and Eastern Europe including, by now, more than 40 governments and 10 international organisations. In recent years, the Budapest Process has increasingly shifted the geographical focus and has addressed challenges of irregular migration in the wider European region, including Russia.

8   The Border Guard Task Force was made up of border guarding experts from the SAP countries, together with national representatives from EU member and non-EU member states, as well as experts from the European Commission and the Council and NATO, UNMIBH and UNHCR. The participating states were Bulgaria, Germany, Hungary, Norway, Romania, Slovenia, Switzerland and the UK.

9   The South-East European Cooperation Process is a non-institutionalised regional cooperation structure founded in 1996, when Bulgaria organised a regional meeting of ministers of foreign affairs. Its *raison d'être* is to provide South-Eastern European states with a regional cooperation framework in domains of common interest.

PART III

The receiving end – governance mode and effectiveness

4

Rule adoption in Croatia

This chapter shifts attention from the EU's policies and strategies to the 'receiving' end of the enlargement process and investigates the dynamics of domestic rule adoption in the case of Croatia. Of the countries subsumed under the Stabilisation and Association Process, Croatia is the most advanced in terms of EU integration, even if its accession process has had its share of controversies and stumbling blocks. The chapter is structured in three parts: first, the procedural and institutional context of EU–Croatian relations is outlined. Next, the analysis presents the ways in which Croatia has reacted to the EU's accession conditions in the field of justice and home affairs. The final part concerns the factors that have driven the country's process of adjusting to the EU.

The procedural and institutional context

Croatia – an 'exceptional' case in the Balkans?

Croatia's history as an independent state began with a war of independence in the early 1990s, with the country struggling for sovereignty and international recognition (see, among others, Magas and Zanic, 2001, Gagnon, 2004). Along with the war in Bosnia, Croatia's war ended with the signing of the Dayton Peace Accords on 14 December 1995.

Following the peace agreement, Croatia ambitiously sought to catch up with the transition countries of Central and Eastern Europe. In economic terms, it indeed made significant progress, managing to achieve rapid growth in its GDP (6 per cent per year from 1995 to 1997, before slowing down to under 3 per cent in 1998). In political terms, however, civil and political rights continued to be seriously restrained under the presidency of Franjo Tudjman. This was the main reason why Croatia remained, in the view and in the treatment of the international community, a subject for the international conflict management framework installed for the entire area of the former Yugoslavia.

According to Romana Vlahutin (2004: 22), an expert on Croatian foreign policy and relations with the EU, Croatia's fear of being pigeonholed in the Balkan region – more concretely, that the country's fate would be closely linked to that of the other former Yugoslav states – derived from this period.

This issue became one of the major political themes in Croatia in the 1990s. Although containing some irrational elements, Croatia's fear was nourished by the EU's lack of a vision for the region. In its Regional Approach, the EU focused more on the region as a whole than on a policy for each individual country. From a Croatian point of view, this meant being hostage to the other Balkan states and trapped in the EU's efforts to re-establish a kind of a 'neo-Yugoslavia' (ibid). The EU's approach even prompted the Tudjman-led country to amend its Constitution to include an article explicitly prohibiting membership in any association of states that may result in a renewal of Yugoslavia or a comparable association of Balkan states (Jovic, 2006: 86).

The year 1999 marked the turnaround with regard to both domestic political transition and the country's international standing. Croatia has improved its political and economic performance at such a pace and to such an extent that political discussions in Europe on the difficult situation in the states of the former Yugoslavia have frequently included the parenthesis 'except for Croatia' (Vlahutin, 2004: 21). Following the death of the Croatian president Franjo Tudjman in December 1999, the consecutive elections brought into power a coalition government under Prime Minister Ivica Racan, and elected Stipe Mesic president of the Republic. The convincing victory of the Racan-led centre-left coalition created a momentum as regards both the internal political transformation and Croatia's relations with the international community, first and foremost with the EU.

In October 2001, Croatia's reorientation towards Euro-Atlantic integration was codified by the signing of a Stabilisation and Association Agreement with the EU. The country's transformation was facilitated by several factors including good macroeconomic data, the absence of unresolved constitutional issues and an improved regional security context (see also, Vlahutin, 2004, Massari, 2005, Jovic, 2006).

Croatia's macroeconomic data
Compared to the other South-Eastern European states, Croatia has established a relatively stable and favourable macroeconomic framework. Croatia was able to start its economic transition from an advantageous level as the country had never adopted communist-style command planning and entry into the market was not dictated by the state alone (Commission of the European Communities, 2004c: 42f). Croatia was, after Slovenia, the second wealthiest province of the former Yugoslavia. Also, Croatian entrepreneurs managed to re-establish the tourism industry as a profitable business branch and to benefit from close economic connections to Western European states, in particular to Germany, Italy and Austria. Croatia's major economic problems were the high trade deficit, the development imbalances between the regions and a deterioration of the purchasing power of the lower income groups (Altmann, 2004: 71, 79). In addition, Croatia's unemployment rate was relatively high, putting a heavy burden on the social system.

Unemployment varied between the different counties, but was particularly strong in some border regions.

In the context of EU integration, the Commission stated early on that Croatia had a 'functioning market economy' that should be able to cope with the EU's competitive pressure and market forces in the medium term, although Croatia was encouraged to make 'sustained efforts' in several areas, particularly regarding the improvement of market mechanisms (Commission of the European Communities, 2004c: 53–54). Also, several Croatian business sectors were believed to be particularly ill-prepared for competing in the single market, notably the shipbuilding and agricultural sectors (ibid). A cross-cutting issue also affecting the economic development has been the weakness of the judiciary system, the reform of which has been an important accession conditionality set by the EU for Croatia.

Table 4.1 Main economic indicators for the Republic of Croatia

	2001	*2002*	*2003*	*2004*	*2005*	*2006*	*2007*	*2008*
GDP per capita (in EUR)	5.752	6.331	6.759	7.380	8.043	8.807	9.656	10.682
GDP – year-on-year rate of growth (in %)	3.8	5.4	5.0	4.2	4.2	4.7	5.5	2.4
Current account balance (as % of GDP)	–3.2	–7.5	–6.3	–4.4	–5.5	–6.9	–7.6	–9.2
Inflation (%)	3.8	1.7	1.8	2.1	3.3	3.2	2.9	6.1
Unemployment rate (%)	15.8	14.8	14.3	13.8	12.7	11.2	9.6	8.4

Source: Croatian National Bank, Economic Indicators (last update: 28 January 2010)

Croatia's GDP per capita has consistently been almost twice that of the other Western Balkan states and in 2008 was still higher than that of several new EU member states in Central and Eastern Europe.[1] The global financial and economic crisis has affected Croatia's macroeconomic performance, with the GDP falling 6.7 per cent in the first quarter of 2009. According to the Croatian government, the GDP saw a record drop of 4.5 per cent in 2009 (Javno, 2009). Inflation rose to 6.1 per cent in 2008. The stability of the banking system was a major concern for Croatia in the context of the crisis. Yet so far, Croatia has proved better prepared to handle the crisis than other countries of the region. According to the World Bank, Croatian monetary and prudential policies established adequate liquidity reserves in the banking system helping withstand the major financial market disturbances (World Bank, 2009). By lifting the marginal reserve requirements for banks' foreign borrowing, Croatian authorities have enhanced their foreign exchange liquidity.

Resolved constitutional issues

Following the Dayton Peace Accords Croatia was able to establish functional state institutions and structures. In line with the Erdut agreement of November 1995, the remaining occupied regions of Eastern Slavonia, Baranja and Western Sirmium were reintegrated into the territory of Croatia in 1998.

After successfully solving the major war-related territorial questions, Croatia could concentrate again on 'normal' political issues, including the performance of the economy, questions in relation to the rule of law, and the functioning of the state administration. The political controversies on these subjects have eventually superseded issues of national identity, statehood and sovereignty (Vlahutin, 2004: 23). In 2000 and 2001, the Croatian parliament amended the Constitution by changing the bicameral parliament into a unicameral parliament and by reducing the presidential powers. These amendments were thought to prevent the re-emergence of an authoritarian style of government and help bring Croatia closer to a modern, democratic, European nation state. Compared to its neighbour Bosnia and Herzegovina, which is struggling to create a functional, multi-ethnic state, or Serbia, which is investing substantial political energy to oppose the breakaway of Kosovo, the territorial and constitutional problems of Zagreb have lost significance. 'With its statehood and territorial framework defined, Croatia was better positioned, after Franjo Tudman's death, to pursue its foreign policy and pro-European and Euro-Atlantic agenda as a rational actor' (Massari, 2005: 264).

The regional security context

According to the Croatian political scientists Visnja Samardzija and Mladen Stanicic, in the late 1990s, the international actors present in the Balkans considered leaving Croatia 'in the position of a security buffer state against a non-transparent and uncertain area to the east of its borders' (Samardzija and Stanicic, 2005: 5). These ideas were dropped, however, when the region's security became increasingly relevant in the context of global threats such as terrorism, weapons of mass destruction, drug and people trafficking. 'It became clear that it would be unrealistic to expect a small country to be able to deal with a combination of autochthonous local and global aspects of security all alone and without institutional support of a wider circle of countries such as full-fledged EU members' (ibid).

With the NATO intervention in Kosovo in 1999 and Macedonia's inter-ethnic conflict in 2001, international peacekeeping activities shifted towards the southern successor states of the former Yugoslavia (Vlahutin, 2004: 24). Croatia was little involved in these conflicts, despite its general interest in maintaining regional stability in South-Eastern Europe. The country remained concerned about becoming too closely associated with problems of Balkan insecurity and instability.

In its foreign policy strategy vis-à-vis its neighbours, Croatia has closely aligned itself to the EU, and its stance on the key question of whether to recognise Kosovo as an independent state was no exception. After Kosovo's declaration of independence on 17 February 2008, Croatia followed the majority of EU member states in recognising Kosovo as a sovereign and independent state. When taking the decision, the Croatian government explicitly referred to the EU accession process. 'In light of the interests of the Republic of Croatia as a country in the process of accession to the European Union, [it] will harmonise its foreign policy decisions with the common foreign and security policy of the European Union and with the approach of other participants in the Euro-Atlantic integration processes' (Government of the Republic of Croatia, 2008a). Croatia was aware that the decision of recognising Kosovo as an independent state was 'a difficult one for Serbia to swallow', according to its Prime Minister Ivo Sanader (quoted in BBC, 2008). 'But I don't expect a worsening of political and economic relations because there is no alternative to good neighbourly relations', the Prime Minister added. Croatia and Serbia have ameliorated their bilateral relations, a process that has been warmly welcomed by the EU. The fostering of regional conciliation and cooperation has always been a key focus for the EU in the context of the Stabilisation and Association Process.

Croatia's state of relations with the EU

Diplomatic relations between Croatia and the EU began in January 1992 when the EU recognised Croatia as an independent country. However, following the 1995 Dayton Peace Accords, EU–Croatian relations were kept at a low level. The EU deemed Croatia's performance with regard to areas such as democratisation and the respect of human and minority rights as too poor to justify an improvement in their relations.

This changed in the year 2000 when the newly elected Croatian leadership committed itself to entrenching democratic values and principles. The Racan-led government, similar to its successor governments, defined the integration into the Euro-Atlantic structures as the key priorities of the country's foreign policy agenda. Satisfied with the new political structures in place, the EU quickly agreed to upgrade relations. In line with the recommendation of the Commission's Feasibility Report (2000), the EU opened negotiations on a Stabilisation and Association Agreement at the November 2000 Zagreb summit and granted Croatia unilaterally autonomous trade concessions. The Stabilisation and Association Agreement was signed in October 2001, with the Interim Agreement entering into force in March 2002.[2] It was the first contractual relationship established between the EU and Croatia; previously started negotiations on a Cooperation Agreement and on a Transport Agreement were never concluded due to the frozen political relations between the EU and the country during the Tudjman era.

The political objective to accede to the EU has been shared by all political parties in the Sabor, the Croatian parliament. In December 2002, the members of parliament adopted unanimously a resolution defining Croatia's accession to the EU as a strategic national objective and authorised the government to submit the country's application for EU membership. In 2003, the national elections brought back into power the former Tudjman party, Croatian Democratic Union (HDZ), now under the chairmanship of Ivo Sanader. Initially the party's victory raised national and international concerns about whether its return to power would imply a return to the condemned practices of the mid-1990s. The Prime Minister Ivo Sanader underlined, however, that the country's reform process should be continued. Membership in the EU and NATO, the improvement of relations with neighbours, developing economic diplomacy and changing Croatia's international image were the five priorities of the foreign policy agenda announced by his government (Government of the Republic of Croatia, 2003a).

When submitting the application for membership in February 2003, high-ranking Croatian authorities visited each of the fifteen EU member capitals to request support for the country's EU accession. Despite these efforts, Croatia's path towards opening accession talks with the EU was not an easy one. After Croatia had filled in a comprehensive EU questionnaire, the Commission (2004c) published its opinion on Croatia's application for membership. In the *avis*, the Commission (ibid: 120) maintained that Croatia was a functioning democracy with stable state institutions and a functioning market economy and concluded that 'negotiations for accession to the European Union should be opened with Croatia'.[3]

Acting on the Commission's advice, the European Council decided in June 2004 that 'Croatia is a candidate country for membership and the accession process should be launched' (European Council, 2004: 8). The start of accession negotiations was scheduled for 17 March 2005, but was contingent on Croatia's full cooperation with the ICTY on delivering the war crime suspect General Ante Gotovina.

When the date approached, the EU was divided how to proceed. Even though Ante Gotovina was not delivered to the ICTY by March 2005, a group of Central European countries headed by Austria argued that Croatia should still be allowed to start negotiations. However, Belgium, the United Kingdom and the Netherlands were particularly insistent that Croatia improve its cooperation with the ICTY before beginning accession negotiations (BBC, 2005). These countries advanced the argument that allowing Croatia to start accession talks would set a negative example in the region.[4] Unable to confirm Croatia's full cooperation, the foreign ministers decided in their Council meeting of 16 March 2005 to postpone the opening of accession negotiations. To soften the blow, they adopted a negotiating framework for accession talks with Croatia, to be applied when the outstanding condition was met.

Croatia was allowed to begin accession talks six months later thanks to the UN's War Crime Prosecutor Carla Del Ponte confirming that Croatia had improved its cooperation with the tribunal.[5] Also, at the General Affairs and External Relations Council meeting of 4 October 2005 the Austrian Minister of Foreign Affairs Ursula Plassnik linked her approval of Turkey's bid for membership to the case of Croatia. Due to the unanimity principle prevailing in the issue, Vienna's approval was pivotal for opening accession negotiations with Turkey. The resulting compromise found in the Council was to offer accession talks to both Turkey and Croatia. Although officially denied, most observers saw this 'deal' as a major reason for the opening of accession negotiations with Croatia.[6]

In October 2005, the Commission officially launched the accession process by screening Croatia's domestic legalisation and assessing its harmonisation with the *acquis communautaire*. Completed within one year, the screening reports confirmed that Croatia would be in the position to assume the obligations of membership in the medium term. From the screening reports the Commission sent to the Council, six resulted in the introduction of 'benchmarks' to be met by Croatia in order to open the respective *acquis* chapter. In October 2006, Croatia was allowed to start negotiations on the thirty-five *acquis* chapters (two chapters more than the candidate countries of the previous enlargements, due to the fact that the chapters on agriculture and judiciary were split into smaller ones to reduce their complexity).

Croatia installed a comprehensive negotiating structure for the accession talks with the EU, with roughly 2,000 Croatian officials working to prepare the country for EU membership.[7] Indeed, the country managed a strong start in the EU accession negotiations (Commission of the European Communities, 2006e, 2007b). In March 2008, the Commission president, José Manuel Barroso, named for the first time a possible date for Croatia's EU accession. According to the Commission president, 'it should be possible to conclude the technical negotiations next year [i.e. in 2009], preferably by the end of the mandate of the Commission' (Barroso, 2008). The date of accession would therefore be either 2010 or 2011, according to the Commission president.

This time schedule proved unfeasible. Croatia's accession negotiations came to a temporary halt in December 2008 when Slovenia decided to veto the opening of new *acquis* chapters due to an open border dispute in the Piran Bay (see below). Rejecting mediating efforts of the French presidency and the Commission, the Slovenian Prime Minister Borut Pahor argued that the veto was necessary because Croatia had presented documents that 'could prejudice the outline of the common border' (quoted in *Agence Europe*, 17 December 2008).

Slovenia's veto caused heated discussions on both sides of the border. The Slovenian Foreign Minister Samuel Zbogar announced that if the border dispute was not resolved in favour of Slovenia's approach, it would be 'quite realistic' that the country hold a national referendum on the ratification of Croatia's accession treaty with the EU (EurActiv, 2009c). In Croatia, the maritime dispute even increased the population's Euro-scepticism. A February 2009 census showed that only slightly more than 25 per cent of

Croatians supported EU membership, referring to the open border issue as a main factor for the decreasing support (Setimes, 2009). The Council presidencies and the Commission eventually withdrew from mediating in the conflict, reacting to several failed proposals, and asked the two countries to come up with a solution bilaterally.

Following the withdrawal of the Croatian Prime Minister Ivo Sanader in July 2009, the efforts toward a solution gained momentum. In September 2009, the two sides reached agreement that the negotiations on the border would continue with international mediation, as proposed earlier by the Commission. The agreement cleared the way for Croatia to re-start accession talks with the EU. The country hoped to be ready to join the EU by 2011 or 2012.

Croatia's border challenges

Since the Eastern enlargement, Croatia has become one of the EU's most strategically important border countries. Croatia's state borders total 3,254.2km in length (670km with the Republic of Slovenia, 355km with Hungary, 335.6km with Serbia and Montenegro, 971km with Bosnia and Herzegovina and 28km with Italy). The nature of these border sections varies considerably. Croatia's lowland borders total around 980km in length; the rest of Croatia's borders stretch through mountain regions or along the sea (875km of Croatia's sea borders are on international waters).

In the context of EU integration, Croatia faced the following border-related challenges. First, due to its geopolitical position and the sheer length and composition of its borders, Croatia has been exposed to flows of irregular migrants and the organised transfer of larger groups across its state borders. Croatia is at the northern end of the traditional Balkan smuggling route, which was revitalised following the Dayton Peace Accords. However, most irregular migrants and asylum seekers view Croatia as a transit country, not a final destination.

Second, some borders have not been marked or definitively demarcated. Croatia has had open border demarcation issues with all its neighbours expect Hungary and Italy. The disputes over how to draw the maritime and land borders with Slovenia, in particular, have obtained high political salience.

Third, cooperation between Croatia and its neighbours in issues of border security and management has been weak. This shortcoming has not been specific to Croatia, however; it has applied to most Western Balkan states. Similar to its neighbours, Croatia was encouraged to strengthen the regional aspects of its border management and to develop a regionally coordinated policy on issues such as readmission and visas. The Croatian, Serbian and Bosnian border guard services were expected to establish close professional links in order to jointly address smuggling activities and other cross-border problems.

Finally, Croatia had to enhance the professionalism of its police in general and its border police in particular. The Croatian police structures have been affected by the wartime system and the armed conflicts of the early 1990s. During the war period Croatia managed to create a local police force that enjoyed high esteem in the population because it was disconnected from the despised Yugoslav militia (Caparini, 2004: 15). However, during this time a paramilitarisation of the police took place, which created strong bonds and loyalties in the police and made the 'subsequent tasks of rooting out police corruption or creating internal controls on misconduct more difficult' (ibid). The key task in view of EU accession was therefore to curtail the high level of corruption among police officers and to reform organisation and staff policies.

EU border security policies: an evaluation of their impact in Croatia

The EU demanded early on that Croatia reform its external border security system. According to the Commission's 2002 Strategy Paper (2002a: 54), Croatia should 'establish greater security at international borders that will diminish cross-border crime and illegal migration, and at the same time facilitate cross border movement of people by developing and implementing asylum and migration policies'. The need to foster regional cooperation was underlined. 'Croatia must cooperate with its neighbouring countries in policing borders and in facilitating the movements of goods' (ibid: 55). In addition, under the heading 'Movement of Persons' the cooperation was contractually regulated in Article 76 and 77 of the Stabilisation and Association Agreement. It committed Croatia to cooperating in the policies of visas, border control, asylum and migration and with regard to the prevention and control of irregular migration, notably by signing bilateral readmission agreements with member states (Council of the European Union, 2005c: 19).

The strengthening of the external border control system
By the negotiations for an SAA with the EU in 2001, Croatia had already begun to implement first reform measures aimed at strengthening its external border control. The activities were not conducted under the auspices of the EU however, but rather within the Budapest Process and the Stability Pact's Working Table III. International experts dispatched by these organisations helped Croatia assess the weaknesses of the external border control system and develop a more strategic approach towards border guarding. The project's most visible result was an evaluation report recommending that Croatia take action in four areas: regulating the existing border disputes with neighbouring countries; resolving the lack of qualified human resources in the border police forces; providing specialised border control training for the border police officers; and intensifying international co-operation with

neighbouring countries to prevent the trafficking and smuggling of human beings (the results of the Budapest Group Report of November 2001 were quoted in ICMPD, 2003: 272).

The evaluation activities tasked the Border Guard Task Force of the Stability Pact to organise a Partnership Project with Croatian authorities. In the project, a regional country team of experts from Germany, Slovenia and Austria was dispatched to Croatia to help the local police draft a national action plan on border policing.[8] The Partnership Project officially ended with the signing of the national action plan in May 2002.

The EU did not ascribe high relevance to these activities. Shortly after the Partnership Project ended, a CARDS programme was launched, which actually repeated some activities of the previous projects. According to a Croatian border police official, the European Commission refrained from approving the national action plan produced by the Stability Pact's Partnership Project and demanded a document with an explicit focus on how to align the Croatian border control system to the EU's integrated border management concept (interview C3, 8 May 2006, Zagreb).

Croatia therefore started the first ever CARDS twinning project, not only for Croatia but for all countries subsumed under the Stabilisation and Association Process. The project, named 'Integrated Border Management: Border Police', officially started on 1 October 2002 and lasted for 16 months. Implemented with German and Slovenian twinning partners, the project focused on four areas: training; review and analysis; organisation and management; and strengthening and upgrading legislation relevant to the Croatian border police. The twinning project's most relevant result was a draft law for border policing that was aligned with EU standards. With the draft law endorsed by both the Ministry of the Interior and the government, the new Border Protection Act was adopted by Croatia's parliament in October 2003 (Commission of the European Communities, 2003a). It was followed by several rulebooks and subordinated acts on how to translate the border policing law into concrete action at the border.[9]

In addition to legal alignment, Croatia agreed to reorganise the institutional structure and hierarchy of its border police. In January 2002, a new Border Police Directorate was created within the General Police Directorate and was tasked to enhance the autonomy of the border police.[10] The European Commission criticised the lack of specialisation of the unit, however. 'As border police officers are therefore part of the general police force, they are in many cases not specialised and act as border police as well as general police. Further specialisation of the border police and specific training to this effect will be required' (Commission of the European Communities, 2003c: 31).

In response to the criticism, Croatia developed a new training schedule. To achieve a higher level of specialisation, border police officers now have to pass a special training of eight weeks, of which six weeks are theory and two weeks practice (in addition to the fifteen months of basic training obligatory to all police officers). Since 2003, 400 to 500 officers have been trained annually under this advanced training programme.[11] Croatia also implemented a 'train the trainer' programme and an English language course.

Croatia's integrated border management strategy
To strengthen the inter-institutional cooperation and coordination among all agencies with a competence at the borders, Croatia was encouraged to develop and implement an integrated border management strategy based on the EU's border management model for the Western Balkans. The IBM strategy aimed, in particular, at improving the cooperation links between the Ministry of the Interior (the Border Police Directorate), the Ministry of Finance (the Customs Administration), and the Ministry of Agriculture, Forestry and Water Management (the Phytosanitary and Veterinary Inspection). The IBM strategy did not focus on a process of border demilitarisation. The EU's objective to demilitarise the borders in South-Eastern Europe was of minor relevance for Croatia, as it was one of the few countries in the region where no military was dispatched at the borders. The exception has been the protection of the maritime border where, if deemed necessary, the Croatian navy may assist the border police. Still, the border police usually maintain the command of maritime border operations.

Croatia created the IBM strategy in the context of the CARDS twinning project 'Inter-agency Cooperation – Development and Implementation of Croatia's IBM Strategy', implemented by a consortium led by the Agency for European Integration and Economic Development (a non-profit organisation under the guidance of the Austrian Ministry of Finance), and with the participation of the Austrian Ministry of the Interior and the ICMPD.[12] The Croatian side was represented by an inter-ministerial group involving officials from the border police, the customs administration and the plant health and veterinary agencies.

During eighteen months of intense work, the international and national stakeholders conducted a gap analysis and established concrete recommendations in relation to three facets of Croatian border management: the legal and regulatory framework; management and training; and technical equipment. Funded with €1.8 million of CARDS allocations, the twinning project ended with an official closing ceremony in May 2006. On this occasion the Croatian ministers involved in border management officially endorsed the IBM strategy and signed memoranda of understanding aimed at formalising and institutionalising the inter-ministerial cooperation. The ministers agreed to permanently install the inter-ministerial working group within the structures of the Ministry of the Interior. This group is chaired by the head of the border police and meets regularly, at least two or three times a year.

The Commission (2004c: 105f) acknowledged Croatia's adjustment steps, yet noted that the country still had to cope with major policy-related challenges. Croatia's technical equipment was insufficient for effective surveillance of the long sea border and large numbers of cross-border roads and paths at the border to Bosnia and Herzegovina remained *de facto* uncontrolled. Therefore, the Croatian government was expected to increase its investments in its border control in general and to improve its central police information system in particular (ibid). The Commission was also concerned with both the speed and quality of Croatia's policy adjustment. The number of border police officers was 'not yet sufficient, particularly considering that parts of Croatia's land border may become part of the EU's external border in future. Recruitment and training of staff, improvement of working methods (risk analysis capabilities in particular) and modernisation of equipment are urgent matters' (Commission of the European Communities, 2004c: 106). There were also serious administrative shortages. In October 2007, only around 5,000 of the 8,500 posts assigned to the border police were filled.

The Schengen acquis

Croatian authorities began their preparations for implementing the Schengen *acquis* by developing a border police development strategy (including an activity plan) for 2005–2009. Whereas the IBM strategy focused on creating closer cooperation between the services and authorities involved in border management, the border police development strategy outlined how the Croatian border police intended to proceed with its reorganisation in view of EU accession. It included a technical equipment acquisition plan for the period 2005–2009 and covered initiatives related to legislative amendments and to improving border police mobility and compatible IT structures (Government of the Republic of Croatia, 2006b: 285). It also contained a plan for the financial expenditures necessary to implement the objectives, underlining that the procurement of technical equipment for the border police was to be mainly conducted through the PHARE 2005 project 'Preparations for the Implementation of the Schengen Acquis'.[13]

In February 2006, the Commission's screening process concerned the *acquis* chapter on freedom, security and justice (Commission of the European Communities, 2006g). The Commission recommended the introduction of a benchmark for the opening of the chapter; however the benchmark they produced was a comparatively easy one. Croatia was asked to submit an updated action plan for the IBM strategy 'with specific activities for mainland and maritime borders, with objectives, realistic deadlines, competent state administration bodies, and a budget estimate for each of the activities demanding more significant investments' (quoted in Government of the Republic of Croatia, 2007a: 361). The Croatian government successfully managed to fulfil this particular benchmark in November 2006 by presenting the upgraded action plan demanded of them. Also, it announced that the document would be updated on an annual basis (ibid).

In general, there was nothing problematic or unacceptable in the

Schengen regulations for Croatia, according to Croatia's chief negotiator for the JHA chapter with the EU, Snjezana Bagic. She advanced the view that the country's alignment process was on track, but that Croatia was still by and large in the initial period of aligning itself with the relevant Schengen standards (Government of the Republic of Croatia, 2006a). In January 2007, the authorities adopted a Schengen action plan outlining all the activities planned through to 2012. This indicative timeframe illustrated how Croatia sought to prepare itself for taking over the responsibility of protecting the EU's external borders. Priority was attached to the quick inclusion of the second generation of the Schengen Information System (SIS II). To this end, the country intended to set up a National Border Management Information System, which was operational at the first border crossing points by 2006.

In short, at the time of writing, Croatia had advanced its adjustment to EU standards in the field of external border control, even though the preparations for entering the Schengen cooperation were still at an early stage. The adjustment steps included the adoption of a new Border Protection Act, the re-organisation and increased specialisation of the Croatian border police and the development of a more 'integrated' approach towards border management. The Croatian government developed strategic documents clarifying the ways in which it sought to strengthen the capacities and infrastructure of border police agencies as well as accomplish better inter-agency cooperation with all services involved in border control (in particular migration and asylum services and customs). The EU's main point of criticism was that the border police was understaffed, and the technical equipment outdated and insufficient (see e.g. Commission of the European Communities, 2008e: 56f).

Regionally coordinated management of the borders

The EU's integrated border management concept aspires to smooth cooperation among border management agencies across national and regional dividing lines. Croatia was therefore required to foster multilateral, bilateral and local cooperation in areas of border management, a demand that included setting up bilateral structures for cross-border operational cooperation, maintenance of the border, etc. According to the IBM Guidelines, the objective of an enhanced regional cooperation was not only to increase the efficiency of border management but also to facilitate trade and to prevent crime and irregular migration (IBM Guidelines, 2004: 33). The commitment to improving regional cooperation in border control and related issues was also contractually regulated in Croatia's SAA with the EU.[14]

Bilateral activities between Croatia and its neighbours

Croatia has institutionalised a high level of cooperation with its northern neighbours Slovenia and Hungary by accomplishing formal bilateral agreements and practical arrangements on customs and border police activities.

Croatian–Slovenian relations have been carried out at local, regional and state level through regular contacts at all levels and the exchange of information. Cooperation between the countries' border police services is formally based on a bilateral agreement on cross-border police cooperation which was brought into force on 16 April 2003 (before the agreement the two police services established cooperation based on written records).

Hungarian–Croatian cooperation is also thought to be functioning well and based on good neighbourly relations, with representatives of the Croatian and Hungarian Ministries of the Interior meeting frequently at an operative level. The countries institutionalised their bilateral cooperation by establishing the Mixed Committee on Cooperation between the Croatian and Hungarian Government dealing with issues such as illegal migration, internal affairs and cross-border traffic (Government of the Republic of Croatia, 2003b: Ch. 24, p. 10f). Together with the Slovenian Ministry of the Interior, the two ministries signed in October 2005 a joint statement on cooperation in the field of internal security focusing on border management, measures against organised crime, terrorism and illegal migration.

Croatia has cooperated with other (non-EU) neighbouring states at a comparatively low level. The country had no formal framework for border police cooperation with Serbia. Croatian officials argued that reaching a formal agreement had been made difficult by the fact that, while Croatia's borders were guarded by its police forces, Serbia's were protected by its military (interview C3, 8 May 2006, Zagreb). This *de facto* absence of cross-border cooperation at the Serbian-Croatian border was a concern for the European partners present in the country. In January 2006, a special border police cooperation project was initiated by the UK government (in conjunction with the International Organisation for Migration and the Austrian Ministry of the Interior) to increase cross-border cooperation by conducting joint training sessions and improving the dissemination and analysis of intelligence and border control equipment. The value Croatia and Serbia attached to the project was reflected by the fact that Serbia agreed to speed up the process of border demilitarisation at this specific section of the Serbian border to ensure a smooth implementation of the project (interview IO5, 10 May 2006, Zagreb).

Croatia's relations with Montenegro were, relatively speaking, better, with the negotiations on a border police agreement starting quickly after Croatia recognised Montenegro as a sovereign state in June 2006. One month later both countries established diplomatic relations. Croatia's relations with Bosnia and Herzegovina have also improved. Their bilateral relations were for a long time overshadowed by some unresolved issues deriving from the dissolution of the former Yugoslavia.[15] Bosnia and Herzegovina and Croatia have defined their border crossing based on mutual consent. For a handful of checkpoints, the countries have arranged for border guards to work at common locations. The two countries formalised their relations by signing an

Agreement on State Border Protection on 22 April 2005. The agreement regulates cross-border cooperation including the exchange of liaison officers, joint patrols, joint contact points, joint working groups etc. Moreover, local units were expected to sign separate agreements or protocols to regulate the cooperation at a local level (interview C7, 27 April 2007, Zagreb).

In addition to these arrangements on border-crossing cooperation, Croatian authorities have signed several local border traffic agreements. A local border traffic regime exists with Slovenia, Bosnia and Herzegovina, Serbia and Montenegro.

The EU's efforts to enhance regional cooperation

The EU's activities to improve regional cooperation and networking in border management among Croatia and its neighbours included in particular the CARDS regional IBM programme 'Support to and Coordination of Integrated Border Management Strategies in the Western Balkans'.[16] Lagging behind the initial schedule, the CARDS regional IBM programme was implemented between January 2005 and April 2007.

The project's official objective was 'to provide technical assistance [...] to support the five CARDS countries in the development or updating of their national Integrated Border Management strategies and ensure that these are coherent and effectively co-ordinated on a regional level, focusing on trade facilitation and border control' (Consortium Implementing the CARDS Regional Programme, 2005). In addition, the participating states should become familiar with EU-relevant border management through specialised training schemes and study visits to one or several EU member states. The project supported the 'integrated' approach promoted by the EU involving a broad range of actors dealing with border management issues (in particular border police, customs, veterinary and phytosanitary inspection).

The regional IBM project was implemented in a series of regional seminars/workshops in which local border authority officials met with international advisers. The regional seminars were thought to provide an opportunity for networking and exchange of experiences. Still, an official of the implementing consortium explained that 'one of the lessons learnt is not to focus on the first regional activities on regional cooperation/networking but to focus more on technical questions in regional activities as "networking" requires trust building. Regional activities dealing with technical aspects serve also as information exchange and thus contribute to regional cooperation' (interview IO7, 11 December 2006, Vienna).

The CARDS regional IBM project was an ambiguous undertaking for the Croatian officials involved. According to one official, they felt they had to repeat several activities from the national IBM project they had just completed (interview C3, 8 May 2006, Zagreb); Croatia was the first country in the region to implement such a project. Another shortcoming was, according to the official, that Croatia could not sufficiently transfer the experience and know-how it had gained to the other SAP participating states, as the institutional set-up of the project prevented such an activity (ibid).

Croatia has concluded a working agreement with Frontex and obtained the status of an observer in the EU Centre for Information, Discussion and Exchange on the Crossings of Frontiers and Immigration (CIREFI). This centre assists EU member and candidate states 'in exchanging information on legal migration, in preventing illegal migration and unlawful residence, on combating smuggling in human beings, improving the detection of false or falsified travel documents and on ways of improving return practices' (Commission of the European Communities, 2008d).

In brief, signs of regionally coordinated border management between Croatia and its neighbours have increased. Croatia has already signed or is in the process of negotiating cross-border border police cooperation and/or local border traffic agreements with neighbouring states. The EU has sought to assist through a comprehensive regional IBM programme aimed at enhancing regional cooperation and networking in border management.

Tackling open border disputes

The EU's strategic paper on the principles governing the negotiations with Croatia stated that the advancement of the negotiations would be guided, among others things, by 'Croatia's undertaking to resolve any border dispute in conformity with the principle of peaceful settlement of disputes' (Council of the European Union, 2005b: 3). It is a basic requirement for a Schengen-like border security system that the national border is either demarcated or agreed upon, or at least properly marked and defined (Niemenkari, 2002: 5). There is no *acquis* on border demarcation, however; candidate countries are expected to solve outstanding border demarcation issues either bilaterally or through international arbitration.

The Croatian–Slovenian border disputes

Croatia and Slovenia have been unable to agree on a number of territorial issues. The most salient border-related issues have concerned the drawing of the maritime border in the Piran Bay (on the north-west tip of the Istria peninsula) and Croatia's intention to establish a fishery and ecological protection zone in the Adriatic Sea. Also, the two countries disagree on the drawing of the border on the Mura River. Although generally receiving less attention, the dispute over the Mura River could potentially have a negative impact on the bilateral relations as well, as shown by an incident in September 2006 when the Croatian police detained a number of Slovenian journalists who were visiting the northern border area of the Mura River (which in the view of the Croatian authorities belonged to their territory) to report on joint Slovenian–Croatian police patrols. The Slovenian government was outraged by this step. The Slovenian police were instructed to take up position in the disputed border zone, erecting barriers and controlling cross-border traffic. The incident could only be resolved through the direct intercession of the two Prime Ministers, Ivo Sanader and his Slovenian counterpart Janez Jansa (Setimes, 2006a).

The disagreement on the maritime border drawing in the Piran Bay originated from the period when Croatia and Slovenia were both Yugoslav provinces without a sea demarcation line. When they became independent, the two countries could not agree on the drawing of the maritime border, more specifically, on whether the demarcation line should run through the middle of the Piran Bay. If this was the case, Slovenia would have no direct access to the international waters. The Croatian side preferred this plan and wanted to divide the northern Adriatic into two main sectors only, a Croatian one and an Italian one. Slovenia, by contrast, insisted that the maritime border should be territorially biased towards the Croatian coast to have a physical corridor between the Italian and Croatian zone onto the international waters. There was also a disagreement on how to solve the conflict. Croatia was in favour of international arbitration, whereas Slovenia preferred the problem to be solved bilaterally. The conflict seemed to be close to a solution in 2001 when the Croat and Slovenian Prime Ministers signed the so-called Drnovše-Račan Agreement which delimitated the entire borders between the two countries, including the Piran Bay. According to the agreement, Slovenia had a corridor to the international waters, whereas Croatia got around 20 per cent of the gulf of Piran and a maritime border with Italy. The Drnovše-Račan Agreement was never ratified by either parliament, however. The failed ratification process closed a window of opportunity, and both countries hardened their respective domestic approach towards the issue.

Moreover, the Slovenian–Croatian dispute over the drawing of the maritime border in the Piran Bay has become increasingly connected to another controversial issue, that is, to Croatia's intention to install an ecological and fishing protection zone in the Adriatic Sea.[17] The zone, covering an area of some 57,000 square kilometres, is intended to protect the Adriatic sea fishing stock which, according to Croatian fishermen, is being depleted by over-extensive fishing on the part of Italy's larger fishing fleet (Setimes, 2007a). To realise the project, Croatia unilaterally declared that it would expand its jurisdiction in the Adriatic Sea in October 2003. The step caused considerable tensions with Slovenia and Italy, which were no longer allowed to exploit the richer, Croatian part of the Adriatic Sea without special permission. These two neighbouring states hence opposed the agreement and prompted the Council of the EU to ask Croatia 'to urgently pursue a constructive dialogue with its neighbour' (quoted in Commission of the European Communities, 2004c: 35–36). When the issue became increasingly linked to the country's EU accession process, the Croatian parliament amended the agreement in October 2004. It now stated that the zone would not be implemented with regard to EU member states until the time when a fishing agreement were finalised between Zagreb and Brussels. By postponing the implementation of the zone, Croatia met a major concern of its neighbours Italy and Slovenia.

The relief of the tensions was only temporary, however. In January 2008, the Law on the Establishment of an Ecological and Fishery Protection Zone entered automatically into force because the new parliament was not yet formed following the 2007 general election. Therefore, the parliament was not in session and no authority was entitled to stop the process. The entering into force of the protected ecological and fishery zone in the Adriatic irritated Italy and Slovenia and both countries threatened to veto Croatia's EU integration process. Slovenia argued that the step 'prejudices a final implementation of the sea border between the two countries and also interferes with the area over which Slovenia has its sovereignty and sovereign rights [...] [the] decision of Croatia's parliament will never be acceptable for Slovenia as it threatens the interests of the country in terms of free fishing on the open sea, i.e. in the international part of the Adriatic' (Government of the Republic of Slovenia, 2008).

In February 2008, the Council of the EU asked Croatia to respect the 2004 amendment and 'not to apply any aspect of the Ecological and Fisheries Protection Zone to the EU Member States until a common agreement in the EU spirit is found' (Council of the European Union, 2008b). Led by Italy and Slovenia, the Council of the EU postponed any further opening of accession negotiations for individual *acquis* chapters as long as Croatia did not refrain from applying the fishing jurisdiction in the pre-defined area. Faced with the choice of either advancing in the accession negotiations or implementing the fishery protection zone, Croatia opted for the first option. The fishing issue would remain 'important for Croatia' but EU membership an 'absolute national interest', according to the Croatian Prime Minister Ivo Sanader (quoted in *IHT*, 2008). On 10 March 2008, the coalition government decided not to apply the protection zone at least until Croatia enters the EU.

Croatia's official stance has been that border-related disputes should not interfere with bilateral relations. According to a former Croatian Minister of European Integration, 'the key approach we have is that we engage in all our efforts not to allow any open [border] issue to actually jeopardise the good relations with our neighbours' (interview C6, 11 May 2006, Zagreb). They have burdened bilateral relations regardless. Being a fully-fledged EU member state has advantageously positioned Slovenia to solve the outstanding border disputes in its favour. In December 2008, Slovenia demonstrated that it was prepared to benefit from this position when it blocked the opening of negotiations for ten new *acquis* chapters due to the open border dispute over the Piran Bay. The Border Arbitration Agreement of 4 November 2009, which brought an end to Slovenia's blockade, again separated the EU accession negotiations from the settlement of the border conflict and defined that the bilateral negotiations should continue under EU supervision. The agreement was warmly welcomed in Croatia, which has always sought to keep the border dispute a bilateral issue 'only' and not to link it to the EU accession process (Government of the Republic of Croatia, 2009).

Croatia's other border disputes

Croatia's border disputes with other countries have been less politically salient than its disputes with Slovenia. Between Croatia and Serbia and Montenegro disagreements have arisen about border definition, particularly in the area of the Prevlaka peninsula. With Bosnia and Herzegovina, the most relevant border-related issue has been the dispute over Port of Ploce.

In the former Yugoslavia the Prevlaka peninsula was a strategically important point. It controlled access to the Kotor Bay in Montenegro which was the only natural harbour where the Yugoslav army could anchor. After the implosion of the former Yugoslavia, Zagreb and Belgrade both claimed that the Prevlaka peninsula would lie within their territory. The United Nations recognised the political importance of the peninsula and demanded a complete demilitarisation of the area. Between 1996 and 2002, the UN dispatched a mission to monitor the process of demilitarisation. The United Nation Mission of Observers in Prevlaka (UNMOP) was actually the smallest UN mission in the entire Balkan region. Regardless of the UN presence, Yugoslav troops entered the demilitarised zone on the Adriatic coastal border between Croatia and Montenegro in 1999. Croatia logged a protest with the United Nations, but the move seemed to be first and foremost a punishment for the government of Montenegro, which had voiced criticisms on Belgrade's Kosovo policy (BBC, 1999).

In 2001, relations between the then State-Union of Serbia and Montenegro and Croatia started to improve. They created an Inter-State Commission on Borders charged to deal with the open border issues, particularly the question of the territorial ownership of the Prevlaka peninsula. In December 2002 when the mandate of the United Nations Mission of Observers in Prevlaka expired, finding a solution to this open issue gained importance. The foreign ministers of Serbia and Montenegro and Croatia therefore signed a protocol on the 'immediate future of Prevlaka', according to which the peninsula would remain a demilitarised zone, controlled jointly by Croatian, Serbian and Montenegrin police patrol boats. Also, they agreed upon a temporary border line at sea and accepted that Croatia assume full jurisdiction over Prevlaka. Although the issue still lacked a permanent solution, the agreement on the immediate status of the peninsula meant a 'great boost for regional stability' (Pop, 2003: 121). The temporary regime was implemented smoothly and Croatian authorities intended to incorporate it as part of a range of bilateral agreements with Montenegro (interview C6, 11 May 2006, Zagreb).

In addition, Croatia and Serbia have disagreed on the exact border delimitation of the Danube River, which draws a section of their common border. The dispute can be regarded as a minor one, as the disagreement has concerned only a few islets. Still, the negotiations on the issue (which have also taken place in the context of the Inter-State Commission on Borders) have so far not yielded concrete results.

The most important border-related issue between Croatia and Bosnia and Herzegovina concerns the Port of Ploce. Although located on Croatian territory, the Port of Ploce is of considerable significance for the economy of Bosnia and Herzegovina, as it represents Bosnia's most important access to the sea. The status of the Port of Ploce was not fully clarified in the 1995 Dayton peace agreements. In 1998, the US Special Envoy to Bosnia and Herzegovina, Richard Sclar, proposed the creation of a Port Management and Executive Council including not only Croatian members but also three Bosnia and Herzegovina members and one from the International Maritime Court. Bosnia was in favour of applying the 'Sclar model' but Croatia was concerned about the negative side-effects of involving foreign experts in the management of the port and refused to ratify the agreement. In 2003, Croatia and Bosnia and Herzegovina agreed on a renewed process of negotiations, which, however, did not materialise (Commission of the European Communities, 2004c: 34f).

The issue on the Port of Ploce gained new momentum in March 2007 when Prime Minister Ivo Sanader submitted a new proposal suggesting that Bosnia would be given favourable status in the Port of Ploce (Government of the Republic of Croatia, 2007b). In exchange for offering Bosnian businesses privileged access to the region Croatia asked Bosnia and Herzegovina to accept compromises on other bilateral issues, notably Croatia's plans for construction of a motorway to Dubrovnik (ibid). Croatia was considering two options for constructing the motorway: either a passage through the Bosnian territory of Neum or a bridge to the Peljesac peninsula. The Bosnian government was not in favour of a bridge to the Peljesac peninsula because they believed it would have a negative impact on the country's economy, effectively cutting off Bosnia and Herzegovina from international traffic. It would make it impossible for large ships to enter the port of the Bosnian city of Neum (although, for the time being, the port of Neum cannot be used for commercial traffic). Bosnia and Herzegovina hence insisted that construction of the bridge should in no way jeopardise Bosnia's access to the sea.

In brief, Croatia has had a range of unresolved border issues with neighbouring states, yet most of them have lost political salience. The notable exception is the dispute over the drawing of the maritime border with Slovenia, which has burdened bilateral relations and slowed the pace of Croatia's EU accession process.

Visa policies

Croatia has enjoyed a unique standing in the EU's visa policy vis-à-vis the Western Balkans, as it was the only country in the region that was never placed on the negative visa list of Council Regulation 539/2001 (Council of the European Union, 2001b).

In preparation for EU accession, Croatia was encouraged to gradually align its national visa regime with the EU's positive and negative visa list. In theory, Croatia therefore needed to introduce visa requirements for the other Western Balkan states which were placed on the EU's negative visa list. But because the EU considered these countries special cases, Croatia was expected to postpone introducing visa requirements for other states in the region until a more advanced stage of its accession process. What is more, Croatia was explicitly asked to foster the free movement of persons within the region (Council of the European Union, 2003d: 8) and to lift its entry restrictions for the immediate neighbourhood, particularly Serbia. The EU considered this aspect of regional integration more important than full compliance with the EU's negative visa list.

The Croatian–Serbian visa regime
Following the 1995 Dayton Peace Accords, Croatia and Serbia established restrictive visa regimes towards one another, complicating the movement of persons between the countries. As illustrated by the Citizens Pact for South East Europe,[18] the visa application was a real annoyance in the late 1990s, with long lines of applicants in the respective consulates who had to accept waiting for up to a month for visa approval from the neighbouring country. The two countries, which in the common Yugoslav state had no state borders, also lacked border crossings for the local population. The newly established borderline deprived inhabitants of several villages of their property and traditional resources by requiring farmers and pupils to cross the state border in order to reach their fields and schools (ibid).

The Croatian President Franjo Tudjman's death in 1999 and the Serbian President Slobodan Milosevic's resignation in 2000 opened the way for the two countries to improve their relations. Serbia and Croatia recognised each other as independent states, established diplomatic relations and voiced their intention to create good neighbourly relations. The authorities started by promoting exchanges in the non-politicised sector and signed several agreements aimed at fostering the exchange of goods and products. In 2000, Croatian enterprises increased their export to Serbia and Montenegro by no less than 656 per cent (VC Experts Group Research, 2004). Despite the progress, Croatian–Serbian relations remain burdened by several open issues, including the return of refugees and displaced persons, as well as the fate of missing persons and the status of minorities.

In light of the gradual improvement in bilateral relations, the creation of visa-free travel became increasingly viewed as an option. In 2002, Croatia and Serbia agreed on first aspects of visa facilitation, introducing the possibility of issuing visas at the borders, allowing multiple visas for businessmen and reducing visa fees. The major leap towards visa liberalisation was made one year later. In June 2003, Belgrade lifted unilaterally its visa requirements for the EU-15 and for most neighbouring countries, including Croatia. The Croatian authorities responded by temporarily lifting the visa requirement for Serbian citizens, but underlined that permanent lifting would depend on cooperation in three areas: the return of birth, marriage and death registers of Croatian citizens that were taken to Belgrade in 1995; replacement of Serbian and Montenegrin military at the Danube border by police; and full cooperation regarding the search for missing persons (Commission of the European Communities, 2004c: 33).

Croatia and Serbia's decision to suspend the visa regime was linked to the EU–Western Balkan Thessaloniki summit, which took place three weeks later on 20 and 21 June 2003. The summit paid attention to the level of commitment shown by each of the Western Balkan states towards enhancing regional cooperation. Since the EU scrutinised Croatia in particular with regard to the improvement of regional cooperation, the country benefited from this step at EU level.

Croatia's further alignment progress of the visa acquis
Following the Thessaloniki summit, Croatia fully aligned its national visa list with the EU's positive visa list of Council Regulation No. 539/2001. Croatia also advanced its compliance with the EU's negative visa list, but maintained a visa-free regime with its neighbouring countries and Turkey. The provisional visa-free regime with Serbia was prolonged several times but not lifted permanently. Russian and Ukrainian nationals might enter Croatia under certain circumstances without a visa (if they could prove that they were in possession of a certified letter of invitation or proof of payment of a reservation).

The acceptance of the EU's positive and negative visa list is likely the most visible conditionality requirement for a candidate country with regard to the visa *acquis*, but there are also several other alignment requirements in relation to procedures for issuing visas and to security features/biometrics in passports and travel documents. The EU sought to familiarise Croatia and the other countries subsumed under the SAP with the visa *acquis* through a so-called Visa Module implemented in the framework of CARDS regional projects.[19] According to an interviewee responsible for its realisation, 'the Visa Module combined a regional approach and common activities for all beneficiary countries with an individual follow-up at the national level. This translates to regional seminars on topics related to visas including the exchange of information combined with national follow-up missions on each of the topics handled in regional seminars' (interview IO8, 11 December 2006, Vienna). The focus on regional cooperation was at the very core of the project and based on the understanding that 'national progress should take place along the same lines and according to the same standards even though every country in the region is on a different level regarding approximation to the EU *acquis*' (ibid).

The Visa Module involved five regional seminars taking place between January 2004 and December 2005 and resulted in the drafting of the visa component of the 'Roadmap for Integrated Asylum, Migration and Visa Management in the Western Balkans'. Through this document, the regional authorities were provided with a practical guide on how to integrate the *acquis* into the domestic legislation. The Visa Module opened discussions about possibilities for consular cooperation between the countries, a subject area that was then transferred to the Stability Pact's MARRI initiative.

In January 2004, Croatia made a major legal adjustment step by replacing the Act on the Movement and Stay of Foreigners with a new Act on Foreigners. Aimed at complying with EU legislation, the new law clarified competent bodies in the visa domain and the deadline for issuing visas, and separated the visa regime for travel purposes from residence and working permits.[20] The Commission was satisfied with Croatia's progress in the visa domain and stated in its opinion for Croatia's application for EU membership that the country has already achieved a 'relatively advanced stage' of conformity with the EU visa *acquis* (Commission of the European Communities, 2004c: 105). The major shortcomings related to Croatia's capacities to detect falsified documents and to ensure proper functioning of the country's consular services in third states. The diplomatic missions and consulates lacked equipment to ensure detection of forged or falsified documents. Also, the staff performing this task needed to be larger and better trained (ibid).

These points did not present a major challenge for Croatia. In February 2005, Croatia introduced new visa labels with increased security features, thereby complying with EU minimum requirements for security features and biometrics in passports and travel documents (Commission of the European Communities, 2006g: 5). Also, the country established an improved IT system linking the diplomatic missions to the national visa register IKOS (Information System of the Foreign Affairs and European Integration Ministry) and gradually introduced a national visa database in all diplomatic missions and consular posts.

Future challenges adjusting to the EU visa acquis

As shown, the EU has endorsed the visa-free regime between Croatia and its neighbours, as 'it has a positive effect on regional integration and stability' (Commission of the European Communities, 2006g: 16). The Commission underlined that 'Croatia must however ensure compliance with EU requirements in this regard on the day of accession at the latest' (ibid).

A possible challenge will therefore be the introduction of new visa requirements for Bosnia and Herzegovina, one of the laggards of the EU's visa liberalisation process towards the Western Balkans (see Chapter 6). Croatia may refrain from introducing new visa requirements for Bosnia and Herzegovina if the country manages to move to the EU's positive visa list by the time Croatia joins the Union. If this is not the case, Croatia will be forced to rely on mitigative procedures to ease the process of introducing new visa requirements.[21] The EU's differential treatment of Bosnia and Herzegovina and Croatia in terms of Schengen visa requirements has always been a sensitive issue. Bosnian Croats, mainly from Herzegovina, have benefited from the liberal EU visa policy towards Croatia as the majority of them are in possession of Croatian passports. In contrast, the Serbian and Bosnian citizens of Bosnia and Herzegovina require visas to travel into the EU and have therefore been at a disadvantage because of their nationality. This has created a *de facto* dividing line in Bosnia.

In short, Croatia has advanced its compliance with EU standards in the visa domain. The adjustment process involved the legal modification of the Croatian visa list and visa procedures, the introduction of new security measures and the establishment of a new information network amongst Croatian consular services. It is possible, however, that a difficult adjustment step still lies ahead. If Bosnia and Herzegovina is on the EU's negative visa list when Croatia accedes the EU, Croatia will have to introduce new visa requirements. According to a high-ranking Croatian politician, this would be 'a quite difficult issue in terms of the normalisation of the regional problems and in terms of the human contacts that will be humbled by the visa regime' (interview C6, 11 May 2006, Zagreb).

Irregular migration and readmission agreements

The EU has closely linked its border management concept to the better control of irregular migration and featured the cooperation in this domain in the context of the Stabilisation and Association Process. The EU accession process has contributed to Croatia increasingly becoming a country of destination, instead of a country of transit for irregular migrants.

Patterns of irregular migration in Croatia

Traditionally, Croatia has been a country of transit for migrants on their way to Western European states. Most migrants entering Croatia have arrived from Bosnia and Herzegovina or Serbia and have sought to transit Croatia in the direction of Slovenia. The highest number of illegal border crossings was registered at the turn of the century. In 2000, the Croatian border police registered 24,180 illegal border crossings, compared to 5,406 in the year 2005. The statistical breakdown shows that most migrants were male (83 per cent) and between 20 and 40 years old.[22]

Croatia's role as an important transit country for the movement of irregular migrants stems from a variety of factors including its position at the northern end of the Balkan route for smuggling arms, illicit drugs and people. Also, the composition and sheer length of Croatia's borders make it difficult to control who and what can legitimately enter the country. Although the country is seven times smaller than Germany, its external borders are only

Table 4.2 Illegal crossings of the state border to and from Croatia

State	2005	2004	+/– (%)	(%)	(%)	To	(%)	From Cro	(%)
Slovenia	3567	3057	16.68	73.81	152	3.15	3415	70.66	
Hungary	22	32	–31.25	0.46	10	0.21	12	0.25	
Serbia	748	364	105.49	15.48	776	16.06	2	0.04	
Montenegro	73	99	–26.26	1.51	73	1.51	0	0.00	
Bosnia and Herzegovina	341	448	–23.88	7.06	288	5.96	53	1.10	
In maritime traffic	82	93	–11.83	1.70	33	0.68	49	1.01	
TOTAL	4,833	4,093	18.08		1,332	27.56	3,531	73.06	

Source: Government of the Republic of Croatia (2006c: 3)

500km shorter. In the past, irregular migration across Croatia's borders was also affected by Bosnia and Herzegovina's comparatively liberal visa regime, which allowed citizens from countries of high migratory risk, such as Turkey or Iran, to enter and stay in Bosnia and Herzegovina. Once in Sarajevo, migrants from these countries often continued to travel with the help of smugglers towards Croatia or, as an alternative, towards Serbia (Kolakovic et al., 2002: 124f). However, migratory pressure from Turkey and the Middle East, as well as from other outside countries, has become less significant since Bosnia and Herzegovina introduced stricter visa requirements vis-à-vis a number of countries.

At the same time, Croatian authorities acknowledged an increase in irregular border crossings for foreign nationals originating from within the region. According to figures from the Croatian Ministry of the Interior (Government of the Republic of Croatia, 2006c), the number of illegal migrants of Albanian ethnicity entering Croatia increased by 300 per cent in 2003. Most illegal crossings were attempted at the border to Serbia, where the number of attempted crossings increased by 105 per cent between 2004 and 2005.

The increase in migratory pressure from within the Western Balkans has been linked to the difficult economic and political situation in the region, particularly in Kosovo, the accession of Slovenia and Hungary to the EU, and Croatia's relatively liberal visa regime towards the successor states of the former Yugoslavia.

EU attempts to control irregular migration from and through Croatia
When irregular migration in Croatia, measured through border apprehensions, grew by more than 40 per cent in the year 2000, the EU became involved in efforts to curb the flow of irregular migration through Croatia. Several activities were launched to regain control over the irregular migration in South-Eastern Europe and to assist Croatia and its neighbours. When asked by the European Commission how many international cooperation forms (regional fora, bilateral agreements, cooperation with the EU) concern-

Table 4.3 Illegal crossings of the state border to and from Croatia: by citizenship

Citizenship	2005	2004	+/– (%)	(%)
Serbia and Montenegro	1534	1010	51.88	31.74
Albania	1014	822	23.36	20.98
Bosnia and Herzegovina	538	476	13.03	11.13
Macedonia	437	424	3.07	9.04
Turkey	332	300	10.67	6.87
Moldova	316	279	13.26	6.54
Croatia	237	247	–4.05	4.90
Rumania	128	263	–51.33	2.65
Slovenia	74	75	–1.33	1.53
Pakistan	16	17	–5.88	0.33
China	4	10	–60.00	0.08
Iran	0	1	–100.00	0.00
Other	203	169	20.12	4.20
Total	4,833	4,093	18.08	

Source: Government of the Republic of Croatia (2006c: 5)

ing the fight against illegal migration it would be involved with, Croatia named twelve initiatives (Government of the Republic of Croatia, 2003b: 104f).

Several initiatives explicitly aimed to bring Croatia closer to EU standards regarding the fight against illegal migration. An illustrating example is the Brdo Process, which was launched in 2001 when the Ministers of the Interior of Croatia, Austria, Italy, Hungary and Slovenia gathered in the Slovenian city of Brdo to develop a regional cooperation forum for the better control of irregular migration flows. The first conclusions highlighted that 'the quickest possible enforcement of the European *acquis*, asylum policy, consistent control of state borders and especially the visa policy towards the non-European states, would contribute to the reduction of illegal flows in the South East European States, through which the flows were running' (quoted in Government of the Republic of Slovenia, 2005). The Brdo Process was hence viewed as a complement to the Stabilisation and Association Process, meant to accelerate the process of EU rule adoption in Croatia. The ministers also agreed to improve the operational cooperation among the states involved, to enhance the exchange of data and to perform joint patrols with the other side of Croatia's borders. The Brdo Process has been gradually enlarged both in terms of participating states as well as in terms of subjects being dealt with. In October 2005, the Brdo Process already encompassed the entire region of South-Eastern Europe and Turkey and envisaged not only a closer cooperation in the field of illegal immigration but also in the fight against organised crime, corruption and terrorism.[23]

In addition, EU member states sought to strengthen their operational cooperation with Croatia and initiated, in direct response to the increase of irregular migration in 2000, a Balkan Border Plan. In March 2001, a team of 40 immigration officers was sent to areas of Bosnia and Herzegovina and Croatia known to be popular with traffickers 'to plug the Balkans' most porous borders' (BBC, 2001). The officers were given the task of assisting and training local immigration staff on how to spot forged passports and visas. The Balkan Border Plan was the main source of reference for the EU's network of member states' immigration liaison officers, which was established in Croatia and other countries of the Western Balkans in the wake of the June 2002 European Council in Seville. The liaison offers were tasked to collect (operational or strategic) information and to 'establish and maintain contacts with the authorities of the host country with a view to contributing to the prevention and combating of illegal immigration, the return of illegal immigrants and the management of legal migration' (Council of the European Union, 2004a). The network of EU liaison officers in the countries of the Western Balkans was the first of its kind and has become a model for similar activities in other regions, particularly Central Asia.

Although the Croatian authorities acknowledged the value added by these initiatives, some officials made reference to the loss of personnel, time and energy that has resulted from involvement in them. A senior Croatian official argued that these initiatives are in some respects even 'counterproductive' for the country:

> Counterproductive as they create two major problems: They do not add value to all the projects we conduct at the EU level. The second problem is that [the involvement] consumes much of Croatia's political energy in terms of human resources and personnel. If you have a police officer who is dealing with illegal immigration in the Ministry of Interior and then involved in EU CARDS, in MARRI, plus the Brdo Process and the Budapest Process and so on. What do you get out of it? A lot of work, mainly coordination and preparation work. (Interview C1, 9 February 2006, Brussels)

Croatia's efforts to fight irregular migration

Article 77 of the Stabilisation and Association Agreement concerns exclusively the topic of 'preventing and controlling illegal immigration'. It suggests that Croatia aligns its legal framework with the EU's *acquis* and improves its domestic standards of accommodation as well as reception and detention procedures for controlling irregular migration.

The first legal amendments, which Croatia introduced to adjust to European and international standards, were not triggered by the SAA however, but by the signing of the UN Convention on Trans-national Organised Crime and the related Protocols on Trafficking in Human Beings and the Smuggling of Migrants in 2000. The UN Convention suggested drawing a better differentiation between smuggling and trafficking in human beings in both legal terms and operational techniques. In December 2002, when the Croatian Parliament ratified the UN Protocol, it also addressed the criminal act of trafficking in persons and slavery by amending Article 175 of the Criminal Code. Perpetrators of trafficking in persons and slavery may now be prosecuted according to the penalties defined in the Palermo Protocol of the UN Convention. A second amendment concerned the Act on the Criminal Liability of Legal Persons, suggesting that companies involved in the organisation of international prostitution and criminal activities connected with trafficking in human beings may be prosecuted as well (Government of the Republic of Croatia, 2006b: 262).

The legal alignment to EU standards was advanced with the adoption of the Act on Foreigners, which entered into force in January 2004. The law provided victims of human trafficking with the status of a temporary resident, if justified under current legislation or an international treaty. At the same time it introduced a new article that facilitated the deportation of foreigners. This stipulation was also meant to respond to operations of smugglers that attempt 'to undermine, delay or obstruct the deportation procedure' (Futo and Jandl, 2004: 44).[24]

Placing particular emphasis on the fight against trafficking, the Croatian government installed a National Committee for the Suppression of Trafficking in Persons in May 2002. The committee was tasked to coordinate training and awareness-raising activities on human trafficking and how to combat it. An interesting feature of the committee was that it included not just ministerial officials but also the state attorney's office, the media and some NGOs. The committee established an operative plan for the suppression of trafficking in persons and introduced a new training system in the policy academy (Government of the Republic of Croatia, 2006b: 261f).

The European Commission was particularly concerned that Croatia lacked the administrative capacities necessary for dealing with irregular migrants. Croatia's major reception centre in Ježevo was considered understaffed and too small (Commission of the European Communities, 2003b: 3). Although the Ježevo centre was established in 1996 to accommodate 80 persons, from 1998 to 2003 it hosted a total of 6,095 irregular migrants from 55 countries (ibid). In the late 1990s, the Ministry of the Interior financed an extension of the centre's capacity to around 250 persons, but the renovation still failed to provide all detainees with adequate accommodation. With the help of EU pre-accession funding, the Ježevo centre was renovated in September 2005. The Croatian Government also built two other transit reception centres to host irregular migrants, located in the area along the state border with Serbia (at the border crossing of Tovarnik) and at the state border with Bosnia and Herzegovina (in Trilj). Both have a capacity to host around 30–40 people.

Improved control of irregular migration was also a concern of the EU's regional Migration Module, which aimed at supporting the Western Balkan countries in the establishment of an EU-compatible national migration system.[25] In this regional framework of cooperation, Croatia underlined the special political and geographic position of their country. According to minutes of the seminars on expulsion, voluntary return and readmission, Josip Paradzik, the Head of the Illegal Migration Department of the Croatian Ministry of the Interior, advanced the view that

> the position of Croatia, both geographically and politically, is different than that of other countries in the region. I am not saying this because I want to put Croatia in a special position, but I am trying to say that we are a transit country for illegal migrants from other countries in the region. I think it is very important to say this. Croatia has been in the position to observe the largest number of asylum seekers and illegal migrants from neighbouring countries, from BiH [Bosnia and Herzegovina] up to Moldova and Albania. (Paradzik, 2005)

With Slovenia and Hungary introducing a Schengen border towards Croatia, the country was confronted with a steadily increasing flow of people trying to cross the Croatian–EU border illegally. Once caught, they were returned to Croatia. Against this background, Croatia was interested in closely cooperating with other countries in the region in order to avoid becoming the final destination of stranded migrants on the way to the EU. The chief means of cooperation have been readmission agreements, which are one of the major themes of the Schengen *acquis*.

Readmission agreements

The aim of a readmission agreement is the mutual taking back of certain categories of persons without any formalities other than those specified in the agreement. In the context of the Stabilisation and Association Process, the EU contractually committed Croatia to 'readmit[ing] any of its nationals illegally present on the territory of a Member state, upon request by the latter and without further formalities' (Commission of the European Communities, 2001c: 48).

The EU accession process obliged Croatia to sign a range of readmission agreements. By October 2007, Croatia had contractual relations with regard to readmission with 24 countries, including Western and Eastern European and other SAP participating states, although seven of these readmission agreements lacked alignment with EU standards (Commission of the European Communities, 2007b: 56).[26] Further readmission agreements were under negotiation with Slovakia, Ukraine, Moldova and Cyprus.

The readmission agreement with Bosnia and Herzegovina (entered into force on 11 May 2001) has proved the most significant. It resulted in roughly 1,000 persons of various nationalities being returned from the Croatian territory into Bosnia and Herzegovina in the first three years. The readmission agreement with Slovenia evoked the second highest number of readmission cases; however the main direction of return was in this case from Slovenia to Croatia (Futo and Jandl, 2004: 45).

As mentioned earlier, Croatia was particularly interested in signing readmission agreements with its neighbours Bosnia and Herzegovina and Serbia. In the late 1990s, Croatia concluded around a dozen readmission agreements with Western European countries, and hence had to accept the return of hundreds of readmission cases. However, the country lacked cooperation with Bosnia and Herzegovina and had not yet clarified whether readmission negotiations would be handled by the central state authority or by authorities at federal level. This problem concerned in particular the cooperation with the Republic of Srpska, accounting for roughly 50 per cent of the joint Croatian–Bosnian border (ICMPD, 1999b: 9). The two countries finally signed a readmission agreement in 2000, after Croatia defined the signing of a readmission agreement as a pre-condition for abolishing its visa requirements for Bosnia and Herzegovina as well as for introducing the possibility of crossing the border using identity cards only.

The initial cooperation between Croatia and Bosnia and Herzegovina was characterised by problems. The return under the readmission agreement took place at one border crossing only, and many individuals who were returned to Bosnia and Herzegovina attempted to re-enter Croatia within a short time due to a lack of effective mechanisms in Bosnia and Herzegovina (Sopf, 2002: 13). These problems have lost salience in more recent years. According to Croatian officials of the Ministry of the Interior, the bilateral cooperation under the readmission agreement has functioned well (interview C8, 8 May 2006, Zagreb).

Also, the readmission cooperation with Serbia was initially ill-functioning due to problems related to unresolved state-building in the region. Croatia signed a readmission agreement with Serbia and Montenegro (in force since June 2004), when Serbia and Montenegro still formed a state union. The two Ministries of the Interior in Belgrade and in Podgorica did not cooperate in the implementation of the readmission agreement. According to a Croatian official, this problem became particularly apparent when Croatia sent a request for the return of an ethnic Albanian from Kosovo. Neither Ministry of the Interior felt responsible (interview C2, 8 May 2006, Zagreb). While Montenegro argued that these cases would not fall within its responsibility, Serbia refused to readmit individuals in possession of an UNMIK document, the official passport issued in Kosovo. As a result, Croatia started to readmit individuals directly into Kosovo (ibid).

In brief, improving control of irregular migration flows from and through Croatia has become an important element of Croatia's EU accession process. Croatia has substantially advanced the alignment to EU standards in the field, a process that included the signing of a range of bilateral readmission agreements, strengthening the administrative capacities of institutions dealing with apprehended irregular migrants and legal amendments to comply with the *acquis* requirements. In 2006, the Commission first announced that Croatia's legislation as regards both legal and illegal migration were largely in place (Commission of the European Communities, 2006e: 54).

Implications for asylum law

The EU's border management policies in the Western Balkans region were only considered successful if supported simultaneously by a clearly defined asylum, migration and visa policy in a regional context (Stability Pact for South-Eastern Europe, 2003: 26). This is due to the fact that 'would-be migrants tend to resort to the asylum procedures in order to achieve their aim of getting into the country of their choice. A harmonised Asylum Policy and Strategy, moulded according to international agreed and accepted standards, could help close these loopholes of exploiting the asylum systems for migration purposes' (ibid).

An introduction into the asylum problematique in Croatia

When talking about asylum in Croatia, a clear distinction needs to be drawn between the refugees and internally displaced persons resulting from the conflicts of 1991 to 1995 and the asylum seekers from outside the region who began arriving in Croatia in 1996.

Between 1991 and 1995, around 300,000 Croatian Serbs fled Croatia and 550.000 Croats became internally displaced. During the same time, Croatia hosted around 500,000 refugees from Bosnia and Herzegovina who either remained in the country (approximately 130,000) or transited through Croatia to another country. From 1995–2006, around 340,000 persons returned to their homes in Croatia. Although the majority were internally displaced Croats, this number also accounts for 120,000 ethnic Serbs who returned to their homes (Commission of the European Communities, 2007b: 13). In 2006, the Croatian Government estimated that approximately 20,000–25,000 persons could still be regarded as returnees (Government of the Republic of Croatia, 2006d: 1).[27]

Ten years after the signing of the Dayton Peace Accords, Croatia, Bosnia and Herzegovina and Serbia sought to finalise the return of refugees and internally displaced persons. In 2005, the three governments signed the Sarajevo Declaration suggesting that the return process should be solved by the end of 2006. This schedule proved unfeasible however, as the signatory states lacked consensus on how to deal with the problems of those refugees who actually returned. In Croatia's case, the problems stemmed from a lack of political motivation 'to deal with compensation claims of those who lost occupancy and tenancy rights (OTRs) in Croatia, and recognition of pensions and other rights for years spent working in Serb-controlled areas of Croatia during the war' (Commission of the European Communities, 2007b: 14).

Over the years, the EU has closely monitored Croatia's efforts regarding the return of refugees and internally displaced persons, yet it has always considered this a separate issue, linked only indirectly to Croatia's adjustment to EU asylum standards.

Asylum seekers from outside the region first arrived in Croatia in 1996, when a total of eleven asylum applications were submitted to the authorities

(UNHCR, 2006). Croatian legislation, more specifically the 1991 Law on Movement and Stay of Aliens, was not sufficiently adapted to deal with the asylum applications (Sopf, 2002: 9f). The law did not outline how to proceed when assessing asylum applications or procedures at borders. Until an official asylum request was made, Croatian authorities generally regarded the asylum seeker as illegal migrants and accommodated them either in the Ježevo detention centre or in a UNHCR funded reception centre in Rakitje (which was in use until 31 December 2002). Despite the small number of asylum seekers, the asylum procedures took a long time (ibid).

Croatia's efforts to align with the asylum acquis
Croatia has initiated a process of aligning to EU asylum standards; however the adjustment has been characterised by a number of problems, both in certain legal aspects as well as in the operational handling of asylum applications.

On 12 June 2003, the Croatian parliament adopted a new Asylum Act. Although the Commission had warned Croatia that 'several provisions of this new draft Law are not yet fully in line with EU standards' (Commission of the European Communities, 2002c: 32), the new law was adopted without major modifications. It was therefore no surprise that the law did not fully meet EU standards. The law did not apply the concept of a safe country of origin, nor did it include legal provisions for accelerated procedures and subsidiary protection. Also, the act did not fully comply with the criteria and mechanisms for determining the responsible member state (Dublin II) (Government of the Republic of Croatia, 2003b: 113f).

Following the Asylum Act's entry into force in July 2004, the EU immediately asked Croatia to amend the law to comply with the asylum *acquis*. Yet it was not until July 2007 that the Croatian parliament introduced amendments to the Asylum Act that resolved its shortcomings. The revised Asylum Act introduced subsidiary protection and accelerated procedures, in addition to several other measures (such as the right to work for asylum seekers after one year in Croatia and the extension of the right to education for asylum seekers) (Government of the Republic of Croatia, 2008b: 391).

Croatia's reception and accommodation standards also lacked compliance with EU standards. The Croatian authorities had at their disposal two reception centres, one for immediate reception and one for long-term accommodation. Certain areas of the reception centre in Ježevo were used for immediate reception, where asylum seekers were given medical examinations, registered and provided with an identity card. From there, they were usually transferred to Šašna Greda where the Croatian Red Cross operated a facility for long-term accommodation of asylum seekers. This system was inefficient and the accommodation substandard. The Croatian authorities therefore sought to improve the reception and accommodation standards and agreed that the accommodation and care for asylum seekers should be provided '*at a single location* till the procedure has been completed' (Government of the Republic of Croatia, 2005: 447–48, emphasis added). The search for a location proved difficult and was accompanied by intense public debates.

In 2005, the Croatian Ministry of the Interior announced its intention to establish the new facility in Stubicka Slatina. The estimated budget required for the development and equipment was HRK13,770,000. Part of the investment, roughly €800,000, was to be covered by the CARDS 2001 programme of reform of asylum policy (Government of the Republic of Croatia, 2005: 448). The CARDS support was not realised, however. According to a European Commission official in Zagreb, the Croatian government dropped the project when the local population opposed it, even though several enterprises were already contracted with the construction work (interview EU11, 11 May 2006, Zagreb). The question of how to accommodate asylum seekers gained priority, and the importance of the issue was reflected by the EU's decision to define the issue as a short-term priority in the country's Accession Partnership (Council of the European Union, 2006a). In June 2006, the Croatian authorities opened a Temporary Reception Centre in Kutina with a capacity of 100 beds.

Croatia's preparations for participating in DublinNet (a communication network supporting the implementation of the Dublin Regulation) and the EURODAC system (which allows the electronic comparison of the fingerprints of asylum seekers) started late. The 2003 Asylum Act provided for fingerprinting and photographing of asylum seekers, but registration was not done electronically. There was no central database to store information about whether an asylum seeker had already submitted an application or other relevant actions. As a result, the Accession Partnership's only medium-term priority in the field of asylum was to develop 'a national database for checking asylum seekers' personal data, including fingerprints, with a view of preparing for participation in EURODAC' (Council of the European Union, 2006a). In August 2007, the twining project Asylum Reform II implemented an investment component to procure equipment for storing the asylum seekers' fingerprints electronically and for connecting to the DublinNET and EURODAC systems. The national system was scheduled for 2009 (Government of the Republic of Croatia, 2008b: 391–92).

The number of asylum applications had been relatively low, with 210 applications in 2005. Interestingly enough, not one of the asylum applications submitted in the period between 1996 and 2005 was approved. The first application was approved in November 2006, when the Croatian authorities granted the right for asylum to a woman from Sudan. According to a Croatian official of the government's asylum department, the lack of asylum approvals was due to the nature of the migratory flows rather than the weaknesses of the asylum legislation.

> Croatia is a country of transit. Most of the asylum seekers leave the country
> before the process is over. Concretely, 90 per cent of the asylum seekers leave

Croatia within 24 days. This is the main reason why Croatia has not approved any request. (Interview C2, 8 May 2006, Zagreb)

In brief, Croatia's initial alignment in the asylum domain was characterised as showing 'no real commitment', according an interviewee of the European Commission delegation in Zagreb (interview EU11, 11 May 2006, Zagreb). The initial legal alignment provided only for partial compliance and the Croatian authorities refrained from improving reception and accommodation standards. Croatia has enhanced its efforts in more recent years by amending the Asylum Act, strengthening its institutional capacities and preparing for participation in the DublinNet and EURODAC systems.

Explaining Croatia's process of adjusting to the EU

This empirical analysis demonstrated that the EU's strategies to invoke rule adoption have been by and large successful in Croatia, with the country strengthening its external border control regime, aligning to the EU's visa and asylum *acquis* and enhancing its efforts to better control irregular migration. Solving open border disputes, notably with Slovenia, has proved to be a particularly challenging issue area. The next section will shift to the explanatory variables that have driven Croatia's process of adjustment to the EU in the field of justice and home affairs, starting with the rational institutionalist argument.

How much explanatory power does the external incentives model of governance have?

The external incentives model of governance maintains, in general terms, that the benefits of EU rule adoption have to exceed domestic adaptation costs in order to make EU rule transfer successful. The cost–benefit calculations of the target government are thought to depend on several intervening variables including the determinacy of conditions, the size and speed of EU rewards, the credibility of conditionality and the domestic size of adoption costs (Schimmelfennig and Sedelmeier, 2004, 2005a).

The determinacy of conditions

A candidate country will refrain from initiating a process of EU rule adoption 'if the EU does not set [these rules] up as conditions for rewards' (Schimmelfennig, 2002: 12). This was not the case in EU–Croatian relations. The EU has ensured that Croatian authorities commit to introducing reforms in the Ministry of the Interior by incorporating at an early stage the EU's justice and home affairs policies and making them a priority in the country's rapprochement process with the Union.

The conditionality principle was provided by the title on justice and home affairs (Chapter VII) of the Stabilisation and Association Agreement, which demanded that Croatia gradually align its policies with the EU's *acquis* on border control, visa policy, migration and asylum. As part of the conditionality principles linked to an eventual EU integration, Croatian actors agreed to introduce reforms in the sensitive policy domain of justice and home affairs. The binding commitment of the SAA to bring the domestic legislation closer to EU standards was very effective in Croatia's case. By the end of 2004, several months before the country officially started its accession negotiations, the Croatian parliament had already adopted around 500 new laws in order to adjust to the EU, meaning that nearly half of Croatian legalisation was harmonised with that of the Community (Kušić, 2005: 439).

The EU's efforts to make Croatia begin focusing at an early stage on compliance with EU policies in the JHA field are reflected in the yearly Progress Reports as well as the Commission's opinion on Croatia's application for EU membership. These documents demonstrate that the EU considers cooperation in justice and home affairs highly important. The *avis* named justice and home affairs as one of the policy fields in which Croatia would need to make 'considerable and sustained efforts' in order to fulfil the accession criteria (Commission of the European Communities, 2004c). Both the European Partnership (Commission of the European Communities, 2004a) and the Accession Partnership (Council of the European Union, 2006a) outlined a number of 'short-term priorities' in particular in the area of border management, judicial reform, equipment procurement and asylum legislation. At the beginning of the accession negotiations, the JHA field was among the policies for which the EU introduced a 'benchmark' to be met before Croatia could begin negotiations on the *acquis* chapter. Croatia faced an EU that was determined to bring the country closer to EU standards in JHA policy.

The EU bolstered its strategy of rule transfer by targeted pre-accession assistance. Between 2000 and 2006, the total EU financial assistance for Croatia (CARDS and the pre-accession instruments PHARE, ISPA and SAPARD) amounted €507 million. The areas that received the most funding were justice and home affairs, democratic stabilisation and economic and social development. When in 2007 CARDS was replaced by IPA, the EU continued to consider assistance in JHA a priority. From the €45.5 million that the EU invested in component I Transposition Assistance and Institution Building of the 2007 IPA programmes, the majority was spent on assistance in eight *acquis* chapters (justice, freedom and security; completion policy; information society and media; agriculture; energy; social policy and employment; environment; and the customs union) (Lynch and Samardzija, 2008: 6).

Certainly the overall progress of Croatia's rapprochement to the EU was determined by issues unrelated to the country's compliance with EU rules in justice and home affairs. Most public and political attention was paid to Croatia's cooperation with the ICTY, particularly on the issue of delivering the war crime suspect Ante Gotovina, the return of refugees and internally displaced persons and the improvement of regional cooperation. In 2009, the unresolved border dispute with Slovenia dominated EU–Croatian relations. The performance of Croatia regarding these subjects has determined, by and large, its pace towards EU accession. That said, Croatia's process in adjusting to EU standards in justice and home affairs has formed an important part of the broader picture. The EU expected Croatia, as a neighbouring country, to take on more responsibility for securing the Union's external borders. Motivated by the prospect of limiting the influx of irregular migrants transiting the Balkans from East Asia and the Middle East, Croatia was urged to establish more effective border security and management systems.

The Croatian authorities did not regard all EU or EU-supported initiatives in the field as useful and sensitive. Rather, some openly questioned the added value of the Ohrid Border Process, which was the attempt of different international organisations to improve border security and management in South-Eastern Europe (see Chapter 3). According to Croatian border officials, the Ohrid Border Process did not present a useful instrument for speeding up the adoption of the EU's integrated border management model.

> To start, one thing has to be clarified: The idea of origin of the Ohrid Border Process was to improve border security on the triangle Kosovo/ Macedonia/Albania. The second main idea was to shift responsibility from the army to the police. With these two ideas, it was finally decided to spread it out and other countries like Croatia became involved. And here is the problem in general: there are several international processes with overlapping agendas and duplications. (Interview C3, 8 May 2006, Zagreb)

From the Croatian point of view, the initiative was considered a chore or a detour on Croatia's road into the EU. Croatian actors would have preferred to concentrate on achieving the most important foreign policy objective, i.e. Croatia's EU accession.

The size and speed of rewards

In the context of Croatia participating in the Stabilisation and Association Process, the first major conditional reward offered by the EU was the signing of a Stabilisation and Association Agreement in October 2001. The decision to offer this EU reward at this particular moment in time was influenced by Croatia's shift towards democratic structures after the end of the Tudjman era. The quick conclusion of the negotiations for the SAA was a means to support the newly installed centre-left Croatian government. The EU sought to create a positive example in the region and possibly initiate a momentum for change in the other Western Balkan states as well. In the late 1990s, the international actors were frustrated with the limited progress in terms of the democratisation of the former Yugoslavia. As one senior Western diplomat stated, 'we were anxious for a change and we were looking for a positive example in the region to make such a change happen' (quoted in Massari,

2005: 268). In their view, the positive example they had looked for was Croatia.

The new Croatian leadership embarked on an ambitious agenda for integrating into the Euro-Atlantic structures, initially even hoping to catch up with the two laggards of the Eastern enlargement, Bulgaria and Romania. With the political support of all parties in Croatia's Sabor, the parliament, the authorities developed an annual National Programme for the Integration of the Republic of Croatia into the EU (the first in January 2003). It clarified the country's schedule and tasks to meet the political and economic criteria linked to EU accession, notably on how to bring the legal framework in line with the EU *acquis communautaire*. The national programme defined its policy priorities according to the short-term and mid-term priorities outlined in the European Partnership and the Accession Partnerships, respectively. Croatia's alignment process of most EU rules under consideration in this analysis can be explained by this institutionalised mechanism of EU integration. According to the Commission's *avis* (Commission of the European Communities 2004c: 5), Croatia's internal arrangements for the implementation of the Stabilisation and Association Agreement seemed to operate effectively.

The second 'reward' relevant for the pace of domestic EU rule adoption was the EU–Western Balkan summit in Thessaloniki in June 2003. The Thessaloniki Agenda adopted at the summit confirmed that each Western Balkan state would enter the EU by its own merit. This statement was particularly well received in Croatia. The EU's lack of differentiation between the countries subsumed in the Stabilisation and Association Process was one of the few points on which Croatia challenged the EU policies (Vlahutin, 2004: 35). As stated by a former Croatian Minister of Foreign Affairs and European Integration,

> a lot of Croats, also political forces, [...] feared that the road to the European Union does not lead directly towards Brussels but that there might be an insistence on a kind of a regional package, even going so far as the recreation of a kind of a third Yugoslav federation. This was the reason why a regional policy was not formulated in Croatia during that time. (Interview C6, 11 May 2006, Zagreb)

The Thessaloniki Agenda reassured Croatia that its accession to the EU would not be linked to the performance of the neighbouring states lagging behind in terms of EU integration. Also, it contributed to Croatia developing a more proactive approach towards regional cooperation, notably with regard to establishing good neighbourly relations with Serbia. As shown, the softening of the rigorous Croatian–Serbian visa regime was among the first measures aimed at improving the bilateral relations. The timing of the Croatian decision was influenced by the Thessaloniki summit, which would take place three weeks later:

> We wanted to [...] cut down the very perception pertaining at that time – the

European view towards Croatia that we were not ready to improve the regional cooperation, to increase the level of our engagement [...] So, when the European Union took a very clear position that all countries of the region have a very clear perspective of EU membership and that this objective can be achieved by individual merits of each state – then we started to be very engaged in the region. This included the suspension of the visa requirements towards Serbia. (Ibid, interview C6, 11 May 2006, Zagreb 31)

In the aftermath of the Thessaloniki summit, Croatia was more constructive towards deepening cooperation in the region. Prime Minister Ivo Sanader's government defined the promotion of regional cooperation as among the key foreign policy objectives. When he entered office in December 2003, one of his first public gestures was to attend the Orthodox Christmas reception party in the premises of the Serb National Council in Zagreb and to visit the Second World War Jasenovac concentration camp in which a high number of Serbs were murdered. These political signs were warmly welcomed by the ethnic Serbs in Croatia as well as in Serbia, opening the door for improved Croatian–Serbian relations (Jovic, 2006: 99).

Regarding the region's EU rapprochement, Croatia sought to assume the role of trailblazer, showing its neighbours how to achieve the objective of Euro-Atlantic integration. In official statements and political discourses, Croatia underlined that it was important for the interest of the country to see the remaining Western Balkan states follow its example. The closer these neighbouring states are affiliated with the EU the better it is for Croatia. Croatian authorities organised a range of activities aimed at transferring the knowledge and best practices they had acquired while advancing in the different stages of the Stabilisation and Association Process to other states in South-Eastern Europe. They invited officials from Bosnia and Herzegovina and Serbia to hold several rounds of technical advisory talks in preparation for the Stabilisation and Association Agreements (House of Lords, 2006: 10). In July 2006, Zagreb organised a regional summit entitled 'Completing Europe's Southern Dimension: The Values That Bind Us' with the official aim of supporting the other countries on their path to the Euro-Atlantic structures.

Croatia increased the pace of EU rule adoption when the country came closer to the accession negotiations with the EU. Several months before the official date for opening accession negotiations was set, the country had finished installing the main negotiating structures. At that time, the government set the objective to become ready for membership by the end of 2007 and to obtain full EU membership by 2009 (Boromisa et al., 2006: 110). So when in 2005 the EU decided to postpone the start of accession negotiations with Croatia due to the country's lack of cooperation with the ICTY, the decision represented not only a setback for Croatia, but also the EU's determination to insist on full compliance with the conditions that had been set.

When Croatia was finally allowed to start the accession talks in October

2005, the country ambitiously sought to break Slovakia's record of two and a half years for completing the EU accession negotiation process. In general, Croatian authorities referred to Slovakia – and not, as one might think, to Slovenia – as a role model with regard to EU accession (interview C5, 11 May 2006, Zagreb). Slovakia was one of the quickest countries to meet EU accession requirements and to finish accession negotiations in the context of the Eastern enlargement. Croatia's eagerness to emulate Slovakia in the accession process was not, however, entirely realised. According to Vladimir Drobnjak, Croatia's chief negotiator with the EU, the information that Slovakia was willing to share about its experience during the accession nego-tiations was of little help to Croatia. The accession process has become different and, in the view of Vladimir Drobnjak, considerably more difficult (quoted in Delevic, 2007). On another occasion, when questioned by the House of Lords, Vladimir Drobnjak underlined that a major difference to previous enlargements was the introduction of benchmarks for opening or closing *acquis* chapters. The benchmarking system has dictated the tempo of accession to the EU and will determine whether Croatia can indeed stick to its pre-defined schedule. Another difference mentioned was that old and new member states were showing the utmost attention to each and every detail (House of Lords, 2006: 5).

The credibility of conditionality
Compared with previous enlargements, the credibility of EU conditionality has decreased for Croatia as a candidate country for EU membership. Compared with the other candidate countries of the present enlargement, however, the EU's conditional rewards have remained the most credible for Croatia. Treated as a special enlargement case, Croatia's prospects of membership have remained plausible, even against the background of the EU's discussions on its 'integration capacity' and a growing enlargement fatigue.

Although building on the experiences of the Eastern enlargement, Croatia's EU accession process has differed in some respects. The EU has increasingly linked its decision of whether to enlarge not only to the perform-ance of Croatia as a candidate country but also to internal developments, notably to the reform of the treaty framework. Because the Treaty of Nice envisaged an enlarged Union of 27 member states, the EU saw the revision of the Nice treaty's framework as a precondition for enlarging beyond this number of member states. The French and Dutch 'no' vote to the European Constitution in May and June 2005 therefore constituted a setback for propo-nents of enlargement. When the EU discussed ways to solve the constitutional crisis, it increasingly considered a revision of the enlargement policies as a contribution to a more favourable public perception of the EU.[28] However, these discussions were particularly concerned with Turkey's continuous case of enlargement, while Croatia's possible EU accession received little attention in the EU's public debate. Croatia was dealt with as a special case in some member states. When on 1 February 2005 the French National Assembly voted on a bill amending the French Constitution so that any further accession to the EU must be submitted to a national referendum, the only candidate country understood to be exempt from this amendment was Croatia. Contrary to other candidates, Croatia's EU accession would not be subject to a national referendum in France.

Despite this favourable treatment, Croatia was concerned with the credibility of the EU membership promises. The domestic political debates centred around the question as to whether, and if so, on which procedural rules, Croatia might enter the EU, now that the project of reforming the EU's institutional framework might fail (Boromisa et al., 2006: 110). The negative referenda on the European Constitution were believed to lower the pace of Croatia's EU accession process (ibid).[29] The idea of a Privileged Partnership promoted by some EU member states as a substitute for full membership was strongly rejected in Croatia. Croatian officials underlined in interviews that it was politically unimaginable for them that the EU would not accept the country if the domestic legalisation was aligned with the *acquis communautaire*. If Croatia would concentrate on the 'homework' necessary for EU accession – no matter how difficult this homework might be – then EU accession was the logical and *only* possible next step.

The EU's adoption of the Treaty of Lisbon in December 2007 to solve the constitutional crisis fostered high expectations in Croatia. Neven Mimica, the president of the Croatian parliamentary Committee for EU Integration, advanced the possibility that the two processes (Croatia's EU accession process and the process of ratifying the Treaty of Lisbon) might be concluded within the same timeframe, that is, by 2009 (quoted in Boromisa et al., 2007: 26). This timeframe proved unrealistic when the Irish people rejected the Treaty of Lisbon in the June 2008 national referendum.[30] Immediately after the Irish 'no' vote, France, Germany and Luxembourg declared that the treaty's entering into force would be a precondition for any further enlargement, explicitly including Croatia in their demand (*Agence Europe*, 21 June 2008). The uncertainty regarding Croatia's EU membership prospects continued to be high.

Croatia reacted to the less favourable enlargement context by reminding the EU of its 'rhetorical action'. This term was developed by Frank Schimmelfennig (2001: 66f) who showed that the EU could be rhetorically entrapped by its shared norms and political promises. If inconsistency between rhetoric and action is exposed in public, 'credibility and reputation suffer'. Croatia applied a strategy of pointing to possible inconsistencies between rhetoric and action in the EU's strategy vis-à-vis South-Eastern Europe. The country portrayed itself as a regional model and a 'showcase' demonstrating how EU integration and the fulfilment of criteria help leave behind a troublesome past (Boromisa et al., 2006: 111). A rejection of

Croatia's bid for membership would have a negative effect on the overall stability of the Western Balkan region, according to the Croatian line of argumentation. If the EU did not reward the frontrunner of the Western Balkans' rapprochement to the EU, how could the other states of the region possibly believe that EU accession would be offered to them?

The EU's institutional problems negatively affected the credibility of the EU membership promises for Croatia; however, they also contributed to an increased threat potential of the EU. In minutes of the EU–Croatian Stabilisation and Association Council and other enlargement documents, Council and Commission officials have frequently referred to a different enlargement context to make Croatia strengthen its reform efforts. For instance, in the minutes of the CARDS Migration Module, Marie-Helene Enderlin, the head of the Justice, Liberty and Security Section of the EC Delegation Zagreb, underlined that 'the first enlargement with ten countries was done quite quickly and with a lot of political pressure; now they [i.e. EU member states] really want benchmarks. If it is not fulfilled you cannot close the chapter. You saw that for Romania and Bulgaria: they have been much tougher on the closing of negotiations' (CARDS Regional Programme, 2005: 13).

The EU has placed more emphasis on the implementation (as follow-up stage to the transposition) of the *acquis communautaire* in Croatia's EU accession process than in previous enlargements. As noted by a Croatian politician, 'we are under more scrutiny by the EU and the Commission when it comes to the implementation of the procedures' (interview C6, 11 May 2006, Zagreb). The Croatian politician attributed the increased emphasis on implementing the *acquis communautaire* to the EU's 'bitter experience' with Bulgaria and Romania's EU accession process, when the issue of implementation was underemphasised.

> This is one of the lessons learnt by the Commission: that implementation is actually the most important one. Therefore, after the fifth enlargement round and with Croatia being the first country of the current enlargement process, we see that the Union insists much more on the implementation performance than it used to do before. In our case, it will not be enough to have fully aligned legislation, but there will be also scrutiny that the existing legislation is fully pursued. (Interview C6, 11 May 2006, Zagreb)

In short, Croatia was among the first countries to experience a more restrictive EU approach towards the admission of new member states. The EU deemed it more important for Croatia to enter the EU well prepared than to enter speedily. In view of this, the EU paid closer attention to how well the country actually enforced and applied the aligned legislative framework.

The extent of domestic adoption costs
In the Eastern enlargement, scholars pointed to the high adoption costs of complying with the EU's border security policies, more specifically with the visa *acquis.* The accession process implied that the then candidate countries

of Central and Eastern Europe had to introduce new visa requirements for Eastern neighbours with which they had close socio-economic and political relations (see e.g. Grabbe, 2002, Kennard, 2002).

In Croatia's case, the alignment with the EU's visa *acquis* has not disrupted good neighbourly relationships. In fact, the EU encouraged Croatia to abolish visa requirements for travel within its immediate neighbourhood, notably with Serbia. The June 2003 decision of the governing coalition under Prime Minister Ivica Racan to ease the visa regime for Serbia was warmly welcomed by the EU, but met with strong domestic criticism. The Croatian Democratic Union (HDZ), the main opposition party at the time, opposed this step on the grounds that the 'resulting "flood" of Serbs moving freely through Croatia would "offend" those Croats who fought in the early 1990s' (quoted in Radonjic, 2003: 2). To counter the criticism, the government launched a media campaign highlighting the fact that the decision was required in order to advance the EU integration process and would also bring economic benefits, in particular in the tourism sector (ibid).

Possibly the strongest implication of Croatia's adjustment process was that the country had to assume greater responsibility to prevent illegal transit migration on the way to the EU. Croatia has become one of the EU's strategically important border countries. Due to its geopolitical position, Croatia seemed to assume this role perfectly, not least in the view of some European politicians. In June 2003, the former UK Prime Minister Tony Blair searched for venues to decrease the political pressure in the asylum domain domestically. He launched plans to process all asylum seekers' claims outside the borders of the European Union. He proposed that so-called Offshore Camps be constructed in nearby third countries. According to his plans, a first camp would be set up in the small village of Trestnik, close to Zagreb. Applications for asylum seekers in Britain would be assessed in this transit processing centre with the EU funding the facility. Successful applicants would then be resettled in the UK or another EU country. Rejected cases would be returned to their countries of origin (*Observer*, 15 June 2003). Faced with Tony Blair's plans, the Croatian government reacted negatively and the idea was soon dropped.

This case was exceptional in the sense that it attracted broad media coverage. However, what should have been achieved by Tony Blair's project immediately is being achieved step-by-step with the EU enlargement process. Croatia has already assumed a greater role in preventing illegal migration flows transiting South-Eastern Europe from entering the EU. According to figures of the Croatian Ministry of the Interior, the number of illegal crossings at the state border has constantly increased in recent years. Croatia's transformation to a buffer zone for preventing irregular migration into the EU has also been influenced by Slovenia and Hungary's introduction of a Schengen border towards the country. As a result, more and more people have been caught while trying to cross the Croatian–EU border illegally.

Croatia's process of aligning with EU standards has therefore produced results comparable to what Heather Grabbe (2002) observed for the Central and Eastern European countries: the alignment of the candidate country's legislation with the justice and home affairs and Schengen *acquis* and, at the same time, giving the candidate country greater responsibility in controlling irregular migration. Similar to their colleagues in Central and Eastern Europe, the Croatian authorities opted for rule compliance in view of the expected payoffs of full membership. A difference of the enlargements was that Croatia was supposed to apply and enforce the adopted legalisation more rigorously and at an early stage. Croatia was expected to become a better-prepared applicant country than any other state before.

How important are alternative explanations?

The external incentives model of EU rule transfer works well to explain Croatia's process of adjusting to EU standards in justice and home affairs. Croatian policies were designed to meet the respective EU rules, which were included at an early stage and in a prominent point in the rapprochement process. The EU managed to establish a credible linkage between domestic *acquis* adoption in Croatia and closer institutional ties with the EU.

Still, a constructivist lens may help explain subtleties of EU rule adoption, as the EU emphasised social learning processes within its strategy of conditionality-based rule transfer. The EU has sought to communicate the legislative, procedural and institutional requirements of the JHA rules in order to decrease problems of non-identification and of legitimacy. 'Conditionality is not important in our daily work in the field of integrated border management', according to an official of the consortium implementing the CARDS regional IBM project. 'We always have to find "carrots" to convince our counterparts' (interview IO7, 11 December 2006, Vienna).

A case in point for the interplay of different dynamics in the EU's external governance approach was the objective of enhancing regional cooperation in border management. The Stabilisation and Association Agreement laid out the conditionality requirement and contractually committed Croatia to establishing cooperation links with the neighbouring border control services (Article 76, Paragraph 1 of the SAA). However, the European Commission was aware that cross-border cooperation cannot be achieved by forcing authorities to do so. A pre-condition for effective cross-border cooperation is a trustful relationship between the authorities. As a result, the EU included confidence-building measures as an important element of the process of EU rule transfer. In the CARDS regional integrated border management project, several workshops were organised in small villages 'where all participants [were] supposed to spend all day and night there and, ideally, come closer to each other' (interview C4, 9 May 2006, Zagreb). Moreover, the participants were supposed to get to know each other and were invited to a three-day study visit in France 'aimed at illustrating how inter-agency co-operation has been organised between border police and customs both at an external EU border and between two EU member states' (Commission of the European Communities, 2005d). Ideally, these activities would translate into a fruitful dialogue on how to share information and data and to cooperate actively.

Also, Croatia's striving for quick EU accession can be better explained by looking at the country's level of identification with the values of the EU. The consensus on the objective of European integration is more pronounced in the Croatian elite than in other Western Balkan states (see Massari, 2005: 264f comparing Croatia, Bosnia and Herzegovina and Serbia). Joining the EU has been seen as 'the ultimate recognition that Croatia no longer represents an exception, but is a normal European state, equal in status and character to others. This is why membership of the EU is now seen as the "second recognition", and is compared to official recognition of independence in January 1992' (Jovic, 2006: 87).

The Croatian political elite perceived of the EU accession process as the completion of the project of nation-state building and as a chance to modernise Croatian society. The EU accession has a particular meaning for Croatia. Coming closer to the EU has been equivalent with distancing itself from the 'Balkans' which is a cultural, historic and geographical term that Croatians have perceived as problematic (Miošaić-Lisjak, 2006: 110). Therefore the accession to the EU not only means the accession to a supranational organisation but rather the ultimate recognition of belonging to a 'European' community. The elite consensus on the objective of European integration was a key for meeting some stumbling blocks on the road towards accession, in particular the improved cooperation with the ICTY and the normalisation of relations with Serbia and Bosnia and Herzegovina (Massari, 2005: 265–66).

Concluding remarks: compliance in times of hardened conditions

This chapter has presented the domestic responses to the EU's external governance approach in the case of Croatia. It has shown that Croatia has made good progress in coming closer to EU standards in the JHA field, even though the EU has hardened the conditions for entering the EU; however, solving the open border disputes proved to be a major stumbling block for Croatia.

The empirical data support an external incentives model of external governance although certain subtleties of the adoption process can be better understood by taking into account the assumptions of the social learning model. The EU defined matters of justice and home affairs, including border management, a priority area for the Croatian government – at an early stage in the accession process. The credible linkage between *acquis* adoption and closer institutional ties with the EU were key conditions for successful EU rule transfer.

Notes

1 According to Eurostat's data on GDP per capita in Purchasing Power Standards, Croatia reached a value of 62.9 in 2008 (EU-27=100). The country's GDP per capita in Purchasing Power Standards was therefore higher than that of five new member states (Bulgaria 41.3, Romania 41.6 (2007 data), Latvia 57.3, Poland 56.4 and Lithuania 61.9). Eurostat data are available at: http://epp.eurostat.ec.europa .eu/portal/page/portal/eurostat/home/.

2 The process of ratification of the SAA in member states was concluded in September 2004 with the agreement entering into force on 1 February 2005. The Stabilisation and Association Agreement meant the establishment of a contractual relationship laying out mutual obligations and commitments. Croatia's performance in the following areas was defined as particularly important for further EU integration: (1) full cooperation with the International Criminal Tribunal for the former Yugoslavia; (2) regional cooperation; (3) return of refugees and internally displaced persons.

3 Together with the opinion on Croatia's application for membership, the Commission presented a European Partnership for Croatia identifying the short- and medium-term priorities for the country (Commission of the European Communities, 2004a).

4 According to the Belgian foreign minister Karel de Gucht, 'an EU climb-down on Croatia would have weakened its power to make Serbia surrender key suspects' (BBC, 2005).

5 The Croatian government had presented an action plan outlining how Croatia seeks to arrest the war crime suspect Ante Gotovina.

6 For instance, see a report by the German newspaper *Frankfurter Allgemeine Zeitung* underlining Austria's role in paving the way for Croatia (*FAZ*, 2005).

7 According to the Croatian Ministry of Foreign Affairs and European Integration, the following bodies were established for the accession talks with the EU: a State Delegation of the Republic of Croatia for negotiations on the accession of the Republic of Croatia to the European Union; a Coordinating Committee for the accession of the Republic of Croatia to the European Union; a Negotiating Team for the accession of the Republic of Croatia to the European Union, supported by 35 working groups for the preparations of negotiations on individual chapters of the *acquis communautaire*; and finally, an Office of the Chief Negotiator and a Secretariat responsible for the negotiating team. Detailed information can be accessed at the homepage of the Croatian Ministry of Foreign Affairs and European Integration: www.eu-pregovori.hr/ (accessed 6 December 2008).

8 The country team was assisted by the secretariat of the Budapest Process, the International Organisation for Migration and the UNHCR. A similar project took place in other SAP participating states.

9 In April 2007, the Croatian parliament amended the law to align it with the *acquis* on passenger data.

10 The process of restructuring the border police included the set-up of other institutions. In January 2005, for instance, Croatia established an additional Mobile Border Unit to combat effectively illegal border crossings.

11 The advanced programme was developed within the working education group in the framework of the twinning project for border police.

12 The Croatian side was represented by an inter-ministerial group involving officials of the border police, the customs administration and the plant health and veterinary agencies. The project started in April 2004 and was funded with € 1.8 million of CARDS allocations.

13 The project concerned the improvement of border police mobility, green border surveillance and equipping of border crossings with devices for the detection of false

travel documents (Government of the Republic of Croatia, 2007a: 363).

14   Article 76, Paragraph 1 of Croatia's SAA outlines that the 'parties shall cooperate in the areas of visa, border control, asylum and migration and will set up a framework for cooperation, including at a regional level, in these fields' (Council of the European Union, 2005c).

15   Before 2000, Croatia had pursued a policy of 'special parallel relationship' with the Federation of Bosnia and Herzegovina (i.e. the Bosnian entity of Muslims and Croats), leaving the Republic of Srpska aside. Following Franjo Tudjman's death, the newly elected Croatian government renounced this policy and established relationships exclusively with the central state authorities in Sarajevo.

16   Funded with €2 million of CARDS allocations, the project was led by the French Service de Coopération Technique Internationale de Police (SCTIP) in conjunction with the French Ministry of Foreign Affairs, the Austrian Agency for European Integration and Economic Development, the OSCE and the International Centre for Migration Policy Development.

17   The ecological and fishing protection zone was initiated by the Croatian Peasant Party (HSS).

18   The Citizens' Pact for South-East Europe is a network of NGOs and municipalities in South-Eastern Europe that launched the visa abolishment campaign with the aim of abolishing all visa requirements within the region and from the region to the EU. For detailed information, see: www.citizenspact.org.yu/novisa/about.htm (accessed 8 January 2009).

19   The visa twinning project was implemented by the International Centre for Migration Policy Development under the supervision of the Swedish Migration Board.

20   An inter-ministerial working group was charged to monitor the implementation of the Act on Foreigners and to propose further legal amendments, if deemed necessary.

21   According to an international expert on visa issues, Croatia's options include 'to certain forms of visa facilitation within the framework of the common consular instructions, such as certain cost reduction in individual cases, faster processing times and simplified procedures, which many countries that have aligned or are aligning to the visa policy of the EU have also done during a bridging period' (interview IO8, 11 December 2006, Vienna).

22   For migration data on Croatia, see Government of the Republic of Croatia (2006c) and Commission of the European Communities (2003b: 2, 2006g).

23   In 2002, Albania, Bulgaria, Romania, Bosnia and Herzegovina and Serbia and Montenegro joined the process, followed by Turkey and Greece in 2004.

24   In April 2005, a working group under the responsibility of the Ministry of the Interior was formed to monitor the implementation of the Act on Foreigners.

25   The Migration Module was financed under CARDS 2002/2003 and implemented by the International Organisation for Migration under the supervision of the Swedish Migration Board.

26   In the first year following the signing of the SAA, Croatia signed a particularly high number of readmission agreements: eight with EU member states, nine with the then candidate countries from Central and Eastern Europe and two with other SAP countries (Commission of the European Communities, 2002b: 29).

27   This number is based on 11,868 individual applications for return, 4,100 reconstruction claims, and 3,880 housing requests submitted by refugees from Serbia, Montenegro and Bosnia and Herzegovina (ibid).

28   Opinion polls revealed that the French and Dutch citizens felt uneasy with the way in which previous enlargements were conducted as well as with which countries may enter the EU in the future (on France, see Dalem, 2006: 120).

29	Croatian politicians were also worried that the process of Croatia's EU accession was linked too closely to Turkey's EU accession, as the two countries started the accession negotiations on the same day (Boromisa et al., 2006: 110).
30	Ireland was obliged by its constitution to hold a national referendum on the EU treaty.

5

Rule adoption in Macedonia

The second case study concerns Macedonia, a country with a background different from Croatia. Macedonia's short history as an independent state has been marked by major challenges and setbacks, the most serious of which was a near-civil war in 2001. As a matter of fact, the EU's policy vis-à-vis Macedonia was characterised by elements of conflict prevention and post-conflict stabilisation, in addition to the pre-accession policy. This chapter analyses the domestic response to the EU's strategy in the field of justice and home affairs and elaborates on the EU's avenues of external influence in this important area of cooperation.

The procedural and institutional context

Macedonia, a country in search of stability

In the wake of its declaration of independence in November 1991, Macedonia faced a difficult and tedious process of consolidation, with its stability jeopardised by conflict spillovers from the war in neighbouring countries to the north. Following independence, the country was *de facto* demilitarised. In addition, the inter-ethnic cohabitation of the young state was fragile and a source of political tension. From a population of 2.1 million, approximately 64 per cent are ethnic Macedonians and 25 per cent ethnic Albanians. There are also other, although smaller, minorities of Turks, Roma and Serbs.[1] The political problems were deepened by a difficult economic situation. Already the poorest province of the former Yugoslavia, its economic transformation was impeded by two embargos, the first imposed by UN resolutions against the entire region of the former Yugoslavia and the second by Greece in reaction to a dispute over the use of the name 'Macedonia'.

The dispute between Macedonia and Greece had its origin in the two countries' diverging views on how to use the name 'Macedonia' and the country's flag (see Tziampiris, 2000, Pettifer, 2001). Greece argued that the name Macedonia implies a geographic region of which 52 per cent is located on Greek territory. Also, Greek politicians publicly advanced that the display of symbols of Greek heritage, such as the Star of Virgina, on the Macedonian flag was an indication of the former Yugoslav Republic's expansionist ambitions over Greece. Macedonia, by contrast, maintained that nothing in its Constitution stating its protection of all Macedonians could be interpreted as a claim for territory in the northern Greek province. With Greece objecting to Macedonia's constitutional name, the country was accepted to the United Nations in April 1993 only under the provisional name the Former Yugoslav Republic of Macedonia (FYROM). This synonym became the official name in EU and UN documents. In bilateral relations, more than 120 states including the US and Russia have recognised Macedonia under the constitutional name Republic of Macedonia, regardless of the protests of Greece.

In 1995, an UN-brokered Interim Accord temporarily relieved the tensions in the name dispute and ended Greece's nineteen-month trade embargo against Macedonia. A permanent solution to the conflict has not yet been found, however. In fact, the bilateral conflict heated up again in April 2008 at the NATO summit in Bucharest when Greece vetoed Macedonia's invitation for NATO membership precisely due to this issue. The decision was bound to have major implications, causing new elections in Macedonia and, as one observer put it, bringing 'Macedonia's multiethnic "success story" [...] to its most profound crisis' (Matovski, 2008).

Macedonia's search for stability has also been challenged by internal tensions between the Macedonian majority and ethnic Albanian minority. In the 1990s, when the country remained uninvolved in the successor wars of the former Yugoslavia, Macedonia managed to build up the reputation of an 'oasis of peace in the Balkans'.[2] This reputation was dismantled as a myth however, when an armed conflict erupted in different parts of the country in 2001. Members of the National Liberation Army (NLA), predominantly Albanian citizens from Macedonia, and Macedonian security forces clashed in the period from February to August 2001. The reasons for the unrest were quite unclear but resulted, according to the Macedonian political scientist Jovan Donev (2003: 228), from a combination of factors including the conditions in Kosovo, the weakness of the state institutions in Macedonia, the difficult economic situation and a high unemployment rate, particularly among the ethnic Albanians.

The EU and US jointly exerted intense pressure on the Macedonian and Albanian parties to agree to a process of negotiations, which contributed to preventing a full-scale civil war. Under the chief negotiators Ali Ahmeti, the Albanian minority's insurgent leader, and his counterpart Vlado Buckovski, the Macedonian Minister of Defence in 2001, a peace accord was brokered and signed on 13 August 2001. Named after the village in which the signature ceremony took place, the Ohrid Framework Agreement defined several constitutional amendments that responded to major grievances of the Albanian minority. The stipulations called for in particular the decentralisation of important parts of the political decision-making processes and better representation of ethnic Albanians in the public administration. Although opposed by radical national circles in Macedonia, the Ohrid Framework

Agreement has stabilised the inter-ethnic relationship and, according to the point of view of the renowned International Commission on the Balkans, 'offers the best way of holding the country together' (Balkan Commission, 2004: 27).

The new constitutional arrangement
The Ohrid Framework Agreement (2001) predefined several constitutional amendments and political reforms, including the development of a decentralised government structure (Principle 3); the principle of non-discrimination and equitable representation of all ethnicities in the public administration and public enterprises (Principle 4); the definition of the Albanian language as an official language in municipalities where it is spoken by at least 20 per cent of the population, in addition to at the central government level (Principle 6, Paragraph 5). Also, the Macedonian authorities sanctioned the presence of NATO troops to collect weapons from the National Liberation Army. In exchange for handing over their weapons, the Albanian insurgents were promised amnesty. Another constitutional amendment concerned the way in which the Albanians have to be referred to in the Constitution ('citizens of Macedonia, who are part of the Albanian nation'). The privileged constitutional status of the Macedonian Orthodox church was brought to an end. The overall objective of the Ohrid Framework Agreement was to transform the Macedonian state into an entity that both ethnic Macedonians and ethnic Albanians could and would regard as 'theirs' (ICG, 2004: 4).

The implementation of the agreement turned out to be difficult. The constitutional amendments and political reforms were salient issues, provoking heated debates on their legitimacy, advantages and possible disadvantages. The major breakthrough in terms of implementing the agreement was achieved in November 2004 when a referendum on the re-territorialisation of the country failed, which was a *de facto* vote on the Ohrid Framework Agreement. The outcome of the referendum demonstrated that a majority of Macedonians and ethnic Albanians had come to accept the new constitutional arrangements. Macedonia's way out of the conflict was considered a success. For instance, inspired by the Macedonian case, the Balkan Commission argued that, 'if the constitutional questions are resolved and if a tangible European perspective is on the table, then Balkan societies have the potential to get out of the cycle of instability and uncertainty. It is not by accident that Macedonia is a success story in Europe's drive to promote multi-ethnic societies in the region' (Balkan Commission, 2004: 27–28).

Not all analysts have shared such an optimistic assessment. Although agreeing that the Ohrid Framework Agreement promoted multi-ethnicity and improved integration of minorities in the Macedonian society, Nadège Raguru maintained that 'decentralisation and recent developments in the educational system are likely to induce greater ethnic separation, if not segregation' (Ragaru, 2008: 51). In her view, the federalisation process has increased the risk of social distance and economic disparities between the communities possibly resulting in strained inter-ethnic relations. Also, the International Crisis Group warned Macedonia in 2005 that it was not 'out of the woods yet' (2005b) since several problems and challenges would still jeopardise the long-term stability of the country. An issue of particular relevance has been the Kosovo final status question and the potential of insecurity spillovers into neighbouring Macedonia.

The context of regional security

The present regional stability in the Balkans has been closely linked to Kosovo's struggle for independence and Serbia's determined opposition to such a step. Kosovo declared its independence on 17 February 2008, which was the final step of years of diplomatic efforts to define the Kosovo final status.[3] The challenges that Kosovo has faced following the declaration of independence have been manifold and complex. Likely the most difficult one is the integration of the Kosovo Serbs into the institutional framework in order to prevent a segregated society and a *de facto* partition of Kosovo (Schmidt, 2008: 33f).

The sensitive handling of Kosovo's bid for independence by the international community is of interest for Macedonia, in particular against the background that 'Macedonia's Achilles heel is Kosovo' (Glenny, 2004a: 6). As long as Kosovo's status remains subject to controversies within the EU[4] and in the region, political forces and organised crime networks will find it easier to destabilise the region for political reasons or to secure their criminal revenues. Radical political forces of the Albanian minority have voiced ideas on a Greater Albanian State, which would also include the Albanian-dominated region of north Macedonia. As will be shown, the border region between Macedonia and Kosovo is an area with a particularly sensitive security situation.

The Macedonian government has closely aligned its position in the Kosovo issue to the EU and NATO mainstream, described as a strategy of 'brac[ing] itself for Kosovar independence from under the Euro-Atlantic security umbrella' (Ordanovski and Matovski, 2008: 2). The question of whether Macedonia should recognise Kosovo as an independent state was contested in the country. According to a March 2008 opinion poll, 95 per cent of the ethnic Albanians favoured the immediate recognition of Kosovo, whereas 60 per cent of Macedonians were against such a step (Centre for Research and Policy Making, 2008). Following several months of hesitation, the Macedonian government recognised an independent Kosovo in October 2008.

In short, the insecurities in relation to the contested nature of Kosovo's independence and an unresolved dispute with Greece over the name Macedonia are key external factors that impact Macedonia's long-term stability. Additional internal challenges also exist, including 'government foot-dragging on implementation of Ohrid, and endemic – and fully multiethnic – corruption that continues to undermine the institutions on which the Agreement must rest' (ICG, 2006). The country has also struggled with a poor economic performance.

Macedonia's macroeconomic data
Already one of the most underdeveloped republics of the former Yugoslavia, Macedonia's transformation from a Communist-based economy into a market economy was troubled by the fact that the country was cut off from its traditional markets through the collapse of the common state. The Greek embargo from the south and the UN sanctions against all successor republics of the former Yugoslavia made the economic situation even more difficult. Despite these unfavourable circumstances, Macedonia implemented some major economic reform programmes in the 1990s, closely assisted and supervised by the World Bank and the International Monetary Fund. The programmes bore their first fruits in the late 1990s, when Macedonia's GDP witnessed a strong growth, yet the economic upswing came to a temporary standstill due to the 2001 conflict (see Table 5.1 below, also Donev, 2003: 231).

Table 5.1 Main macroeconomic indicators for the Republic of Macedonia

	2000	*2001*	*2002*	*2003*	*2004*	*2005*	*2006*	*2007*	*2008*
Per capita GDP (in EUR)	1,925	1,890	1,962	2,028	2,130	2,298	2,491	2,834	–
GDP – year-on-year rate of growth (%)	4.5	–4.5	0.9	2.8	4.1	4.1	4.0	5.9	4,8*
Current account balance (as of % GDP)	–2.7	–6.9	–10.0	–4.0	–8.4	–2.7	–0.9	–7.5	12.7
Inflation (%)	5.8	5.5	1.8	1.2	–0.4	0.5	3.2	2.3	8.3
Unemployment rate (%)	32.2	30.9	31.9	36.7	37.2	37.3	36.0	34.9	33.8

* preliminary data for 2008
Sources: National Bank of the Republic of Macedonia, basic economic data (last update: 29 January 2010) Data on 'Per capita GDP' retrieved from the Commission Progress Report (2009a: 77).

Macedonia's objective was to achieve macroeconomic stability with low inflation, balanced public finances and low public indebtedness. Between 2003 and 2008, the country did indeed achieve a significant GDP rate, reaching a peak of 5.9 per cent in 2007. An impediment to its economic advancement has been the particularly high unemployment rate. Large sectors of the population have been excluded from the regular employment market (33.8 per cent in 2008) and threatened by impoverishment. Although the global financial crisis had a negative impact on Macedonia, the slowdown of the Macedonian economy has been 'limited', according to European Commission data (2009a: 25). Still, the crisis slowed the GDP growth of Macedonia, reduced the budget revenues and negatively affected Macedonia's foreign exchange reserve and external debt (ibid).

The process of creating a functioning market economy has not yet been completed. The European Commission maintained that 'despite important progress in improving the business environment, the still slow speed of judiciary procedures and sometimes insufficient resources of supervisory and regulatory agencies are still impeding the rule of law, contract enforcement and the creation of a level playing field for market participants, which are crucial elements for fully functioning markets' (Commission of the European Communities, 2008g: 28). It was questionable if the country's economy would at this stage sustain the competitive pressures in the EU's single market.

To sum up, Macedonia managed to consolidate as an independent and sovereign state although several challenges, in particular the 2001 inter-ethnic conflict between Macedonian security forces and insurgents from the National Liberation Army, jeopardised the stability of the country. After this conflict was prevented from escalating into a full-scale war, Macedonia agreed to sign a peace accord that revised its Constitution, initiated a process of decentralisation and laid the basis for an improved multi-ethnic coexistence. The country's long-term stability, however, has remained fragile and depends on several endogenous and exogenous factors such as the Greek–Macedonian dispute over the name for the country. The analysis now shifts attention to Macedonia's state of relations with the EU, an important factor of influence throughout the country's short history as an independent state.

Macedonia's state of relations with the EU

EU–Macedonian relations started officially in the year 1996 when Macedonia became eligible for funding under the PHARE programme. Between Macedonia's declaration of independence in 1991 and 1995, any improvement in EU–Macedonian relations was vetoed by Greece, taking the EU institutions hostage for the Greek–Macedonian name dispute (Tziampiris, 2000). In January 1998, a first Cooperation Agreement and an agreement in the field of transport entered into force.

When the EU launched the Stabilisation and Association Process in May 1999, Macedonia was the first Western Balkan country to forge closer ties with the Union. The main reason for doing so was Macedonia's constructive role during the 1998–1999 Kosovo conflict. The country had to shoulder most of the refugee burden, with around 360,000 people fleeing from the conflict into neighbouring Macedonia. EU member states deemed the country's handling of the refugee crisis exemplary. After the end of the Kosovo war, the Council quickly approved the Commission's Feasibility Report (1999) and gave the go-ahead to open the negotiations for a Stabilisation and Association Agreement, explicitly underlining the 'positive record achieved by the country, its exemplary role in the region and its compliance with the relevant conditionality' (Council of the European Union, 1999a).

The process of negotiating the EU–Macedonian SAA coincided with the time period in which the tensions between the Macedonian majority and the Albanian minority increased significantly. The EU quickly concluded the negotiations and allowed Macedonia to sign the SAA on 9 April 2001 (Council of the European Union, 2001d) – a point in time when the Macedonian inter-ethnic conflict was on the edge of erupting into an open civil war. The EU made Macedonia's EU rapprochement process conditional on its peaceful handling of the internal security crisis. Since the conflict was portrayed as a 'test case' for successful EU foreign policy-making (Ahlbrecht, 2004), the EU sought keenly to prove that its evolving CFSP/ESDP was finally capable of stabilising the area of former Yugoslavia. In view of criticism that the EU's involvement in the previous successor wars of the former Yugoslavia was a policy failure (see e.g. Cafruny, 1998, Lucarelli, 2000), the newly emerging conflict provided the EU with an opportunity to demonstrate its capacity of preventing another Balkan crisis from further escalation.

The EU employed a range of civilian and military crisis management capabilities available across the pillar temple structure. Within its first pillar, the European Communities, substantial financial aid packages were announced in the case of a peaceful conflict resolution. The signing of the Stabilisation and Association Agreement at the peak of the conflict was thought to be an incentive for ending the violence. When the actors involved in the conflict signed the Ohrid peace accord, its implementation was defined as a precondition for the country's further progress in the EU accession process. The farthest-reaching involvement took place within the second pillar, the EU's Common and Foreign Security Policy. The CFSP's High Representative Javier Solana travelled frequently to Macedonia to exert pressure for a peaceful conflict resolution, and was assisted by Special Permanent Envoys that were dispatched to Skopje to achieve a higher degree of visibility and presence on the ground.[5] Furthermore, the EU and NATO closely coordinated their activities and tabled very similar proposals for conflict resolutions. All activities combined contributed to the EU's success of preventing a civil war and brokering the Ohrid Framework Agreement as a peace accord acceptable to the conflict parties (Ahlbrecht, 2004).

When the activities for conflict prevention proved successful, the EU also sought to assume responsibility in stabilising the post-conflict situation. In May 2003, the EU deployed to Macedonia its first military operation, named

Operation Concordia, under the European Security and Defence Policy. It took over command of the NATO mission Essential Harvest as well as the smaller successor missions Amber Fox and Allied Harmony, which were dispatched in the immediate aftermath of the conflict to supervise the Ohrid Framework Agreement and, in line with the stipulations of the peace accord, to disarm the Albanian insurgents of the National Liberation Army. Operation Concordia was established to further monitor the implementation of the peace accord and to contribute to the overall stabilisation of the security situation in the country.[6] During its dispatch, progress in implementing the Ohrid Framework Agreement and a successful government change gave reason to believe that Operation Concordia had effectively fulfilled its mandate.

However, Macedonia's internal stability remained fragile. In October 2003, the International Crisis Group published a report with the meaningful title 'No Room for Complacency' arguing that the peace process lacked sustainability and might still be jeopardised. The conclusion of the ICG report, stating that 'Macedonia still needs security assistance' (ICG, 2003: ii), was shared by the EU. In December 2003, the EU dispatched the Police Mission Proxima as a follow-up to Operation Concordia. With a strength of 200 police officers and civilians, Proxima was tasked 'to monitor, mentor and advise the local police, thus help to fight organised crime more effectively and consolidate public confidence in policing' (Council of the European Union, 2003c). Proxima remained in Macedonia for two years and was replaced by the smaller EU Police Advisory Team (EUPAT), which completed its mandate in June 2006.

The EU relied not only on mechanisms of conflict prevention and post-conflict stabilisation but also on the incentive of membership. Macedonia was allowed in advance the step-by-step process towards EU accession. On 22 March 2004, the country officially submitted its application for EU membership. The Commission asked Macedonia to fill in a questionnaire of more than 3,000 questions relating to the political system, economy, legislation, administration and social affairs. In February 2005, less than four months later, Macedonian authorities completed the process of answering the questions and presenting the state of play of each policy sector on roughly 700 pages.[7]

Despite progressing European integration, Macedonia's internal consolidation suffered a setback when the Macedonian President Boris Trajkovski died in a plane crash on 26 February 2004. Boris Trajkovski had been appreciated well beyond the Macedonian borders for, as the European Commission (2004b: 5) put it, his 'constructive role in building consensus on issues of national importance, including European integration and security matters, as well as the implementation of the Framework Agreement'. The subsequent presidential elections brought into power Branko Crvenkovski, the former Prime Minister. The country's internal consolidation was also challenged by the intense debates in the run-up to the referendum on the decentralisation programme as mandated by the Ohrid Framework Agreement. The then main opposition party VMRO-DPMNE tried to make political hay of the referendum and featured the general halt of the decentralisation process. The failed referendum of 7 November 2004 demonstrated, however, that the campaign was not successful, thus clearing the way for further implementation of the Ohrid Framework Agreement.[8]

When the peace accord was fully implemented in July 2005, the European Commission (2005b) published its opinion on Macedonia's application for EU membership. The Commission's *avis* recommended granting Macedonia the status of a candidate but emphasised that Macedonia lacked progress in some areas, in particular regarding the electoral process, police and judiciary reform and the fight against corruption. The Brussels European Council of 15 and 16 December 2005 followed the Commission's advice and granted Macedonia the status of a candidate for EU membership. However, the heads of state and government of the EU made no mention of when the country could possibly begin the negotiations for EU membership, calling for further progress in implementing the Copenhagen criteria and the SAA provisions (European Council, 2005).

In three consecutive Progress Reports (2006–2008), the European Commission deemed the efforts of the Macedonian government insufficient and recommended against opening accession talks. According to the EU's Accession Partnership for Macedonia, the country would not take the next step in the accession process unless eight benchmarks were met. These benchmarks related to the establishment of a track record in implementing judicial reform, ensuring an impartial and non-politicised police force, improving the fight against corruption, and the recruitment of civil servants in a more objective manner based on professional criteria (Council of the European Union, 2006c, 2008a).

The poor performance of the June 2008 elections presented a major setback to Macedonia's aspirations to start EU accession negotiations, as 'key international standards were not met' (Commission of the European Communities, 2008g: 7). The elections were won by Prime Minister Nikola Gruevski's VMRO-DPMNE and his 'For a Better Macedonia' coalition, yet overshadowed by serious irregularities in the election process. There were cases of violence, and also family voting (where the head of a family influenced or determined the vote of other family members) and voting without papers. A re-vote had to be held at nearly 200 polling stations on 15 June 2008.[9] Following the election, the EU introduced an additional benchmark for opening accession negotiations, that of conducting elections without irregularities. In the 2009 Progress Report, the Commission finally suggested opening accession negotiations with Macedonia (Commission of the European Communities, 2009a), yet the European Council delayed the decision to 2010 in reaction to Greece's opposition to an early start of accession negotiations (EurActiv, 2009b).

In brief, the EU has developed an active foreign policy approach towards Macedonia, particularly in the years following the 2001 security crisis when the EU contributed to stabilising the fragile post-conflict situation and allowed Macedonia to advance in the EU accession process. Macedonia's progress in the Stabilisation and Association Process has slowed down in more recent years, as reflected in the country's difficulties in receiving an official date for the start of EU accession negotiations.

Macedonia's border challenges

Macedonia is a landlocked country with a total border length of 748km (151km with Albania, 148km with Bulgaria, 246km with Greece and 221km with Serbia). The country's external border is a difficult one to control as the borderline frequently passes through rural and mountainous provinces following the ridge of mountain ranges.

In the context of EU integration, Macedonia has faced several border-related challenges. The border control system that Macedonia established in the aftermath of its independence was inefficient, weak and guided by outdated doctrines (Bolton, 2005). To comply with EU standards, Macedonia was not only asked to strengthen its existing border control system (as was the case in Croatia) but to entirely transform its internal arrangements on border policing. The reform process included discharging the army from its border protection responsibility and replacing the military conscripts with professional police officers.

Similar to other Western Balkan countries, Macedonian border control was characterised by weak (if any) levels of cooperation and coordination across institutional and national dividing lines. Several well-established trafficking routes have traditionally passed through Macedonia's porous borders, including a 'central' route through the Presovo Valley section of the border north-east of Skopje, in the direction of Belgrade, and another 'Italian' route from the Tetovo area over to Prizen (Hills, 2004c: 60). Corruption has been a phenomenon among the poorly paid and ill-equipped border guards: as one international adviser noted, border-guarding personnel have been 'happy to take bribes to turn a blind eye to illegal border crossings' (Bolton, 2005: 9).

The border triangle of Macedonia, Kosovo and Southern Serbia has been characterised by a fragile security climate. Criminal groups or networks have benefited from the enduring insecurity in the region and have sought to maintain a relatively lawless environment in which they can pursue their criminal activities. They are generally well armed and willing to use their weapons. Macedonian authorities consider criminal and insurgent activities originating outside the state territory to be among the country's biggest border-related challenges. From the perspective of the EU, however, the problem is more complex and relates also 'to the country's legacy and the Macedonian government's inability or unwillingness to deal with the country's troubling socio-economic realities, such as corruption' (Hills, 2004c: 60).

Finally, there has been a lack of consensus on the demarcation of the border between Kosovo and Macedonia which has been not only a problem in terms of effectively protecting the borders but also a source of political tensions between the Kosovar and Macedonian authorities.

EU border security policies: an evaluation of their impact in Macedonia

When the country gained independence in 1991, the Macedonian Constitution tasked the army to provide security and territorial integrity for the state. The 1st Army Border Brigade was established to patrol the green border (the borderline between the official border crossing points) whereas the crossing points came under the charge of police forces of the Macedonian Ministry of the Interior. In strategic terms, Macedonia started to approach border security from the perspective of militarily protecting a linear feature. This 'linear feature approach' has been criticised as an 'antiquated and ineffective approach to borders which places the emphasis on security rather than management and efficiency' (Bolton, 2005: 3). Indeed, the country's border guarding system manifested several shortcomings in the context of the 2001 security crisis. Albanian insurgents belonging to the National Liberation Army managed to cross the Macedonian–Kosovar border without any difficulty.

In the aftermath of the crisis, the EU considered the transformation of the external border control policies an important factor in stabilising the overall security situation of Macedonia. As argued by Alice Hills, Macedonia had few strategic options at that time. It essentially could have opted either to continue to 'place poorly trained military forces and ineffective police on its insecure borders, or [to] gain international credibility by reforming its border system according to Schengen standards' (Hills, 2004c: 61).

The transformation of the external border control system

The overall reform objective in the area of border management was to establish a specialised, professional civilian border police in Macedonia in line with European standards. Starting with the signature of the Stabilisation and Association Agreement, the reform was centred around two activities: first, the creation and implementation of a national integrated border management strategy and second, the transfer of border protection responsibility from the Ministry of Defence to the Ministry of the Interior.

The drafting and the implementation of the national IBM Strategy

The Macedonian government began the process of drafting a national IBM strategy in accordance with the EU's IBM Guidelines by establishing an inter-ministerial working group made up of experts from seven ministries, all of which were already involved in border management.[10] The Ministry of the

Interior took the lead in the process and carried out the overarching coordination work. Ahead of the official schedule, the working group finished the national IBM strategy in only nine months. The strategy's adoption on 22 December 2003 was warmly welcomed by the European Commission and the European Agency for Reconstruction, which praised Macedonia as 'the first country in the Western Balkans to develop a national integrated border management strategy that is in line with Schengen rules' (EAR, 2005a).

In the IBM strategy, a booklet of fifty-five pages published in conjunction with the police reform strategy, the Macedonian government defined each element of the reform of Macedonia's external border control system, including stipulations for legislative changes, a more exact delineation of competences, and plans to improve management procedures as well as operational facilities. According to the IBM strategy,

> in the future, border management in Macedonia will be *radically different* from that of today with its linear orientation [...] This integrated border management concept will provide greater security through better intelligence, more effectively coordinated responses, and unprecedented inter-agency and international cooperation against the threats posed by international crime and terrorism. (National IBM Strategy, 2003: 79, emphasis added)

The major change foreseen, which would indeed make Macedonia's border management 'radically different' (see quotations above), was to establish a new national Border Police Service and to withdraw the 1st Army Border Brigade from its responsibilities on Macedonia's state border. The new Border Police Service was to become the equivalent, yet non-military, border guarding structure in the Ministry of the Interior, tasked to 'absorb the responsibilities of the Sector for Border Crossings of the Ministry of the Interior in addition to those of the army Border Brigade. It [would] therefore be responsible for the control and the checking of persons of all points of the country's borders, including airports and lakes' (National IBM Strategy, 2003: 85). The strategy defined that the military should be released from border management at the latest by 31 December 2005.

The transfer of responsibility for protecting the state borders to the Ministry of the Interior

Similar to the drafting of the IBM strategy, transferring responsibility for state border protection from the military to the Ministry of the Interior was supervised by an inter-ministerial working group made up of officials from the two ministries. The working group was charged to clarify the necessary administrative structures in the Ministry of the Interior and to develop time schedules for the transfer of responsibility. The lead section for Macedonia's border policing became the Department of Border Police, which was legally created on 7 May 2004 and became operational in 2005.[11] It operates at a central state level and is supported by four Regional Coordination Centres, each of which is responsible for securing one border section to the four neighbouring states: Greece, Bulgaria, Albania and Serbia.

The process of border demilitarisation included the recruitment of new cadets and the re-training of the military personnel from the Ministry of Defence. The soldiers were trained in three seminars, conducted by the Macedonian police with the participation of OSCE experts, and their chain of command was shifted from the Ministry of Defence to the Ministry of the Interior. The process of transferring the border protection responsibility started with the border to Greece (May 2004) followed by Bulgaria (October 2004), Serbia (May 2005) and finally Albania (November 2005). The demilitarisation process was finished in August 2006 when the Border Police assumed the sole responsibility for protecting all state borders, including airports and lakes.

The National Border Management Coordination Centre
A key element of the EU's IBM concept has concerned the improvement of cooperation and coordination links among the agencies involved in border management. Macedonia was asked to delineate the exact competence of each agency with an authority at the border and to bring these agencies together at a single location. With this step, they should be capable of sharing resources and information in real time. An EU official in Skopje put it bluntly that 'you learn painfully that ministries do not talk to each other [...] The only way in which you can force them to share resources is to put them physically in one location' (interview EU9, 3 May 2006, Skopje).[12] This would be the main rationale behind the idea of creating a common coordination centre.

For the setup of the National Border Management Coordination Centre (NBMCC) Macedonia received a €1.7 million subsidy from the CARDS programme, as well as technical assistance from France to develop the unit's operational capacities. It was to become the 'focal point for mutual support and facilitation of information and should reduce duplications of efforts and improve coordination of all of the operational aspects of border management' (EAR, 2006). According to Macedonia's national IBM strategy, the NBMCC was scheduled to open 'by 30 June 2004, to be fully operational by 31 December 2004' (National IBM Strategy, 2003: 89). The Macedonian authorities did not manage to stick to this timeframe. The centre's opening ceremony ultimately took place on 10 April 2006, two years behind schedule.

The border-related activities of the EU Police Mission Proxima
The transfer of the responsibility for protecting Macedonia's state borders was embedded into the broader reorganisation of the Macedonian police, one of the reform objectives agreed upon in the Ohrid Framework Agreement of August 2001. The peace accord defined that new police cadets, particularly of Albanian ethnicity, should be recruited, trained and integrated into the Macedonian police.

The reform of the police was a politically salient issue of the EU–Macedonian relations and a 'key priority' of the EU's Accession Partnership for the country (Council of the European Union, 2008a). The reform of the police was also part of the mandate of the EU Police Mission Proxima, which started to operate in Macedonia in December 2003. The EU's police mission was tasked to supervise reforms introduced by the Ministry of the Interior and to support the local police in confidence-building activities with the population (see Ioannides, 2006).

Proxima also dealt with issues related to border management. Within Proxima's border police branch, approximately 20 officials were located at the Ministry of the Interior and the four Regional Headquarters of the country's border police structure. According to Proxima's Deputy Head of Programme Department, Giorgio Butini (2005: 2), the objective was to have 'the grip on the Host Country Chain of Command and to be able to clearly identify possible shortcomings as well as to be able, for example, to track the flow of information, the delegation of tasks and so on'. Proxima provided support for the implementation of the integrated border management strategy and for the creation of the civilian border police structures in the Ministry of the Interior. Another focus was the transfer of know-how and management skills. Typically, the seconded European policemen were involved in projects that aimed at detecting forged documents and developing plans to prevent and control trans-border crime.

Proxima had a two-year mandate operating in Macedonia from December 2003 to December 2005 and was subsequently replaced by the smaller mission EUPAT. With a mandate of six months, EUPAT was made up of 30 police advisors who were expected to mentor and monitor 'the country's police on priority issues in the field of border management, public peace and order and accountability, [and] the fight against corruption and organised crime' (Council of the European Union, 2005a: 1).

Problems in the transformation of Macedonia's border control system
At first glance, the border demilitarisation process took place without major difficulties and at an impressive pace. A total of 1,470 employees underwent the training course at the Police Academy and were transferred to the Department of Border Police. Together with new recruits, the newly created border police amounted to a total of approximately 2,700 employees (Government of the Republic of Macedonia, 2005). The devil is in the details, however. According to independent experts who assessed Macedonia's justice and home affairs sector for the European Commission, the three-month training programme foreseen for the military personnel was not sufficient to transform them into a professional non-military unit. In the conclusions, these experts stated that 'there is a huge need for additional and continuous training' (quoted in Commission of the European Communities, 2005a: 3). A Skopje-based official of the European Agency of Reconstructions advanced a

similar view by stating that the training programmes did not change the military-style behaviour of the new border police, who 'are still behaving like soldiers' (interview EU9, 3 May 2006, Skopje). According to his point of view, 'the priority was to achieve the transfer on paper – that the border security is now in the hands of the Ministry of the Interior. The operational reality is somewhat different' (ibid).

A second challenge concerned Macedonia's ability to apply and enforce EU rules upon completing the transposition process. Macedonia was believed to face a gap between the transposition and the actual implementation of these rules.

> Unfortunately the practical implementation of the [integrated border management] strategy lags far behind. And this is a general pattern: the focus is too much on the legislative issues that are to bring the control of the state border in line with the *acquis* requirements. But the pattern we see is that there is a great gap between what is written on paper and what actually happens on operational level (interview EU9, 3 May 2006, Skopje).

An example of such delays in the implementation of the national IBM strategy can be found in Macedonia's efforts to reform its legislative framework. The Macedonian IBM strategy stated that the twenty-one laws and sixteen regulations affecting border management in Macedonia were to be combined in a single legal act in accordance with European Schengen standards (National IBM Strategy, 2003: 83f). The timeframe for adopting this new law proved unfeasible, however. Rather than being adopted by the end of 2003 – as foreseen by the Macedonian IBM strategy – the new Law on State Border Control the was approved almost three years later in May 2006, to be applicable as of April 2007. The main reason for this long delay was the close link between the new border control law and the new police law, which was intended to re-regulate the appointment system for police chiefs and decentralise the police force's organisational structure. These police-related reforms were salient issues and subject to political controversies in the media and the National Assembly. The EU strongly pushed for the adoption of the new police law, which it considered a milestone in the country's decentralisation process initiated by the 2001 Ohrid Framework Agreement. When the new police law was finally approved, the EU underlined that the 'adoption of the new law met a key priority of the European Partnership' (Commission of the European Communities, 2006f: 9).

Although it received less public attention, the new Law on State Border Control was an important step in JHA policy alignment, allowing Macedonia to come closer to EU standards in the field of border security. It regulated the surveillance of the state border, the cooperation between the state authorities responsible for border management, the competencies of the police in the Ministry of the Interior and the international police cooperation (Government of the Republic of Macedonia, 2006a: 264).

A final challenge in the process of transforming Macedonia's border control system concerned financial expenditures. The upgrade and modernisation of Macedonia's frequently outdated and rudimentary equipment and technologies was cost-intensive. The lack of proper equipment limited the country's ability to verify the validity of passports, to detect forged travel documents and visas and to trace criminal activities. In addition, the absence of an IT culture negatively impacted Macedonia's border surveillance capabilities (ICMPD, 2003: 335). The reform costs were substantial. According to the International Crisis Group, Macedonia adopted more than fourteen new laws and amended more than one hundred legal acts for the police reform, in which the reorganisation of the border police was embedded. 'The complete reform of the police is estimated to cost between euro 100,000,000 and euro 120,000,000. The 2005 reforms alone are estimated to cost euro 39,300,000 euros, a small part of which will be paid out of the State Budget with the rest coming from international donors' (ICG, 2005b: 9). In 2004 Macedonia allocated €3.2 million of its state budget to police reform and a similar amount again in 2005.

The EU contributed to covering these expenditures. Shortly after the 2001 security crisis, the Commission applied for the first time for the Rapid Reaction Mechanisms (RRM) which included accelerated implementation of the CARDS programmes and additional funds under a CARDS emergency assistance programme (Commission of the European Communities, 2003e). Among others, the RRM established a European Commission Justice and Home Affairs Team (ECJHAT) to advise the Macedonian Ministry of the Interior. This team focused on the development of national action plans as key strategic documents.

The EU's assistance has continued by way of IPA funding. In the 2008 IPA national programme for Macedonia, a total of €5.4 million was allocated to integrated border management, making it the single most funded policy area. The objective of the IPA project was to consolidate the progress, to improve the existing radio communication systems and to upgrade the country's border posts at the border to Serbia, Kosovo and Albania (Commission of the European Communities, 2008a). The European Agency for Reconstruction provided the Macedonian border police service with patrol vehicles, communications and data management equipment to other supplies. In June 2005, the agency supplied the Macedonian Ministry of the Interior's border police service with 115 vehicles worth €2.8 million (EAR, 2005a). Additionally, individual EU member states made contributions on a bilateral basis. Italy, for example, donated computer equipment worth €60,000 to Macedonia's border police service.

In short, following the 2001 inner-Macedonian security conflict the country subscribed to a comprehensive reform of its police system, which included the creation of a specialised and professional border police under a civilian, non-military chain of control. For this task, Macedonia established new border police structures within the Ministry of the Interior, implemented several training programmes, revised the existing legislative framework and strengthened inter-institutional cooperation by creating the National Border Management Coordination Centre. Macedonia's preparations for EU membership in the area of external borders have been 'advanced', according to the European Commission (2009a: 65). Several challenges have persisted, however, including the possible gap between the transposition and implementation of EU rules as well as the need to change the military-style behaviour of border guards.

Regionally coordinated management of the borders

The EU has encouraged Macedonia to establish close bilateral, regional and international cooperation links in the area of border management. Contrary to other SAP participating states, the promotion of regional cooperation has not been a difficult issue in EU–Macedonian relations. The EU has never seriously questioned Macedonia's commitment towards regional cooperation and integration. In light of its small geographical size and economic interdependence, Macedonia has considered it important to participate in regional activities and initiatives.

The promotion of the regionally coordinated management of the borders

Macedonia's IBM strategy set priorities for establishing regionally coordinated borders management. Under the heading 'Regional Cooperation and Coordination', the strategy outlined that 'measures will be adopted to strengthen and improve cooperation with our immediate and regional neighbours covering the whole spectrum of cross-border cooperation, exchange of national liaison officers, risk analysis, exchange of experience, cooperation on training and cooperation on investigation' (National IBM Strategy, 2003: 113). Other measures put forward to forge closer ties with neighbouring countries included holding regular coordination meetings at the border crossing points and at the regional coordination centres.

In theory, the IBM strategy therefore provided Macedonia with a clearcut plan on how to improve cross-border cooperation and coordination with neighbouring border police services. In practice, however, the implementation of these points turned out to be difficult. The UK adviser Henry Bolton, one of the co-authors of the IBM strategy, stated in 2005 that, as far as it concerns the enhancement of regional cooperation, 'the Macedonian Border Police have failed to apply the strategy to date' (Bolton, 2005: 9).

This criticism was probably too harsh, as Macedonia has implemented several measures of the IBM strategy. Macedonian liaison officers were appointed to exchange information with Bulgaria and the UNMIK administration in Kosovo. With Greece, Macedonia has held regular meetings between the services at the borders. With Albania, such meetings have been held at local, regional and central levels. A joint Macedonian–Albanian project sought to train the border guards of both countries in the border-related legislation of their neighbouring countries (Government of the Republic of Macedonia, 2005: 5). Moreover, the Macedonian government signed bilateral agreements and protocols on enhancing border management cooperation and data sharing with Albania, Bulgaria, Greece, Serbia, Romania, Turkey and Ukraine. Other bilateral agreements with Bulgaria, Albania and Greece have concerned the prevention and resolution of incidents on state borders and defined how to cooperate on issues of border control and prevention of irregular migration (Government of the Republic of Macedonia, 2006b, 2007). The only neighbouring country with which Macedonia adopted a local border traffic agreement was Albania. This has provided for the opening of some local border crossing points and has defined the manner of movement in the border zone (Government of the Republic of Macedonia, 2005: 35/44).

The EU's efforts to enhance regional cooperation in border management
To facilitate regional cooperation in border management, the EU financially assisted Macedonia, along with Albania, Bosnia and Herzegovina, Croatia, Montenegro and Serbia, through the regional CARDS project 'Support to and Coordination of Integrated Border Management Strategies in the Western Balkans' (January 2005–April 2007). Macedonian authorities used this CARDS project to update the national IBM strategy and align it with the regional IBM Guidelines that were released in conjunction with the project.

The EU's Police Mission Proxima also implemented projects aimed at enhancing regional cooperation in border management. The police mission advised on and fostered the professional exchange between Macedonian and Greek authorities in the South, and with the Bulgarian partners in the East. Proxima was less successful at enhancing cooperation at the Macedonia–Kosovo border, although, according to the Deputy Programme Manager of Proxima, Giorgio Butini, 'contact with UNMIK and KFOR develops steadily. Proxima particularly works on this subject' (Butini, 2005: 4). However, Proxima was dispatched in the country for a relatively short period of time, prompting scholars to ask whether the activities of Proxima would indeed be sustainable – or if their effect on the Macedonian police would be 'temporary and limited' (Hills, 2004c: 67).

Cooperation with the EU's border agency Frontex was strengthened in March/April 2008 when Frontex representatives met with Macedonian authorities to develop a Working Agreement for Operative Cooperation. This agreement, which entered into force on 20 January 2009, outlined that the cooperation between Frontex and the Ministry of the Interior should be gradually developed, including information exchange and risk analysis, common training and joint operational measures (Frontex, 2009).

In short, Macedonia advanced the regionally coordinated management of its borders, but did so in a less comprehensive way than foreseen in the national IBM strategy. The country fostered the exchange of liaison officers with neighbouring countries and signed several bilateral agreements and protocols on enhancing border management cooperation and data sharing. The EU assisted these activities and aimed at fostering professional exchange between the Macedonian Ministry of the Interior and its border management agency, Frontex, as well as among border management authorities of the region.

Macedonia's Achilles heel: the border between Kosovo and Macedonia
The border region between Kosovo and Macedonia has one of the most sensitive security climates in South-Eastern Europe, characterised by political tensions, potential insurgency and illegal smuggling and trafficking activities.

Background and context of the vulnerability of the Kosovo–Macedonia border
Following the breakaway of Macedonia from the former Yugoslavia, Serbia and Macedonia established a new international borderline, drawing through the predominantly Albanian border communities of Kosovo and Macedonia. In view of the vulnerability of the border, the United Nations dispatched the United Nations Protection Force (UNPROFOR) Macedonia Command in 1992, which was the first UN peacekeeping mission with a preventive mandate. The mission was tasked to monitor the borders with Kosovo, southern Serbia and Albania in order to prevent conflict spillovers from the Yugoslav successor wars. In 1996, UNPROFOR was replaced by the United Nations Preventive Deployment Force (UNPREDEP), which was provided with a similar mandate. The UN peacekeeping activities in Macedonia came to a sudden end in 1999 when the Macedonian government decided to recognise the independence of Taiwan for a business deal. Macedonia's recognition of Taiwan outraged China which, in consequence, exercised its UN Security Council veto on the extension of the UN peacekeeping presence in Macedonia (Koveca, 2004: 30). Despite the abrupt end of the mandate, the UN peacekeeping missions were regarded as a success. During the time of dispatch, the missions were able to fulfil the mandate of preventing conflict spillovers and contributing to the stabilisation of the country.

Security in the border region remained fragile. Several Albanian dominated villages were *de facto* beyond the control of the central state authorities and thus developed into focal points for smuggling activities and the recruitment and training of Albanian extremists (Hills, 2004c: 61). In fact, the outbreak of the 2001 conflict between Albanian insurgents and Macedonian security forces was caused to some extent by a border dispute. On 22 February 2001, Macedonia signed an agreement with Serbia on the delineation of the common Yugoslavian–Macedonian border. The agreement was internationally welcomed, as it ended the open border dispute between the two countries. However, the agreement outraged the Albanian communities on both sides of the border, which were not consulted during the negotiations. The Kosovar Albanians resented that the Serbian authorities took it upon themselves to decide on their behalf (Karpat, 2006: 1).

The nationalist outcry that followed the signing of the border demarcation agreement was fed by organised crime networks who saw that their criminal business interest was at stake and used nationalism as a convenient tool to mobilise against the agreement (Glenny, 2004b: 251). These local organised crime groups were interested in protecting their profitable smuggling chains from Macedonia into Kosovo, which continued further on to Montenegro and Bosnia and Herzegovina and ultimately into the EU. When Macedonia began to control the border section four months later, the conflict escalated (Hills, 2004c: 61).

Macedonia's efforts to solve the outstanding border dispute
Following the August 2001 Ohrid Framework Agreement, which brought an end to the violent conflict, Macedonia sought to downsize the political salience of the open demarcation issue with Kosovo. Similar to the EU's official standpoint, Macedonia presented the open border demarcation as a purely 'technical' problem that should be solved as soon as possible, preferably within the context of the Kosovo final status decision.

At certain moments, the politicised nature of the border demarcation issue was apparent despite Macedonia's official policy. In April 2006, the Macedonian Prime Minister Vlado Buckovski demanded that 'closure on this "open border question" [be] a pre-condition for Kosovo's independence' (quoted in MacDonald, 2007). In his opinion, there was no need to restart negotiations on the drawing of the Kosovo–Macedonia border, as the previously agreed-upon border delineation agreement between Serbia and Macedonia was a perfectly valid international agreement (ibid). By contrast, Kosovar Albanians insisted on amending the border delimitation agreement, as they considered it an illegal act of Serbia against Kosovo. According to the Kosovo Prime Minister Agim Ceku, 'Serbia does not have any right to sign anything related to Kosovo because they have no authority over Kosovo' (quoted in Karpat, 2006: 1).

The missing border demarcation was a subject of concern to the EU. In the CARDS 2001 programme, a project called 'Demarcation of the Northern Border' was scheduled to clarify the demarcation of the Northern Macedonian border. However, as a European official in Skopje stated, this project was cancelled 'due to political reasons – [it was] too sensitive' (interview EU9, 3 May 2006, Skopje). The uncertainty about the border's exact location has contributed to a worsening of the already fragile security situation. The security standards of this border region have been undermined by a high intensity of illegal activities, notably by smuggling and trafficking activities and by large-scale illegal logging operations. These criminal activities have been firmly in the hand of local organised crime networks and 'the police will not get involved in those things. By no means is the rule of law consolidated on that border' (interview EU9, 3 May 2006, Skopje).

Against this background, the European Commission welcomed any progress. When the Macedonian authorities opened eight border crossing points to facilitate local border traffic between Kosovo and Macedonia, the European Commission stated that 'such a pragmatic approach is to be welcomed' (Commission of the European Communities, 2003d: 14). In general, the EU was rather low key about the open border demarcation subject and demanded only that Macedonia 'continue to be constructive' towards the Kosovo status issue, including towards the demarcation of the Kosovo–Macedonia border (Commission of the European Communities, 2006f: 17).

Following Kosovo's declaration of independence in February 2008, Kosovo and Macedonia intensified their efforts to solve the open border demarcation issue. As mentioned, Macedonia had closely aligned its standpoint on Kosovo's final status to the Western mainstream, and was therefore in favour of recognising Kosovo's independence. The Prime Minister Nikola Gruevski publicly supported the plan for a 'supervised independence' of Kosovo as presented by the UN Special Envoy to Kosovo Martti Ahtisaari. The Prime Minister considered it an 'acceptable solution' which may 'contribute to the stability of the region and help the countries in the region in their preparations for the European Union and NATO membership' (quoted in Ragaru, 2008: 55). Martti Ahtisaari's plan also included a proposal on how to demarcate the common border between Kosovo and Macedonia. A joint technical commission was to be created within 120 days of the entry into force of Kosovo's supervised independence, and was to be tasked to find a solution to the border demarcation issue within a one-year timeframe.

Kosovo and Macedonia agreed to implement this plan; the negotiations were positively influenced by improved bilateral relations. Following Kosovo's independence, Macedonia decided to accept the new travel documents issued by Kosovar authorities. Most importantly, Macedonia recognised Kosovo as an independent state in October 2008, despite the protests of Serbia. These factors allowed the border demarcation process to progress. By October 2009, the demarcation of the northern border was close to completion and a new bilateral border agreement was in the final preparation stages (Commission of the European Communities, 2009a: 64). A longstanding problem in Macedonian-Kosovar relations was close to settlement.

Visa policies

Under Council Regulation No. 539/2001, Macedonia was placed among the countries 'whose nationals must be in possession of visas when crossing the external borders' of the EU (Council of the European Union, 2001b). Achieving removal from the EU's negative visa list was a politically salient goal in Macedonia and was ranked high on the country's foreign policy agenda.

Aligning with the EU negative and positive visa list
In the context of EU rapprochement, Macedonia was encouraged to bring its national visa list in line with the EU's negative and positive visa lists according to Council Regulation No 539/2001. Compliance with the EU's visa lists was an important conditionality requirement for policy alignment. The Macedonian authorities were asked to introduce new visa requirements for several third countries that previously enjoyed visa-free travel into Macedonia and to accept asymmetrical visa regimes vis-à-vis EU member states. Until December 2009, the EU member states refrained from reciprocating visa-free travel to Macedonian citizens.

When the country gained independence in 1991, Macedonia simply took over the inherited visa regime of the former Yugoslavia. The country hence kept visa-free travel with all former Soviet Republics, the successor states of former Yugoslavia and Turkey. In 2002, when Macedonia started the process of adjusting its visa regime to EU standards, it introduced new visa requirements for most former Soviet Republics, including Kazakhstan, Kyrgyzstan, Tajikistan, Turkmenistan, Moldova, Georgia and Russia. The country maintained visa-free travel for countries in the immediate neighbourhood (Bosnia and Herzegovina, Serbia and Montenegro) and Turkey.[13] In the alignment process, Macedonia introduced particularly strict visa requirements for Moldovan citizens. The application procedures, which requires that Moldovans attain visa approval in advance from the Macedonian Ministry of the Interior is 'presumably a policy to address Moldova's prominence as a source country for trafficking in women' (Baldwin-Edwards, 2006: 7). Compliance with the EU's positive visa list was achieved in June 2006, when the Macedonian government abolished all visa requirements for the remaining new EU member states in Central and Eastern Europe (Government of the Republic of Macedonia, 2006b: 14).

Although the EU member states did not immediately reciprocate the visa-free travel, the EU allowed Macedonia to enter a visa liberalisation process. The first step in the process toward visa-free travel was the negotiation of an EU–Macedonian visa facilitation agreement which would provide certain categories of Macedonian citizens with facilitated travel opportunities. The EU made the conclusion of this agreement conditional on the acceptance of an EC readmission agreement and the fulfilment of several policy-related conditions. The exact categories of Macedonian citizens who would benefit from the agreement were not pre-defined but instead subject to the negotiations, which started in September 2006. Macedonia's chief negotiator with the EU, Antonio Sanev, announced that Macedonia's negotiation objective was to facilitate the visa procedures for as many Macedonian citizens as possible and to get a realistic perspective as to when full visa liberalisation might take effect (Mak Fax, 2007).

The negotiations on visa facilitation and readmission between the EU and Macedonia were finalised on 13 April 2007. Macedonia, together with

Albania, Bosnia and Herzegovina, Serbia and Montenegro, signed the EC visa facilitation and readmission agreement in September 2007. The visa facilitation agreement fixed the price for processing visa applications for *all* Macedonian citizens at €35, and waived the fees for certain categories of persons. In Macedonia's case, the categories of citizens eligible for facilitated visa procedures included business people, journalists, pupils, tourists and others (Council of the European Union, 2007a). Each category needs documentary evidence regarding the purpose of the journey (e.g. tourists needed a voucher from a travel agency or a tour operator).

Defined as an intermediary step towards visa-free travel, the EC–Macedonian visa facilitation agreement entered into force on 1 January 2008. On 8 May 2008, the European Commission gave Macedonia a roadmap specifying the measures that needed to be taken in order to further proceed towards visa-free travel. The roadmap included four thematic blocks (document security; illegal migration, including readmission; public order and security; and external relations and fundamental rights), each of which contained a detailed list of benchmarks to be met (Visa Liberalisation Roadmap, 2008). According to the European Commissioner Jacques Barrot, the roadmap for Macedonia 'will encourage the country to continue implementing the relevant reforms and reinforcing cooperation at the regional level and with the EU in areas such as strengthening the rule of law, fighting organised crime and corruption' (Agence Europe, 14 May 2008). The implementation of the measures outlined in the roadmap was supervised in the EU–Macedonian Visa Liberalisation Dialogue. The Commission underlined that the pace towards visa liberalisation depended on Macedonia meeting the conditions of the roadmap.

Macedonia indeed managed to be the first Western Balkan country to meet all roadmap criteria for visa liberalisation (Commission of the European Communities, 2009b: 5). In July 2009, the European Commission proposed to the Council the lifting of visa requirements for Macedonian citizens, as well as for Serbs and Montenegrins (ibid). Upon the Council's approval of the Commission's proposal, the citizens of Macedonia (and of Serbia and Montenegro) were able to travel without a visa to the Schengen area as of 19 December 2009.

The regional impact of adjustment to EU visa standards
Macedonia's adjustment to the EU visa *acquis* had an impact on several aspects of regional cooperation. An example of this was seen when the EU asked Macedonia to abandon the widespread practice of issuing visas at the borders. In 2003, Macedonian authorities issued a total of 67,764 visas at the borders, most of which were for citizens of Albania and Kosovo (Government of the Republic of Macedonia, 2005: 76). The European Commission criticised this system because 'it makes no sense in terms of effective pre-clearance and thus failed to meet European standards' (Commission of the European

Communities, 2003d). A European expert on visa policy explained in a research interview why the EU opposed the practice of issuing visas at the borders:

> Issuing visas at the borders concerns the border guards and misses the point visas were thought for. The instrument of visas is aimed at providing for immigration control. In recent years, there is a common understanding that the first line of border control starts in third countries and the second line is the border itself. Issuing visas at the borders should be done just in exceptional cases as it is against the original principle of pre-control in third countries. Issuing visas at the borders does in the normal case not correspond to the same security require- ments as when visas are issued at consulates, especially regarding security checks and vetting procedures. (Interview IO8, 11 December 2006, Vienna)

In 2004, Macedonia stopped the disputed practice, with the exception of local border traffic with Albania. In 2008, when Albania and Macedonia agreed on a visa-free travel regime, the practice of issuing visas at the Macedonian borders ceased to be applied.

The EU's visa regime also had an impact on Macedonian–Bulgarian relations. When Bulgaria entered the EU on 1 January 2007, it was obliged to introduce visa requirements for Macedonian citizens, as Macedonia was still on the list of countries whose citizens required a visa to enter the EU. Bulgaria waited until an advanced stage of accession preparations and introduced the new visa restrictions two months before its EU accession, on 3 November 2006. Moreover, the country sought to mitigate the resulting negative side effects by offering concessions to Macedonian citizens, including free short-term visa applications, one-year business visas and speedy procedures for emergency cases. Bulgaria's visa regime for Macedonia lasted for exactly two years and was lifted on 19 December 2009, when Bulgaria and the other EU member states jointly removed the visa requirements for Macedonian citizens.

The Macedonian–Greek visa regime has always been characterised by several peculiarities deriving from the fact that Greece has refused to recognise its neighbour under the name Republic of Macedonia (Baldwin-Edwards, 2006: 13–14). Therefore the Greek authorities do not accept Macedonian passports and declined to issue a visa inside them. Instead, they put the visa stamp on a blank sheet of D4 paper. The result is that no record of Greek border crossings can be found inside a Macedonian passport. Despite this highly unusual procedure for issuing visas, the Greek liaison office, which acted as a consulate in Skopje, was highly important for Macedonian travellers. It annually issued around 100,000 one-year multi-entry visas and some observers believed that the actual numbers were at times even higher (Baldwin-Edwards, 2006: 14). Therefore, the Greek liaison office was clearly the most frequented EU member state authority for those Macedonian citizens who sought to enter the Schengen area.

Other adjustment steps to the EU's visa acquis

In addition to a common list of countries whose citizens need or do not need a visa to enter the EU, the EU's visa policy suggests a common visa format and common rules for issuing visas. Macedonia was assisted in complying with these EU standards through the regional CARDS programme 'Establishment of an EU compatible legal, regulatory and institutional framework in the field of asylum, migration and visa matters'. The project resulted in a Roadmap for Visa Management that provided Macedonian authorities with detailed recommendations on how to implement the visa *acquis*.

On 14 March 2006, the National Assembly of Macedonia adopted a new Law on Aliens (entered into force in March 2007) which explicitly aimed to adjust to *acquis* requirements (Government of the Republic of Macedonia, 2006b: 15). In 150 articles, the new law comprehensively regulates the conditions for entry, exit and stay in Macedonia, provides details on a new visa categorisation system and the form and content of visa stickers, and specifies which authority will decide upon and issue visas. It also outlines how to extend, shorten and annul the validity of visas (Government of the Republic of Macedonia, 2006b: 13). The main organisation to advise the Macedonian authorities in the drafting of the Law on Aliens was the Norwegian Directorate for Immigration. According to an official of IOM-Skopje, this created a challenge because Norway, as a non-EU member state, did not place priority on full alignment with EU standards: 'As [the law] was drafted by the Norwegian government, it was nothing like EU standards' (interview IO1, 28 April 2006, Skopje). The draft law established by the process had hence to be revised with assistance from IOM-Skopje to align with EU standards (ibid).

Macedonian authorities also sought to improve the administrative capacities of the Department for Consular Affairs and to strengthen IT support and technical equipment. There were serious inefficiencies and problems with information exchange, as Macedonia's diplomatic and consular missions were not permanently connected with the Ministry of Foreign Affairs (Damjanovski and Vurmo, 2004: 33). To resolve this, Macedonia began building a central database, and a network that both interfaces the Ministry of the Interior with the border crossings and provides an IT connection between the Ministry of Foreign Affairs and the diplomatic and consular offices. In May 2006, the Minister of the Interior Ljubomir Mihajlovski announced that the preparatory work for this computer networking was close to completion. The minister added that Macedonia had also begun to improve the quality of travel documents and would be able to issue new biometric passports as of November 2006 (Setimes, 2006b).

Improvement of document security was a priority for the EU, as Macedonian passports and IDs offered insufficient protection against forgeries. Document falsification was a well-known phenomenon in the country. Macedonia sought to become one of the first non-EU countries to issue ID documents fulfilling the security specifications of EU standards. On

6 December 2005, the German company Giesecke and Devrient was awarded a contract worth €23.5 million to supply 1.5 million electronic passports, 1.8 million personal ID cards and around 500,000 driving licences (Setimes, 2007b). Managed and supervised by the Macedonian Ministry of the Interior, issuance of the new passports began in April 2007. In the two years that followed (until April 2009), more than 417,000 new biometric passports, 330,000 ID cards and 140,000 driving licences were issued. The Macedonian authorities plan to complete the process of replacing old travel documents with new biometric passports by 1 April 2012 (Commission of the European Communities, 2009c: 1). The Commission mentioned positively that 'no cases of corruption regarding document security have occurred' (ibid).

To sum up, Macedonia has achieved an advanced level of alignment with the EU's visa *acquis*. The process of adjustment included the alignment of the Macedonian visa list to the EU positive and negative visa list (some exceptions have been maintained for citizens of countries in the region, which was endorsed by the EU), the adoption of the new Law on Aliens with a focus on meeting *acquis* requirements, the installation of a new IT system and the replacement of old travel documents with new biometric passports. The EU responded to Macedonia's 'significant progress' (Commission of the European Communities, 2009a: 63) in visa policy (and in related policy-areas) by removing Macedonia from the EU's negative visa list. Since 19 December 2009, Macedonian citizens have enjoyed visa-free travel to the Schengen area.

Irregular migration and readmission agreements
The better control of irregular migration has been a central objective of the EU's border security policies. This policy field has been particularly relevant for Macedonia, as progress on irregular migration and cooperation on read-mission were among the benchmarks set by the EU for attaining visa-free travel.

Patterns of illegal migration in Macedonia
Macedonia is not traditionally a source or destination country for irregular migrants but rather a country of transit, thus placing the phenomenon on a regional scale. Macedonia has fallen into the position of a strategic crossroads on the Balkan route by which migrants transit South-Eastern Europe on their way to Western Europe. According to Macedonia's IBM strategy,

> Macedonia suffers from its geographical location. It is at the crossroads of ancient trading routes leading from Persia, Eastern Europe and the Caucasus. These trading routes still exist and given the economic differential between the states in these regions and those of Western Europe, the trade in drugs, cigarettes, human beings, weapons and contraband goods is prolific in the southern Balkans. (National IBM Strategy, 2003: 82)

The two major channels for crossing Macedonia's territory have traditionally been the route from Kosovo or southern Serbia towards Greece via Macedonia; and the route from Turkey and Bulgaria across Macedonia in the direction of Greece or Albania (as a connection to Italy). At the end of the 1990s, many illegal migrants apprehended at the Bulgarian–Macedonian border were from African or Asian states (ICMPD, 1999a: 330). According to the ICMPD, 'the problem of illegal migration and trafficking in and smuggling of persons in and through Macedonia constitutes an immense threat for the security in the whole region of South Eastern Europe' (ibid).

Published in 1999, this ICMPD report is a good example of the alerting wording applied by international actors when talking about irregular migration in South-Eastern Europe. At the turn of the century, the irregular migration flow from the Balkan region into Western Europe reached a peak. Following 3,736 cases of illegal border crossings in 1999, Macedonian law enforcement bodies apprehended 9,771 illegal migrants in 2000 and a similarly high number in 2001 (9,262 cases) (Government of the Republic of Macedonia, 2005: 96). The number of illegal border crossings dropped significantly in 2002 and 2003[14] but has been on the rise again in more recent years. In 2007, the Macedonian border police identified 1,086 illegal border crossings (compared to 3,302 in 2006) and prevented 1,919 attempts to illegally cross the green border (compared to 1,866 during the previous reporting period) (Commission of the European Communities, 2007c: 53, 2008g: 60). Albanians have been in the majority, if the numbers of irregular migrants are broken down by nationality.

Table 5.2 Illegal Crossings of the state border to and from Macedonia: by citizenship

Citizenship	2002	2003	2004 – 10 months
Albania	332	553	999
Romania	62	41	38
Moldova	58	26	11
Bulgaria	26	27	8
Serbia and Montenegro	31	27	6

Source: Government of the Republic of Macedonia (2005: 97)

Albanian migrants enter Macedonia not only for purposes of transit but also for reasons of irregular labour. During the spring and summer months, they come to Macedonia to work illegally in agriculture and at the end of season, they return to their home country. The same pattern has been observed with Macedonian citizens migrating to Greece to work illegally in agriculture.

Trafficking in human beings, especially women, has been a particularly worrying facet of the broader irregular migration problem in Macedonia. The country's legal system and administrative capacities have demonstrated serious shortcomings in dealing with trafficking in human beings (IOM, 2006). In the past, Macedonia has prosecuted these criminal activities based on the articles of the criminal code that relate to illegal crossing of state borders, pimping and mediation of prostitution, with the result that 'legal prosecution was essentially limited to local perpetrators caught in action, without concern for the international aspects of trafficking in human beings' (IOM, 2006).

In caring for victims of human trafficking, Macedonian authorities have been assisted by the Skopje-based branch of the International Organisation for Migration (IOM). According to IOM-Skopje, the organisation had assisted 740 victims of human trafficking in Macedonia by April 2006 – most of them coming from abroad, mainly from Moldova and Bulgaria (interview IO1, 28 April 2006, Skopje). IOM-Skopje only had the mandate to deal with international victims of human trafficking, even if a national dimension of the human trafficking problem was also present. The national dimension was seen as neglected, mainly due to concerns of the Macedonian Ministry of the Interior's concerns regarding the country's reputation vis-à-vis the international community (ibid). The number of trafficked persons has decreased in Macedonia, a development 'which is of course good but also bad because IOM-Skopje thinks that the victims are here yet that the methods and ways [in which] the girls are hidden are more refined now' (ibid).

Macedonia's EU policy alignment process
The first major reforms towards improving control of irregular migration and trafficking in human beings were triggered by the UN Protocol to Prevent, Suppress and Punish Trafficking in Persons, Especially Woman and Children (the Palermo Protocol was a supplement to the UN Convention against Transnational Organised Crime) which was signed by the Macedonian government in December 2000. Pursuant to Article 5 of the Palermo Protocol, which suggested drawing a clear distinction between human smuggling and trafficking in human beings, the Macedonian National Assembly amended the Criminal Code in 2002 and defined trafficking in human beings as a separate criminal offence. With the opening of a transit centre for aliens on 4 April 2001, victims of human trafficking were also provided with a more adequate shelter. Operated in cooperation with IOM-Skopje, the transit centre included facilities for social assistance and phsychological counselling and sought to lodge victims of human trafficking until a solution for their status was found (Government of the Republic of Macedonia, 2005: 91).

The process of developing legislative alignment and EU-adjusted policy frameworks started in 2001 when a National Commission for the Fight against Trafficking in Human Beings and Illegal Migration was established. The commission's most visible result was a National Programme for Fighting Trafficking in Persons and Illegal Migration, which recommended taking action in six areas: (i) legislative amendments, (ii) prevention work, (iii) education of personnel, (iv) improved assistance to victims, (v) international coordination in the implementation of the laws and (vi) an information campaign to influence public opinion in the fight against human trafficking. The programme also identified the institutions and bodies responsible for implementing the objectives.[15]

Although acknowledging these efforts, the European Commission was concerned about Macedonia's reform pace. In its 2003 Progress Report, the Commission stated that 'in the field of trafficking in human beings, reports suggest a worrying increase'. Macedonia was instructed that 'the changes made by the Criminal code to criminalise trafficking in human beings should be followed by prosecutions and the National Action Plan for Combating Illegal Trafficking in Humans and Illegal Migration adopted by the government on 5 February 2002 must be swiftly implemented' (Commission of the European Communities, 2003d: 28). Other reform objectives set by the EU included the strengthening of administrative capacities and more specialised training programmes (ibid).

A particular challenge for Macedonia related to a low level of specialisation among law enforcement officials dealing with victims of human trafficking. Victims of human trafficking were frequently equated with criminals. There was little knowledge of how to treat these persons (interview IO1, 28 April 2006, Skopje). To tackle this problem the Macedonian government and the EU jointly developed training programmes that aimed to enhance the professionalism of involved agencies. In the framework of the Migration Module, personnel from ministries and agencies were trained in migration management over a period of 12 to 18 months and guided 'in instituting a more co-ordinated, inter-departmental approach to asylum and migration issues generally' (EAR, 2002).[16] Further training programmes were implemented by the OSCE, which concentrated on the issue of gender and human trafficking, and by the ICMPD, which developed a regional training manual for personnel involved in trafficking in human beings.

In January 2005, the Ministry of the Interior opened a specialised organised crime department tasked to improve the country's performance in fighting various forms of organised crime. Within the broader structure of this department, a Section for Trafficking in Human Beings and other Violent Crimes has assumed the lead responsibility for 'prevention, detection, documenting and processing criminal offences in trafficking in human beings and illegal migration' (Government of the Republic of Macedonia, 2005: 91). The section has helped collect operative information for a trafficking database and has supported the public prosecutor in taking legal measures against the perpetrators of human trafficking. Another specialised unit (the Human Trafficking and People Smuggling Unit) was established within the border police in May 2004 to improve the effectiveness of counter-trafficking operations at the borders.

In terms of legal alignment, Macedonia adopted a new Law on Aliens in March 2006 which re-regulated migration-related issues in the country, notably on stay and residence, expulsion and voluntary return, irregular migration, trafficking in human beings, migration statistics and data protection (Government of the Republic of Macedonia, 2006c). The stipulations of the new law brought 'the legislation [...] largely in line with the *acquis*', according to the Commission's 2006 Progress Report (Commission of the European Communities, 2006f: 48). Data collection on legal and illegal migration has been carried out both at the central (the Statistical Bureau) and the regional level (the Regional Centres for Border Management). In November 2009, 48 persons were responsible for measuring migration movements and for preventing irregular migration (Commission of the European Communities, 2009c: 9).

The actual impact of these reforms on Macedonia's performance in better controlling irregular migration and the fight against human trafficking is difficult to assess. According to the country's Minister of Interior, Gordana Jankuloskva, the number of human trafficking cases solved by the police in Macedonia grew by 46 per cent in 2007 compared to the preceding year (Setimes, 2008b). The Macedonian police have made some spectacular cases in the fight against trafficking. In March 2008, they arrested a group that allegedly was complicit in human trafficking and smuggling illegal migrants to Western Europe for many years. The police had cooperated closely with authorities in the smugglers' destination countries and had infiltrated and observed the group for over one year (ibid). Macedonia's progress in the fight against trafficking has also been acknowledged in the US State Department's yearly Trafficking in Persons Report (TIP-Report), which is one of the most important performance ratings worldwide. Since 2008, Macedonia has been ranked in Tier 1 meaning that the government fully complies with the minimum standards of the Trafficking Victims Protection Act.[17]

Readmission agreements

In Article 76 of the Stabilisation and Association Agreement, the EU committed Macedonia to concluding bilateral readmission agreements with any EU member, if requested. Even before the readmission issue could be raised at the first meeting of the EU–Macedonian Stabilisation and Association Council, Macedonia sought to speed up the procedures for signing these agreements. This is a rather surprising fact, when considering that the main benefit of signing readmission agreements is not attained by the Macedonian government but by EU member states as the main returning parties.

In 2003, the Macedonian government adopted a declaration of intent to intensify the procedures for signing readmission agreements. The declaration asked the Macedonian Ministry of the Interior to establish a template for bilateral readmission agreements and a protocol for their implementation.

The draft bilateral agreement was delivered to the EU member states with which Macedonia had not yet signed a readmission agreement (with the exception of Cyprus and Malta with which Macedonia had no diplomatic relations). Turkey and Moldova were provided with the same document. At the same time, the Macedonian Ministries of the Interior and of Foreign Affairs installed a common working group to provide a coherent and fast procedure in concluding readmission agreements (MARRI, 2006).

The efforts of the Macedonian government yielded quick results. Eight readmission agreements were signed in the first six months of 2006 alone. In 2007, Macedonia had ratified fourteen readmission agreements with sixteen EU member states and six agreements with non-member states. Negotiations for a readmission agreement were initiated with the EU member states Finland and Latvia and with the non-EU member states Bosnia and Herzegovina, Ukraine, Turkey, Montenegro, Moldova and Serbia. Great Britain, Lithuania, Estonia and Ireland informed Macedonia that there would be no need for concluding this type of agreement. Greece and Portugal did not respond to the initiative of the Macedonian government (MARRI, 2006: 5f, Government of the Republic of Macedonia, 2007: 245).

These readmission agreements, which Macedonia signed bilaterally, did not result in the return of large numbers of irregular migrants or rejected asylum seekers to Macedonia. The only agreements that evoked the return of a larger number of persons were the ones with Germany and, less significantly, with Switzerland. In 2005, Germany requested the return of a total of 685 persons with Macedonia agreeing in 521 cases. To draw a comparison, the total number of readmitted persons from all other states to Macedonia amounted to 2,050 in the same year. The reason for the relatively high number of readmission cases was that the Macedonian readmission agreement with Germany contained some unusual provisions. Whereas the other agreements concerned only citizens of Macedonia and their underage children, the agreement with Germany included the obligation to readmit marital partners with citizenships of a third country and persons who were born in Macedonia (even if they have no Macedonian citizenship) (MARRI, 2006: 11, Government of the Republic of Macedonia, 2006b: 17).

The previous bilateral agreements that Macedonia had signed with EU member states lost significance or were reconsidered when Macedonia agreed to sign a horizontal readmission agreement with the European Community. The EU set the signing of an EC readmission agreement as a condition for achieving facilitated travel opportunities for Macedonian citizens. The EC–Macedonian negotiations on readmission started in November 2006 and lasted until November 2007, with the readmission agreement entering into force on 1 January 2008. The agreement covers procedural provisions regarding return procedure, transit return arrangements, responsibility criteria, standard of proof, time limits and cost distribution (Council of the European Union, 2007b). In the first six months of 2008, the EC readmission agreement and bilateral readmission agreements with non-EU member states led to the return of 269 people to Macedonia, with the Commission underlining that the 'readmission agreement with the Community worked well' (Commission of the European Communities, 2009a: 63–64).

In short, Macedonia has made 'significant and continuous progress' (Commission of the European Communities, 2009c: 4) in the fields of irregular migration, including readmission. Because the EU ascribes a great deal of importance to this issue area, Macedonia has sought to quickly come closer to EU standards in the field. The country even actively sought to accelerate the process of signing readmission agreements with EU member states and, in November 2007, accepted the signing of a readmission agreement with the European Community.

Implications for asylum law

Regarding asylum, the EU asked Macedonia to develop a functional asylum system, to uphold the standards of the Geneva Convention and to guarantee refugee rights and the principle of non-refoulement in accordance with European and international standards.

Macedonia's process of alignment with the EU's asylum acquis

Macedonia had already signed the 1951 Convention Relating to the Status of Refugees (and the 1967 Protocol that removed geographical and temporal restrictions from the Convention) in 1994, yet the country refrained from incorporating some key principles into its domestic asylum legislation.

The Macedonian asylum system revealed its shortcomings in the context of the 1998–99 Kosovo crisis when more than 360,000 refugees from Kosovo arrived in Macedonia. The local authorities provided these refugees with the status of Temporary Humanitarian Assisted Persons (THAP). Most of them returned home after the end of the conflict but approximately 3,500 persons, mainly Roma from Kosovo, stayed in Macedonia. The existing legislative framework made no mention of how to deal, under the temporary protection regime, with those refugees who refused to return home (Damjanovski and Vurmo, 2004: 3f). Although the Macedonian government had extended the temporary protection regime several times, it was not until the Macedonian parliament adopted a new Law on Asylum and Temporary Protection in July 2003 that these refugees were given the right to submit individual asylum applications (ibid).

Established in cooperation with the UNHCR, the Law on Asylum and Temporary Protection contained the conditions and procedures for obtaining asylum in Macedonia and defined the rights as well as duties of asylum seekers and persons granted asylum in Macedonia. The different stipulations clarified the responsibilities between the Ministry of the Interior and the Ministry of Labour and Social Policy; introduced a differentiation between normal and accelerated procedures; laid out the chain of command in the process of decision-making; aligned with several key European principles (the principle of manifestly unfounded application, the principle of safe country of origin, the principle of safe third country or first country of origin); and clarified the status of asylum seekers, refugees and temporarily protected persons (Government of the Republic of Macedonia, 2005: 100f). Although the European Commission (2004b: 29) positively noted that Macedonia's Law on Asylum and Temporary Protection was in line with EU standards, it criticised the fact that the procedures for the management of asylum seekers and refugees were still inadequate and that asylum issues were not incorporated into the country's integrated border management system.

The Macedonian government foresaw short- and medium-term measures to address these gaps and modified the Law on Asylum and Temporary Protection in November 2008 to ensure full harmonisation with European standards. A major amendment concerned the introduction of the status of subsidiary protection.

A lingering deficiency of the Macedonian asylum system was the absence of a facility that allowed for separating persons in need of international protection from illegal migrants who were not allowed to stay in the country. The right to accommodation in a reception centre or at another accommodation facility was provided in Article 48 of the Law on Asylum and Temporary Protection. Financially assisted with EU CARDS funding, the Macedonian government thus began creating a Reception Centre for Asylum Seekers in the vicinity of Skopje in 2005. The centre, which became operational in 2008, is staffed with 10 employees and provides asylum seekers with language training, schooling for children and psychosocial and social care for persons with special needs. Until the end of February 2009, the centre hosted a total of 24 asylum seekers (Commission of the European Communities, 2009c: 8). In a separate institution-building project, the European Agency for Reconstruction provided funding for the development of an IT platform that allows for easier communication and coordination among the ministries dealing with asylum (EAR, 2005b).

A central database for aliens that also covers asylum has not yet been developed. The lack of proper equipment, together with insufficiently trained staff and budgetary support, have been the major remaining challenges for Macedonia in the asylum area (Commission of the European Communities, 2008g: 62).

So far, Macedonia has received a relatively small number of asylum applications. In 2006, only 10 individuals submitted an application for asylum in Macedonia. The notable exception was the year 2003 when the number of asylum seekers in Macedonia amounted to a total of 2,373 persons. This statistical outlier was caused by the decision of the Macedonian government to allow the remaining Kosovo war refugees to individually submit applications for asylum following the entry into force of the new Law on Asylum and Temporary Protection.

Table 5.3 Asylum data of the Republic of Macedonia

Year	Number of asylum seekers	Refugee status	Humanitarian protection	Expiry of humanitarian protection	Suspended procedures	Rejected requests	In process
2002	118	1	0	0	15	102	0
2003	2,373	17	1,131	216	454	521	34
2004	46	0	3	0	19	23	1
2005	19	0	1	0	8	10	0
2006	10	0	0	1	1	5	3

Source: Government of the Republic of Macedonia (2006b: 15)

In brief, Macedonia created a new Reception Centre for Asylum Seekers and has advanced its legislative harmonisation with EU standards. Even though 'the asylum system [became] fully operational' in May 2009, certain challenges remain, including the strengthening of institutional capacities and technical equipment and the increase of budgetary support for the asylum sector (Commission of the European Communities, 2009a: 64, 2009c: 8).

Explaining Macedonia's process of adjusting to the EU

The empirical findings have shown that Macedonia was very ambitious to come closer to EU standards in justice and home affairs. In certain issue areas, especially in the field of readmission, Macedonia sought to comply with EU requirements at an even quicker pace than requested by the EU. The present section shifts attention to the causal factors that have driven Macedonia's EU adjustment process.

The explanatory power of the incentives model of external governance
As outlined, the rational institutionalist argument of EU external governance maintains that the use of EU conditionality is not automatically effective in terms of evoking external EU rule adoption but instead depends on several factors (Schimmelfennig et al., 2003: 496f). The first factor, which is seen to impact rational-cost-benefit calculations of the actors involved, refers to the determinacy of conditions, meaning that a candidate country will only adopt EU rules if the EU sets them as conditions for rewards (ibid).

The determinacy of conditions
In EU–Macedonian relations, the determinacy of EU conditions was particularly high. The EU set adjustment to EU border security policies as a condition for two rewards: the first to advance in the process towards EU membership; the second to achieve visa liberalisation.

Similar to the case of Croatia, the EU established early on a link between

JHA policy reform and EU rapprochement. In the wake of the 2001 security crisis, the EU considered the transformation of Macedonia's justice and home affairs sector, particularly the police system, imperative for stabilising the post-conflict situation and improving relations between the different ethnicities. The police was to be transformed into a 'capable, depoliticised, decentralised, community-based, multi-ethnic police service which is responsive to citizens' needs, accountable to the rule of law and transparent' (Ioannides, 2006: 71). In the police reform process, the reorganisation of the external border control system was defined as an important component. The EU aimed to enhance regional security by helping Macedonia develop a functioning border control service, thereby improving the country's ability to control irregular migration and fight organised crime in border regions.

The principle of conditionality was established by Title VII of the Stabilisation and Association Agreement which provided for an intense cooperation in JHA-related issues. Moreover, the EU incorporated into the SAA those provisions of the 2001 Ohrid Framework Agreement that dealt with the reform of the police and related areas. In doing so, they transformed these reform objectives into conditions to be met by Macedonia in the EU accession process. The fact that Macedonia was the first Western Balkan country to sign a Stabilisation and Association Agreement with the EU gave Macedonian authorities extra incentive to harmonise with EU legislation.

> In 2001, we signed the Stabilisation and Association Agreement. This was a big step for the Macedonians and the first time when we realised that we have to work in the approximation [of the legislation]. Everything started since then, with the conflict, of course, slowing it down. (Interview M6, 28 April 2006, Skopje)

As shown, the EU engaged comprehensively in Macedonia's reform process following the 2001 security crisis. Among other measures, the EU dispatched the Police Mission Proxima (followed by the smaller EUPAT mission) to supervise and mentor Macedonia's reform process. The missions had a strong mandate to deal with JHA-related issues, including border management. From the Macedonian point of view, the police missions provided useful assistance, but were also harmful to the country's international reputation. According to a senior official of the Macedonian Ministry of the Interior, 'the mission [EUPAT] was basically good. But it is very important for us that the mission leave the country. If a country has such a mission, it can be very bad for the country's rating' (interview M4, 4 May 2006, Skopje). Evidently, Macedonia preferred to be dealt with as a candidate country for EU membership rather than a country still in need of post-conflict stabilisation.

The EU increased the determinacy of conditions by linking successful rule adoption to a second incentive at a more subordinated level: visa-free travel. Following the June 2003 Thessaloniki summit, the EU promised

Macedonia visa liberalisation, once certain conditions have been met. In interviews, Commission and Council officials emphasised the strength of this avenue of external influence.

> In Macedonia visa liberalisation is the issue which is the most relevant for the daily life of the population [...] EU member states now say that they have to comply with certain standards concerning illegal migration etc. before they qualify for a visa liberalisation. This is a tremendous incentive to speed up things. (Interview EU3, 6 February 2006, Brussels)

A Commission official even stated that Macedonian authorities were 'prepared to do almost everything' to get rid of the visa requirements (interview EU2, 6 February 2006, Brussels).

The EU increased the value of this policy reward by introducing a two-step procedure towards visa-free travel and linking a comprehensive list of conditions to the reward (measures against illegal border crossing and the spread of fake travel documents, the signing of an EC readmission agreement, an aligned visa regime, a new policy framework for preventing and fighting financial crimes, a strengthened anti-drug policy, etc.). This strategy gave Macedonian authorities a strong motivation to comply with EU rules. The promise of achieving visa liberalisation was frequently named as the strongest single incentive to speed up reform efforts in Macedonia's justice and home affairs sector.

Also, it is worth noting that Macedonia's willingness to subscribe to the reform objectives of the Ohrid Border Process was related to these two EU rewards. Since EU-compatible border management was defined as a prerequisite for both closer institutional affiliation with the EU and visa-free travel into the EU, the Macedonian authorities considered the Ohrid Border Process a useful additional project that would provide them with clear ideas on how and when they should reform their external border control system. The short- and medium-term commitments of the Ohrid Border Process were widely accepted and implemented in a timely manner. To the Macedonian border police, the Ohrid Border Process represented the launch of the demilitarisation process of the country's external border control system:

> When the Ohrid Summit took place, our country did not have a border police. We were starting with the reform in Ohrid. And in the last year, we finished completely with the change of authority from the Ministry of Defence to the Ministry of the Interior. (Interview M4, 4 May 2006, Skopje)

The size and speed of rewards

The size of EU conditional rewards and the speed at which they are granted are seen as possible causes for variation in whether, and how quickly, a candidate country adopts EU rules (Schimmelfennig and Sedelmeier, 2005b: 13). To trace the influence of this explanatory variable, an analytical distinction will be drawn between the two types of conditional rewards with which the EU has sought to evoke rule adoption in Macedonia.

For Macedonia, the first major reward relating to closer institutional affiliation was the Stabilisation and Association Agreement, which it signed at the peak of the 2001 security crisis. The EU successfully linked the peaceful settlement of the conflict to Macedonia's membership ambitions by giving clear indication that the country's prospect of EU integration would depend on the prevention of full-scale war and the establishment of peaceful inter-ethnic cohabitation. Failure in either of these areas would permanently exclude Macedonia from EU integration. This assertion proved effective, as joining the EU has been among the national objectives shared across party and ethnic dividing lines. Only upon the end of the conflict and the signature of the August 2001 peace accord did EU member states ratify the SAA and allow Macedonia to proceed towards EU accession. The link between conflict resolution and the reward of signing the SAA hence provided the EU with powerful external leverage at a crucial moment.

The EU kept little temporal distance between the offering of the next major membership reward and the successful implementation of the Ohrid peace accord set as a condition for Macedonia. The extensive reforms, including the police reforms and the constitutional changes prescribed by the 2001 Ohrid Framework Agreement, were politically salient and controversial in Macedonia. Six months after the implementation of the peace agreement, the EU awarded these efforts and the 'important progress made since 2001' (Commission of the European Communities, 2005b: 4) by upgrading Macedonia's status from a potential to a real candidate country for EU membership. The Macedonian government considered the reward of candidacy for EU membership a major political success. In the National Programme for the Adoption of the *Acquis Communautaire* established shortly after the EU decision, Macedonia ambitiously defined 2010 'as a deadline for meeting the criteria required for membership in the European Union' (Government of the Republic of Macedonia, 2006a: 15).

A general characteristic in Macedonia's EU rule adoption process is the impact of the timing at which the EU offers the conditional rewards. In 2001, when the Stabilisation and Association Agreement was signed, Macedonia prepared the first 'National Programme for the Approximation of the National Legislation with that of the European Union', thereafter updated annually. The document outlined the agenda for Macedonia's EU integration and was then complemented with the 'National Strategy for European Integration', first adopted in September 2004. In response to the candidate status, Macedonia drafted the 'National Programme for Adoption of the *Acquis Communautaire*', defined as the core strategy for activities relating to the preparations for EU accession (Government of the Republic of Macedonia, 2006a).

The EU has become less willing to swiftly provide Macedonia with conditional rewards in relation to EU accession since 2005. Following the Dutch and French 'no' vote on the European Constitution in May and June 2005, Macedonia seemed to have 'become hostage to political considerations that have nothing to do with Macedonia's progress in implementing reforms' (ESI, 2005: 4). The decision whether to grant Macedonia the status of a candidate country was already subject to controversies among EU member states. In December 2005, when the European Council was deliberating on the Commission's favourable opinion of Macedonia's application for EU membership, France opposed granting Macedonia the status of a candidate country. Two days before the European Council summit, the French Foreign Minister Philippe Douste-Blazy said that such a decision would be 'premature', as it would send a 'political signal' to the public that a 'new wave of enlargement' was about to take place (quoted in Beunderman, 2005). Thus, the French opposition to the Commission's opinion was not based on Macedonia's lack of reform or cooperation, but on internal political considerations about how to react to the negative referenda on the European Constitution.

At the December 2005 European Council summit, France accepted the compromise offered by the Dutch presidency suggesting that extra safeguards would be included in Macedonia's accession process and that granting the status of a candidate would not automatically lead to the start of accession talks with the EU. When the Dutch Foreign Minister Bernard Bot announced the results of the summit, he underlined in relation to Macedonia's accession process that 'it should be clear that the next step could be very far away' (ibid). Although a candidate country for EU membership, Macedonia entered into a period in which it was not clear when the EU would reward rule adoption with the next integration step, the opening of EU accession talks.

Though the EU slowed the pace at which it offered EU membership rewards, the conditional reward of visa-free travel became more tangible for Macedonia. In November 2006, the Council of the EU provided the Commission with a mandate to start the EU–Macedonian negotiations on visa facilitation. The Macedonian authorities had impatiently waited for this decision. When Macedonia was placed on the EU's negative visa list in 2001, the country had hoped for a quick visa liberalisation plan. This hope did not materialised however, as the EU refrained from specifying the conditions for visa liberalisation. In July 2005, the Macedonian Foreign Minister Ilinka Mitreva remarked in the EU–Macedonian Stabilisation and Association Council that 'regretfully, I would have to conclude that two years after the adoption of the Thessaloniki Agenda the only issue regarding which there is still no evident progress is the start of a dialogue on the visa regime liberalisation' (Stabilisation and Association Council, 2006: 10). According to Macedonian officials, they had frequently asked their EU colleagues to provide them with clear roadmaps or timetables on how to achieve visa facilitation; however, their requests were rejected:

Macedonia already proposed an agreement for visa facilitation two years ago. We

> liberalise the visa regime with the new member states, implement some other things and get something back in exchange. It was proposed already two years ago but we still do not have any response to it. We were then offering a roadmap on what exactly we should do [...] When we are through all the tasks [...] we can go to the European Commission and say: look, we have this agreement and have done all the required things, so it is up to you to liberalise the visa regime. But they do not like those roadmaps and such commitments. In the end [visa liberalisation] is a political question. (Interview M3, 27 April 2006, Skopje)

The reason for the EU's reluctance to specify the conditions for visa liberalisation was that the EU did not want to treat Macedonia separately from other Western Balkan states but sought to develop a common approach on visa facilitation, within the context of its readmission policy (see Chapter 6, also Trauner and Kruse, 2008).

The launch of the negotiations on visa facilitation in November 2006 was therefore a much-anticipated moment in Macedonia, and it prompted the Macedonian authorities to step up their efforts on policy alignment. The EU applied strict conditionality in the process of granting the reward of visa-free travel and outlined around fifty conditions that Macedonia and the other Western Balkan states needed to meet to join the EU's positive visa list (ESI, 2008a). Macedonia was the first Western Balkan country to conclude the negotiations on visa facilitation in 2007 and then, following the launch of the Visa Liberalisation Dialogue in February 2008, was the first to finish the implementation of the tailor-made benchmarks set by the EU for the country (Commission of the European Communities, 2009b). The EU succeeded in transforming the leverage that derived from the prospect of visa liberalisation into a major stimulus for successful EU rule adoption in Macedonia's justice and home affairs sector.

The credibility of EU threats and promises

Macedonia was aware that the EU's threats of withholding or delaying membership rewards were credible. Given Macedonia's small size, economic weakness and political fragility, the country's bargaining power has been very asymmetrical in favour of the EU, increasing Macedonia's incentive to present itself as a worthy candidate for EU accession. As shown earlier, before 2005, the EU swiftly delivered on its promise to provide membership rewards in case of rule compliance with the 2001 Ohrid peace accord and the Stabilisation and Association Agreement. At the December 2005 European Council summit, the EU heads of state and government already found it difficult to agree on whether to grant Macedonia the status of a candidate country; and in the years following the summit, the EU's willingness to deliver rewards related to closer institutional affiliation has decreased. From October 2006 to October 2009, the Commission continuously advised in its Progress Reports against opening EU accession negotiations, and Macedonia's political elite became increasingly nervous that the country would fall victim to the EU's internal crisis.

One of the main reasons, however, for Macedonia's increased scepticism about the EU membership promise had nothing to do with the application of more rigorous conditionality. Rather, it stemmed from its failure to receive an invitation to join NATO. Until the April 2008 NATO summit in Bucharest, Macedonia believed that the country would enter the EU on the basis on which it had entered other international institutions – as the Former Yugoslav Republic of Macedonia (FYROM). When Greece vetoed Macedonia's invitation for NATO membership at the Bucharest summit, despite protests from the other NATO member states, Macedonia realised that Greece would no longer sustain this compromise.[18] Following the event, Greece announced that it would block any attempt to open EU accession negotiations with Macedonia until the dispute over the country's name has been resolved (Agence Europe, 30 July 2008). This dispute has run the risk of bringing Macedonia's EU accession process to a complete halt or even jeopardising the stability of the country (ICG, 2009).

The credibility of EU's threats and promises was quite the opposite when it came to EU visa liberalisation rewards. When the June 2003 Thessaloniki summit first defined visa-free travel as a reward to be achieved in exchange for sustained reform efforts, it was questionable whether the EU would indeed be willing to deliver it.

Introducing the possibility of visa-free travel for Macedonia and other Western Balkan countries was contested in European capitals. The political actors of several EU member states have been hostile towards a softer stance on any migration-related issue, including on the question of whether to move any Western Balkan country from the negative EU visa list onto the positive one. A senior European official in Skopje explained in 2006 that 'the real problem for a possible suspension of the visa requirements is that in Europe, politicians think the circumstances are the same in Macedonia [as] in Romania and Bulgaria' (interview EU8, 2 May 2006, Skopje). Several EU member states considered the experiences gained in the wake of the visa liberalisation for Bulgaria (April 2001) and for Romania (January 2002) as predominantly negative. In the case of Romania, the effect of the country's inclusion onto the EU's positive visa list 'appears to have been a mass illegal migration for work within the Schengen zone, allegedly reaching over a million temporary migrants per year' (Baldwin-Edwards, 2006: 1). Afraid of facing similar problems with other South-Eastern European states, the EU refrained from specifying how the reward of visa-free travel might be achieved following the 2003 Thessaloniki summit.

The member states opposing visa-free travel could only be convinced by installing a visa liberalisation process based on strict and rigorous conditionality, in combination with a refined assessment procedure. To ensure objectivity in the assessment reports, a series of meetings were held and expert missions involving experts from EU member states were sent to Macedonia.

Starting with the negotiations on visa facilitation in November 2006, the promise of visa-free travel gained increasing credibility in Macedonia and was no longer only an abstract possibility without palpable political implications.

The domestic size of adaptation costs

In research interviews, Macedonian officials frequently responded to the question on the domestic adaptation costs and controversies surrounding the adjustment process by referring to what it meant in their daily lives to be placed on the EU's negative visa list. The combined cost of visa fees, travel insurance, and translation and notarisation of documents made travelling into the EU too expensive for many Macedonian citizens. A letter from the Macedonian Foreign Minister Illinka Mitreva to the European Commissioner Franco Frattini reflected the widespread perception of isolation and exclusion caused by the EU's visa regime by stating that 'an entire generation of young people, who are building Macedonia's European future, has been facing diffi-culties to even physically communicate with citizens, companies, schools, and other institutions in the EU member countries' (Mitreva, 2006).

Also, the EU's visa policy was believed to reinforce a trend that might ultimately undermine an important feature of the country's statehood. To avoid the tedious EU visa application procedure, Macedonian citizens have searched for different ways of travelling, without restrictions, into the EU. An increasing number of Macedonians have applied for a Bulgarian passport. Bulgaria's vice president Angel Marin announced in January 2008 that 'between 2002 and 2007, some 39,000 Macedonians and as many Moldovans applied for Bulgarian passports [...] Of those, some 13,925 Macedonians and 10,613 Moldovans were granted passports' (quoted in Spongenberg, 2007). In Moldova, there is a Bulgarian minority of 60,000 to 80,000 people. As for Macedonia, Bulgaria considers the country's Slavic population Bulgarian in origin and therefore easily grants passports (ibid). EU officials were aware of the seriousness of this problem. In an interview, a senior diplomat of an EU member state voiced concern that

> the Bulgarians will come sooner or later to claim territory from the Macedonian state when one day the majority [in some border regions to Bulgaria] will possess a Bulgarian citizenship. Once, they will even somehow understandably pose the question: What is the foundation of statehood in these areas? (Interview EU8, 2 May 2006, Skopje)

Against this background, visa liberalisation became an issue of highest political salience in the country. The EU promise of a more relaxed visa regime in exchange for rule compliance unified the domestic political actors and societal forces in their efforts to integrate in the justice and home affairs sector. By speedily adjusting to EU standards, Macedonian authorities hoped to convince their European counterparts that the country is capable of effec-tively guarding its external borders. Rather than a country of origin or transit of unwanted migration flows, Macedonia wanted to be regarded as a partner country in the EU's broader efforts to control irregular migration flows in Europe.

The Macedonian government felt the reform pressure not only from the EU but also from within the country. Several NGOs and student organisations initiated a campaign for eliminating the visa requirements and demanded that their government speed up their efforts to achieve visa-free travel as soon as possible.[19] The fulfilment of the criteria relating to visa-free travel became a shared national objective which superposed all 'purely' national agendas in the field. When the Commission proposed to grant Macedonia visa-free travel in July 2009, the domestic reactions were therefore exuberant. In a play on Neil Armstrong's famous words, the Macedonian Prime Minister Nikola Gruevski called the Commission's proposal 'a small step for the EU, but a giant leap for Macedonia' (EurActiv, 2009a). The Prime Minister added that 'it wasn't an easy process [but] our strong will helped us overcome the problems'. Having received the long-anticipated objective of visa-free travel, the country would now step up efforts to advance the EU accession process and to get a date for launching EU accession negotiations (ibid).

How important are alternative explanations?

Can Macedonia's process of EU rule adoption be explained by reasons other than rational cost–benefit calculations? Did Macedonia opt for EU rule adoption in the JHA field because it was persuaded of the appropriateness of these rules?

Persuasion and social learning processes have played a role in Macedonia's adjustment process, with Council and Commission officials confirming that the day-to-day cooperation of EU–Macedonian relations has not been characterised by coercion. Macedonian authorities remained deeply convinced of the benefits that an eventual EU accession would bring to the country. 'They are willing to do whatever it takes' to achieve the objective of EU accession, according to a Commission official (interview EU2, 6 February 2006, Brussels). As noted by the International Crisis Group, 'the prospect of EU integration gives [Macedonian] politicians their main motivation for pursuing reform policies and helps guarantee peaceful coexistence of the main ethnic groups' (ICG, 2004: 1). EU integration has been a shared national commitment 'declared since [Macedonia's] independence and permanently and strongly supported by the political parties and the citizens' (Government of the Republic of Macedonia, 2004: 3).

There has been a difference in the EU's resonance between the more political and the more technical level, however. At hierarchically lower levels, Macedonian authorities have more frequently deemed that 'their own system is just fine. At that level, it is more coercive, but at the same time we need to ensure ownership. There is no point to give them a rule book if the rules are not applied correctly' (interview EU2, 6 February 2006, Brussels).

Although relevant, the EU's persuasion and social learning activities were not the decisive elements in Macedonia's adjustment to EU standards. In interviews, Macedonian officials did not place great importance on discussions and principled debates for their willingness to comply with EU rules in the JHA field. 'We have very open and friendly discussions. The European experts know very well our [Macedonian] position. They basically agree with us, but they always refer to problems in some member states' (interview M1, 8 February 2006, Brussels). The Macedonian official is referring to the difficulties Macedonia initially faced in getting a visa liberalisation scheme from the EU. As shown, the EU was internally divided about whether to grant visa-free travel to Macedonia and the other Western Balkan states. The EU's internal division actually strengthened the credibility of conditionality threats in relation to visa-free travel. Macedonian actors were aware that they would not receive the policy reward, should they not fully implement the benchmarks set by the EU.

The 'visa problem' was one of the topics which was treated with great interest by the Macedonian media and public (Nelkovski, 2006: 14), particularly against the background that Macedonian citizens travelled without restrictions in former times. The visa regime of the former Yugoslavia was one of the most advantageous in the world. Yugoslav citizens were allowed to travel to both the former Soviet states in the East and the democratic states in the West. It was therefore difficult for Macedonians to understand and accept that they were allowed to travel without restrictions to Western Europe under the Communist era but no longer to do so under the newly established democratic structures. As a result the domestic political debates and discourse were not dominated by questions about the legitimacy or effects of the aligned domestic legislation but rather by the question of how to achieve the coveted perspective of visa liberalisation as soon as possible.

Concluding remarks: visa-free travel as an extra incentive to speed up EU rule transfer

This chapter has shown that the EU's influence on policy-making in the JHA field has been considerable in Macedonia, which has subscribed to far-reaching reforms in the Ministry of the Interior and in border policing. The rationalist explanation provides for strong explanatory power to understand Macedonia's process of EU rule adoption. By linking visa-free travel to the signing of an EC readmission agreement and to meeting a comprehensive list of policy-related requirements, the EU has used its visa regime to increase its influence and speed up the process of transferring EU rules to Macedonia. Although the prospect of EU membership was relatively loose, the Macedonian government accepted the EU's demands because it wanted to achieve a closer institutional affiliation with the EU as well as facilitated travel opportunities for its citizens.

Notes

1　See the Macedonian State Statistical Office, 2002 Census results: www.stat.gov.mk/english/glavna_eng.asp?br=18 (accessed 18 April 2009).

2　This quotation was framed by the former Macedonian President Kiro Gligorov. It was widely used by the international community and the media in the 1990s (see Dimitrova, 2004b: 172).

3　These efforts were supervised by the UN Special Envoy to Kosovo, Martti Ahtisaari, but did not bear fruit due to the diverging views of Serbia and Kosovo. Serbia strongly opposed granting any form of sovereign statehood to Kosovo and insisted that the province remain within the territory of Serbia. Serbian politicians believed that Kosovo would present a historical heartland for the Serbian Republic. Whereas they wanted to offer a broad and extensive autonomy within the state structures of Serbia, Kosovars contented themselves with nothing less than full independence from Serbia. In March 2007, the negotiations between the Serbian and Kosovar delegations unsuccessfully came to an end. The UN Negotiator Martti Ahtisaari presented a plan to the UN Security Council, which concluded that a compromise would not be possible and that a form of internationally supervised statehood for Kosovo would be the best solution for Kosovo (Ahtisaari, 2007). In the UN Security Council, however, the Russian Federation refused to back the plan.

4　The EU member states have been divided regarding Kosovo's final status. Not all EU member states were willing to recognise Kosovo as an independent state, mainly due to fears that domestic separatist movements get a boost (as e.g. the Basque separatists in Spain). The EU agreed, however, to launch its biggest civilian mission ever in the former Yugoslav province. The European Union Rule of Law Mission in Kosovo (EULEX), headed by the retired French army general Yves de Kermabon, should help the Kosovo authorities in all areas related to the rule of law, especially in the police, judiciary and customs areas.

5　The first Special Permanent Envoy appointed by the Council of the EU on 25 June 2001 was the former French Defence Minister Francois Léotard.

6　The mission was regarded as a test for both the EU's military crisis management capabilities and the future deployment of the European Rapid Reaction Force.

7　The answers to the questionnaire are available at the homepage of the Macedonian government: www.sei.gov.mk/prasalnik/ (accessed 13 October 2008).

8　In the referendum, the turnout was just over 26 per cent and failed to meet the 50 per cent threshold.

9　Even before the elections, the Commission criticised irregularities in the political dialogue between the government and the opposition (one of the key priorities of the Accession Partnership). Between April and May 2007, the opposition ethnic Albanian Democratic Union for Integration (DUI) had boycotted parliament due to differences with the government on the proper functioning of the Committee for Relations Among Communities and the application of the double majority mechanisms.

10　The ministries involved were the Ministry of Education and Science, the Ministry of Foreign Affairs, the Ministry of Finance, the Ministry of Defence, the Ministry of the Interior, the Ministry of Transport and Communication and the Ministry of Environment and Physical Planning.

11　On 24 March 2004, the Macedonian Parliament amended the Law of Internal Affairs and adopted the Law on Alterations on the Law of State Border Crossings and Border Area Management. These changes provided the legal framework for the transfer of border security competences to the Ministry of Interior.

12　The EU official maintained, however, that a lack of intra- and inter-ministerial cooperation between agencies and ministries involved in border management is not unique to Macedonia, as the problem also concerns several member states in the EU (interview EU9, 3 May 2006, Skopje).

13 The prolongation of visa-free travel to these states was in accordance with the 2003 Thessaloniki Agenda, which explicitly defined a visa-free travel zone in the Western Balkans as a political objective. The document encouraged the SAP countries to abandon the visa requirements in the region (Council of the European Union 2003d).

14 In 2002 and 2003, only 641 and 781 illegal border crossings were registered at Macedonian borders (ibid).

15 Another Action Plan on Migration and Asylum was adopted in the framework of the Stability Pact's Initiative on Migration and Asylum in December 2002.

16 The Migration Module was part of the CARDS 2002/2003 project Establishment of an EU Compatible Legal, Regulatory and Institutional Framework in the Field of Asylum, Migration and Visa implemented by the International Organisation for Migration under the supervision of the Swedish Migration Board.

17 The Trafficking in Persons Report of the US State Department is available at: www.state.gov (accessed 13 January 2009).

18 Bilateral relations between Macedonia and Greece also deteriorated following the decision of Nikola Gruevski's government to rename Skopje Airport after Alexander the Great. According to the International Crisis Group (2009: 5), this step 'seemed calculated to bring back to the surface all the Greek angst about the alleged appropriation of the Hellenic heritage'. Considering the decision a violation of the 1995 Interim Accord, Greece lodged an (unsuccessful) protest against its neighbour. The decision to rename Skopje Airport also helped raise the name issue in the Greek parliamentary elections of September 2007 when the Greek Prime Minister Kostas Karamanlis publically announced that 'Skopje will not join any international organisation, including NATO and [the] EU, if a mutually agreeable solution for the name is not found' (quoted in ICG, 2009: 6).

19 See the Macedonian campaign 'Visa, forget about it' (www.aegee-skopje.org.mk/) and the Schengen White List Project of the European Stability Pact (with a more regional focus) (www.esiweb.org/index.php?lang=en&id=342).

6

Cross-country discussion and outlook

The previous chapters traced the dynamics of EU rule transfer in justice and home affairs in two of the Western Balkan states. This chapter opens up the analytical lens by discussing the findings in a comparative perspective and embedding them in the regional context. It advances the argument that the key to understanding sectoral integration in justice and home affairs in the Western Balkans is to take into account policy-related conditionality deriving from the prospect of visa-free travel in addition to membership conditionality. The chapter concludes by considering the broader implications of these findings and asks whether the EU's use of policy-related conditionality in the Western Balkans can be considered exemplary for the European Neighbourhood Policy.

Assessing the EU's pre-accession framework

By providing the Western Balkan states with the prospect of membership, the EU hoped to repeat the success of the post-communist transformation and adaptation of Central and Eastern Europe. Croatia and Macedonia's processes of adjustment to the EU have shown that the incentive of membership has indeed remained a powerful source of external influence. Since the principle of membership conditionality includes the obligation to implement the EU's *acquis* in justice and home affairs in full, theoretically it has not been a question of whether these countries would adhere to the *acquis*, but rather when and how. The EU has assisted them with substantial pre-accession funding in the CARDS and IPA programmes, in which issues relating to justice and home affairs have been included in a prominent manner. In some Western Balkan countries, the JHA field has actually become *the* most prominent area of cooperation. Still, the Stabilisation and Association Process has differed from previous enlargements in some respects, contributing to an altered dynamic of EU rule transfer in the JHA field.

The altered enlargement context for South-Eastern Europe
The EU has tried to maintain a delicate balance in its foreign policy approach towards the Western Balkans. On the one hand, the EU has understood that

these countries' stability, transformation, and successful reform depend greatly on the EU's maintaining a European perspective in the region. On the other hand, the EU's commitment to enlarge to South-Eastern Europe has decreased against the background of an internal enlargement fatigue following the accession of ten new member states in 2004 and Bulgaria and Romania in 2007, the difficulties in reforming the EU's institutional framework and increasingly hostile public opinion towards further enlargement.

Although the EU's overall objectives of stabilisation, transformation and integration have been the same for the Western Balkans and the Central and Eastern European states, the emphasis has changed in the present enlargement round. 'While in the CEE the phases of stabilisation, transition and integration indeed overlapped, they did basically follow one another. In the Western Balkans, EU integration is a *condition* of stabilisation, rather than the other way round' (Batt, 2004a: 19). The stabilisation of the region has remained challenged by war legacies and unresolved status questions, most notably Kosovo's bid for independence and Serbia's determined opposition to it.

The EU considers Kosovo a key to stabilising the region in general, and to achieving the strategic JHA objectives in South-Eastern Europe in particular. The unsettled and disputed status of Kosovo has prevented Serbia from consolidating its statehood and may also have a destabilising effect on Macedonia. Also crucial to regional stability is Bosnia and Herzegovina, which has faced difficulties in becoming a viable state since the 1995 Dayton Peace Agreement. Although the agreement successfully brought the violent conflict to an end, it also burdened Bosnia and Herzegovina with a complicated confederative political order that split the country into the Serbian dominated Republika Srpska and the Bosniak-Croat Federation of Bosnia and Herzegovina. Political leaders from all the constituent peoples, most frequently from the Republika Srpska, have applied a strong nationalist rhetoric and have challenged the constitutional order of Bosnia and Herzegovina.[1] It is still questionable whether Bosnia is able to stand alone, that is, without international presence. Another issue that has become a potential source of insecurity is the name dispute between Macedonia and Greece, which has escalated to an extent that it may even put at risk the broader NATO/EU strategy for stabilising Macedonia and the region (ICG, 2009). Overall, the political landscape in the Balkans has remained volatile and unstable, regardless of the fact that a major conflict is improbable in the foreseeable future. European integration is among the few political objectives shared across ethnic and political dividing lines and that has helped reform and stabilise the political environment.

At the same time, the political dynamics and debates have changed in the present enlargement. While the Eastern enlargement was portrayed as a project ending the Cold War division of Europe, the arguments for enlargement to the Western Balkans were framed in predominantly negative terms – 'if we don't let them in, we will be threatened by an impoverished neighbourhood, wracked by criminality and the ever-present threat of bloody conflicts, which means endless costs to the EU in security missions and financial aid' (Avery and Batt, 2007: 2). This or similar lines of argumentation have reinforced a negative image of a 'Balkan enlargement' and increased public opposition to further enlarging the EU. The opposition is particularly strong in the old member states. In 2009, only 38 per cent of the respondents in the EU-15 were in favour of the inclusion of other countries, while 52 per cent opposed the idea.[2]

The EU has reacted to the less favourable enlargement context by making its enlargement policies more restrictive. In the wake of the failed European Constitution, the Commission suggested that three lines of action were to provide guidance for further enlargement: stricter conditionality, consolidation of the existing commitments and a better communication of the benefits of enlargement in order to improve the legitimacy of the process (Commission of the European Communities, 2005c). The EU's application of fair and rigorous conditionality implied that 'the EU must remain rigorous in demanding fulfilment of its criteria, but fair in duly rewarding progress. Aspirant countries can only proceed from one stage of the process to the next once they have met the conditions for that stage' (ibid: 3). Thus, rather than judging whether applicants fulfil the minimal requirements for membership at a more or less one-time occasion, applicants come under permanent scrutiny in all spheres of their legal, political and economic reforms (Kochenov, 2005: 14). The Union reserved the right to interfere more directly and comprehensively in the applicant's policy-making than in previous enlargements. Also, the aspiring candidate countries of the Western Balkans were not given an automatic right to accede even if all conditions are met. 'A new institutional settlement should have been reached by the time the next member is likely to be ready to join the Union' (Commission of the European Communities, 2006c: 15).[3]

The revised EU enlargement strategy has contributed to the fact that the Western Balkan states are moving towards EU membership in a more open-ended and uncertain process. While the existing EU rules are still predetermined and non-negotiable, not all countries of the Western Balkans have to adopt the whole *acquis* within a clearly specified timetable. In December 2006, the European Council declared that 'the Union will refrain from setting any target dates for accession until negotiations are close to completion' (European Council, 2006). This was different from previous enlargements, most notably from Bulgaria and Romania's EU accession process when the European Council had already confirmed in 2002 that 'the objective is to welcome Bulgaria and Romania as members of the European Union in 2007' (European Council, 2002).[4] Croatia is the only Western Balkan country that has managed to reach this advanced stage of EU integration.[5] In general, the economically advanced Croatia has been the least controversial candidate of the present enlargement round. As shown in the case study, EU member states have treated Croatia in some respects as an exceptional enlargement case, although the conditions for entering the EU are stricter for Croatia as well when compared to previous applicant countries.

Table 6.1 Major differences between previous enlargements and the Stabilisation and Association Process

	Previous enlargements	*Stabilisation and Association Process*
Prospect of membership	Credible promise of membership	Questionable promise of membership
Timeframe for membership	Clearly circumscribed deadlines	No target dates for accession, open process
Rigidity of EU rules	Non-negotiable	Non-negotiable
Scope of EU rules and regulations for transfer	Whole EU acquis	Selected policy fields within the EU acquis

Source: Renner and Trauner (2009: 453)

The Western Balkan states have faced more uncertainty as to when compliance with EU rules would be rewarded. Since the accession horizon has been relatively remote and/or uncertain, the credibility of EU threats and demands could be questioned. In this respect, one has to distinguish between controversial and non-controversial areas of cooperation. In several interviews for this analysis, ministerial officials of the Balkan countries have underlined that the EU's pre-accession assistance programme has helped upgrade substantially (or, even to create) domestic justice and home affairs systems. This result particularly applies to policy areas in which no real domestic reform steps are required (as in, for instance, the technical upgrading of border control equipment). The challenge for the EU relates rather to its capacity to induce changes in areas in which real (and hence, painful) reform steps are expected or considered necessary. Because the membership prospect is remote, the EU's repeated insistence on far-reaching reforms in, say, Croatia's judiciary sectors trailed off with a promise to do so at a later stage in the rapprochement process (interview EU11, 11 May 2006, Zagreb).

Overall it can be said that the Western Balkan states have faced a European political arena in which public opinion and political support for the region's full integration have been fading. For the EU, in turn, this indecisive stance has a concrete impact on the possibilities for setting deadlines and demanding far-reaching reforms in certain sectors. However, as shown in the case of Macedonia, the EU benefited from an additional, this time essentially exclusive instrument to speed up reform efforts in the Western Balkans' justice and home affairs policies: the liberalisation of the visa regime.

Developing policy-related conditionality: the role of the EU's visa regime

The EU's cooperation in justice and home affairs is guided by the principle of safeguarding internal security. A 'safe(r) inside' is contrasted with an 'unsafe(r) outside', 'with the EU's frontiers as the dividing line and law enforcement and border controls as key instruments to maintain and further enhance the distinction' (Monar, 2001a: 762). EU justice and home affairs cooperation has therefore created a strong dynamic of inclusion and exclusion between inside and outside countries (Monar, 2000, Lavenex, 2005). In the Western Balkans, the EU has used this dynamic to propose inclusion in terms of facilitated travel opportunities in exchange for enhanced efforts in reforming domestic justice and home affairs.

The EU's visa regime and the Western Balkans

In the EU's understanding of an effective border control, visa policies take an important role. The visa issuance procedure should allow for separating worthy from unworthy guests, thus preventing unwanted migration flows into the EU. For the EU, the first line of border control starts directly in third countries, whereas the second line is the border itself. Visas therefore play an important role in what scholars called 'policing at a distance' (Bigo and Guild, 2005a: 1).

The Amsterdam Treaty transferred far-reaching competences in the visa domain to the European Community, which were then used to differentiate the world in four categories of citizens: first, European Union citizens who have the right to move and reside freely within the territory of the European Union (limitations to this right are allowed only in a few cases); second, citizens of countries participating in the European Economic Area enjoying privileged relationships with the EU and having equivalent rights; third, favoured third-countries, e.g. Israel, which are placed on the EU's positive visa list of Council Regulation 539/2001, meaning that their nationals do not require a visa to enter the EU; and finally, third-countries that are placed on the negative visa list of Council Regulation 539/2001, meaning that their citizens do require a visa to enter the EU (Bigo and Guild, 2005b: 235–36, Council of the European Union, 2001b). In Council Decision 539/2001, all Western Balkan states with the exception of Croatia were placed onto the list of list of countries whose citizens require a visa for the EU.

This decision was bound to have major implications. When the EU decided on the positive and negative visa list in 2001, the South-Eastern European countries hoped for more preferential treatment in view of the EU's rhetoric of the region's significance for Europe (ICG, 2005a: 6). The decision was therefore regarded by the region as a detrimental signal of the EU's actual level of commitment (Kacin and Lax, 2006).[6] In the South-Eastern European countries placed on the negative visa list, the impression that the EU was establishing a 'fortress Europe' or a 'Schengen wall' was reinforced. A study by the International Crisis Group demonstrated that the EU visa policy negatively affected the image of the EU in the region and even caused an increasing European alienation effect. The EU's approach was seen as 'fostering resentment, inhibiting progress on trade, business, education and more open civil societies, and as a result contributing negatively to regional stability' (ICG, 2005a: i).

The political salience of the visa issue increased in the Western Balkans when the eight Central and Eastern European countries joined the EU in 2004. As part of membership conditionality, the CEECs had to impose visa requirements on all countries placed on the EU's negative visa list, including the target Western Balkan countries. This step was politically contested, as some CEECs had minorities on the other side of the border (e.g. the Hungarian minority in Serbia) and/or close economic and socio-political relations (e.g. Bulgaria–Macedonia). After the fall of the Berlin Wall, the governments of the Central European states had pursued an open borders policy as an important element to maintain good relationships with neighbouring countries. Sustained by Western European states as part of regional and bilateral integration, these countries have build up intense relations across borders and allowed citizens of Eastern and South-Eastern Europe to travel easily to the candidate countries of Central and Eastern Europe (Apap et al., 2001: 2–3). The Eastern enlargement led to the end of the liberalised movement of persons in the region.

Against this background, the objective of visa-free travel was among the most politically salient issues in EU–Western Balkans relations. The visa issue eventually became a common cause in the Western Balkans and mobilised NGOs and other members of the civil society in pursuit of the common objective of visa liberalisation (as a prominent example, see the Schengen White List Project of the European Stability Initiative).[7] Sometimes the issue even became a catalyst for cooperation among different groups in this fractious region. For instance, the Catholic, Jewish, Muslim and Orthodox communities in Bosnia and Herzegovina have started to work together in an effort to gain more travel opportunities for the country's citizens. Perhaps most remarkably, the common cause has brought together Serbian and Albanian experts. They have jointly published a study entitled 'A joint European Vision: Free Movement for Goods and People in Kosovo and Serbia' (Setimes, 2006c). A similar study was published by the Citizens' Pact for South-Eastern Europe, which functions as a network of NGOs and municipalities throughout South-Eastern Europe (VC Experts Group Research, 2004). These initiatives were only a few of a whole range of activities launched in the region in order to achieve visa free travel.

The EU's visa liberalisation process

Even if the Western Balkan states were lobbying for a quick visa liberalisation proposal after 2001, the EU recognised visa-free travel only as a long-term objective. The 2003 Thessaloniki Agenda first introduced the prospect of a liberalised visa regime, if certain conditions were met.

> The EU is aware of the importance the peoples and governments in the Western Balkans attach to the perspective of liberalisation of the visa regime. Meanwhile, progress is dependent on these countries implementing major reforms in areas such as the strengthening of the rule of law, combating organised crime, corruption and illegal migration, and strengthening their administrative capacity in border control and security in documents. (Council of the European Union, 2003d)

Despite the promise of the Thessaloniki Agenda, EU member states were reluctant to accept the prospect of visa liberalisation for the Western Balkans. As illustrated in the case of Macedonia, granting visa-free travel for any Western Balkan state was controversial in the EU, as some member states were dissatisfied with their experiences in the wake of the visa liberalisation for Bulgaria and Romania. A comparatively high number of their citizens overstayed the permitted three months, and it was rather complicated to 'collect them again and repatriate them' (interview EU3, 6 February 2006, Brussels). The proponents and the opponents of visa liberalisation for the Western Balkans had intense discussions in the Council (ESI, 2008b: 4), and the International Crisis Group (2005a) reported at the beginning of 2005 that the Council Working Group (COWEB) was unable to agree on possible first steps for visa facilitation for the Western Balkans. This would reflect 'a general hardening of the political environment following the negative result of the referendums in France and the Netherlands on the EU Constitution. Paris argued that the region remains a security threat' (ICG, 2005a: 7).

Against this background, the governments of the Western Balkans were aware that the EU would not soften the tight visa requirements unless they met the pre-conditions as defined. The EU, in turn, installed a very demanding process towards visa-free travel. Visa liberalisation should not be achieved at once, but only in a graduated approach with the signing of a visa facilitation and readmission agreements as the most important intermediary step. Moreover, any improvement in the strict visa regime should only be achieved through 'substantial efforts by the countries in question' (Commission of the European Communities, 2006d: 9). The final decision on visa-free travel would be taken on a 'case by case basis' and depend on the performance of each target country in meeting the pre-defined conditions. The countries' status as candidates or potential candidates should also be taken into account (ibid).

The go-ahead for the Commission to launch negotiations on an EC visa facilitation and readmission agreement was granted at the Council meeting held on 13 and 14 November 2006. The Commission initiated the negotiations with the countries in November 2006, except for Albania whose readmission agreement with the EC entered into force on 1 May 2006. In this case, the negotiations on a visa facilitation agreement started on 13 December 2006. All agreements were officially signed in September 2007 and entered into force on 1 January 2008.

It needs mentioning that the use of visa liberalisation as a means to exert external influence was not first introduced in the Western Balkan states (on the cases of Bulgaria and Romania, see Grabbe, 2005). Even the incentive of facilitated travel opportunities was not used for the first time in South-Eastern Europe, but in the negotiations on an EC readmission agreement with the Russian Federation and Ukraine. When the EU proposed visa facilitation, the two countries finally agreed to sign the EC readmission agreement. Nevertheless, the EU's visa liberalisation approach in South-Eastern Europe was unique in some respects, and it may become a standard model for other neighbouring countries.

With the exception of Albania, the Western Balkan states were the first countries with which the EU commonly negotiated visa facilitation and readmission right from the start. What is more, the EU linked a very comprehensive list of conditions to the reward of visa-free travel and placed an emphasis on the fact that these conditions would be fully accepted and implemented by the partner countries. After the visa facilitation and readmission agreements entered into force, the EU provided each target Western Balkan country with a roadmap specifying the exact conditions to be met to achieve visa abolishment.[8] The roadmaps were tailor-made for each country, covering four broad areas of cooperation: document security; illegal migration and readmission; public order and security; and external relations and fundamental rights. The benchmarks set in the roadmaps have been comprehensive, and according to a Council official, they have been in some cases just as comprehensive (and in exceptional cases even more comprehensive) than the JHA accession conditions the Central and Eastern European countries were required to fulfil in the 2004 and 2007 enlargements (interview EU12, 17 March 2009, Brussels).[9]

Their implementation has been supervised in so-called Visa Liberalisation Dialogues between the EU and the respective country. The progress made by each of the countries in fulfilling the conditions was assessed in a series of special expert missions involving officials from the Commission and individual member states. In the assessment reports produced by May 2009, the Commission concluded that Macedonia had met all the benchmarks; Montenegro and Serbia had achieved important progress and should also benefit from visa-free travel on the condition that a limited number of outstanding benchmarks should be met; and that Albania and Bosnia and Herzegovina had made progress yet failed to implement a series of benchmarks (Commission of the European Communities, 2009b: 5). It was suggested that these two countries remain on the EU's negative visa list until they have fulfilled the necessary benchmarks set by the EU.

After the European Parliament (2009) adopted its (non-binding) report on the Commission's visa proposal, the JHA Council (Council of the European Union, 2009a) voted in favour of abolishing the visa requirements for Macedonian, Montenegrin and Serbian citizens with biometric passports beginning on 19 December 2009. The decision was eagerly awaited in the three countries; however, it also met with criticism regarding its implications for Bosnia and Herzegovina. Since ethnic Serbs can hold two passports in Bosnia and Herzegovina, the preferential treatment of Serbia may put the already fragile stability of Bosnia and Herzegovina further at risk. In an attempt to address such a concern, the Council underlined that it would treat an eventual Commission visa proposal concerning Bosnia and Herzegovina and Albania 'as a matter of urgency' (Council of the European Union, 2009b: 17).

Due to the division between member states about recognising Kosovo's independence, Kosovo has been a special case in the EU's visa liberalisation process for the Western Balkans. Like Bosnia and Herzegovina and Albania, its citizens do not have the benefit of visa-free travel. Even the holders of a Serbian biometric passport who have been residing in Kosovo or whose citizenship certificate has been issued for the territory of Kosovo have been excluded from visa-free travel for Serbia. To fulfil a benchmark set by the EU, Serbia has started to issue passports to Kosovo residents exclusively at a specific Coordination Directorate in Belgrade, making this category of Serbian passports easily recognisable. The JHA Council of November 2009 made a first step towards formalising the EU–Kosovo cooperation in the visa domain by adding Kosovo to the EU's negative visa list of Regulation (EC) 539/2001 (Council of the European Union, 2009a: 3). The visa issue for Kosovo was resumed by the General Affairs Council of 6–7 December 2009 stating that 'Kosovo should also benefit from the perspective of eventual visa liberalisation[10] once all conditions are met' (Council of the European Union, 2009c: 16). This was the first time that the EU officially envisaged the prospect of visa-free travel for Kosovo.

In brief, the EU has used the regional setting of the Western Balkans to develop a more refined approach to leveraging the prospect of visa-free travel. Now that the Western Balkan states have either successfully completed the Visa Liberalisation Dialogue or are in the process of completing it, the question is: Have these states been exceptional cases in the EU's visa policy or has the EU's application of policy-related conditionality in this region been exemplary for other neighbouring states? What is the importance of the EU's visa regime in the context of the European Neighbourhood Policy?

Outlook: the EU's visa policy in the European Neighbourhood Policy[11]

The European Neighbourhood Policy (ENP) has been the attempt of the EU to associate its Eastern and Southern European neighbours as closely as possible, without offering them full membership (for an overview, see Johansson-Nogués, 2007). The former President of the European Commission Romano Prodi famously phrased this principle as 'sharing everything but institutions' (Prodi, 2002). In the context of the ENP, the EU has embarked on a strategy of using facilitated travel opportunities as an avenue of external leverage, making explicit reference to the Western Balkan states as a test case. As noted by the former European Commissioner Franco Frattini, the EU sought to enhance the EU's internal security 'through global visa facilitation and readmission agreements aimed in the longer term at the Union's neighbourhood countries, on the model currently being developed in the Balkans' (Agence Europe, 4 May 2006).

Similar to the Western Balkan states, the EU's visa policy has become a politically salient issue in many ENP participating states, in particular in the countries neighbouring the EU to the East. With the exception of Israel, all countries subsumed under the ENP have been placed on the EU's negative visa list of Regulation (EC) 539/2001. The EU's visa policies have become a source of serious discontent in these states, with the Commission acknowledging that 'the length and cost of procedures for short-term visas (e.g. for business, researchers, students, tourists or even official travel) is a highly "visible" disincentive to partner countries, and an obstacle to many of the ENP's underlying objectives' (Commission of the European Communities, 2006b: 3–4).

At the same time, the EU has faced serious problems and challenges with obliging neighbouring countries to conclude an EC readmission agreement, as these agreements mainly bring about negative consequences and difficult challenges of varying dimensions for countries of origin or transit (Kruse, 2006). Since the Treaty of Amsterdam has conferred competences for readmission to the EU, the EU has sought to sign such agreements with a range of ENP participating and other third states;[12] however, it became clear that successful negotiations would depend on the EU's offer of some concessions or incentives in exchange. Against this background, EU member states have increasingly accepted the link between visa facilitation and readmission for ENP participating states. EC visa facilitation and readmission agreements were seen as beneficial to both sides. They provide the EU with a strong lever to make third countries sign an EC readmission agreement and increase the reform efforts in their domestic justice and home affairs sector, while they also meet major grievances of the neighbouring countries by easing the tight visa regime and fostering facilitated travel opportunities for bona fide travellers (for a detailed account of these agreements, see Trauner and Kruse, 2008).

Following the negotiations with the Western Balkan countries, Moldova was the first ENP participating state with which readmission and visa facilitation were negotiated right from the start. The EC–Moldovan negotiations on visa facilitation and readmission started in February 2007 and lasted until November 2007, with both agreements entering into force on 1 January 2008. The Commission underlined that Moldova should not remain the only ENP country but that the 'Union should be willing to enter negotiations on readmission and visa facilitation with *each neighbouring country* with an Action Plan in force, once the proper preconditions have been met' (Commission of the European Communities, 2006b: 6, emphasis added).

Hence, a major precondition is that an ENP Action Plan be in force. Most participating states now fulfil this requirement. Action Plans were agreed upon with Israel, Jordan Moldova, Morocco, the Palestinian Authority, Tunisia and Ukraine in 2005, with Armenia, Azerbaijan and Georgia in 2006, and with Egypt and Lebanon in 2007. The other countries neighbouring the EU do not yet have such an agreement: Belarus, Libya and Syria are still excluded from the ENP structures; Algeria has decided not to negotiate an ENP Action Plan yet; and Russia refrained from participating in the ENP but agreed with the EU on a Strategic Partnership covering four 'common spaces'.

Table 6.2 shows that even though, theoretically, each neighbouring state may conclude an EC visa facilitation and readmission agreement, their concrete actions in this field differ. In the visa domain, the clauses are most often rather vague, referring to commonplaces such as 'establish constructive dialogues' or 'exchange views'. In its 'common approach on visa liberalisation', the EU specified the concrete factors that impact the decision to open negotiations:

> whether an readmission agreement is in place or under negotiations; external relations objectives; implementation record of existing bilateral agreements and progress on related issues in the area of justice, freedom and security (e.g. border management, document security, migration and asylum, fight against terrorism [...], organised crime and corruption); and security concerns, migratory movement and the impact of the visa facilitation agreement. (Quoted in Commission of the European Communities, 2008h: 2)

The Commission suggested that three countries in particular meet these pre-conditions: Georgia, Armenia and Azerbaijan (ibid: 9). Georgia was the first of these countries to conclude the negotiations on a visa facilitation and readmission agreement in August 2009. Achieving facilitated travel conditions with the EU has become a priority for Georgia following the entering into force of the EU–Russian visa facilitation agreement in June 2007, which was considered by Georgia to possibly provide Georgian citizens living in the breakaway provinces of South Ossetia and Abkhazia with an extra incentive to apply for a Russian passport.

Table 6.2 Specific action on visa facilitation and readmission in the
ENP Action Plans

	ENP Action Plan	*Specific action on visa facilitation in ENP Action Plan*	*Specific action on readmission in ENP Action Plan*
Algeria	No		
Armenia	Yes	'exchange views on visa issues'	'initiate dialogue on readmission which could possibly lead to an EC–Armenia readmission agreement'
Azerbaijan	Yes	'exchange views on visa issues'	'initiate dialogue on readmission which could possibly lead in the future to an EC-Azerbaijan agreement in this area'
Belarus	No		
Egypt	Yes	'Cooperate in the field of improving the movement of persons, including to facilitate the uniform visa issuing procedures for certain agreed categories of persons'	'Develop the cooperation between Egypt and EU on readmission, including negotiating readmission agreements between the parties, building on Article 69 of the Association Agreement'
Georgia	Yes	'exchange information on visa issues'	'Strengthen the dialogue and cooperation in preventing and fighting against illegal migration, which could possibly lead in the future to an EC-Georgia agreement on re-admission'
Israel	Yes	No short stay visa requirements	No specific action
Jordan	Yes	'In order to facilitate the circulation of persons, examine … possibilities of facilitation visa issuing (simplified and accelerated procedures in conformity with the acquis)'	No specific action
Lebanon	Yes	'Cooperate on facilitating the movement of persons … in particular examining the scope for facilitating visa procedures for short stay for some categories of persons'	'Improve cooperation … on all forms of readmission including the possibility of negotiating a readmission agreement'
Libya	No		
Moldova	Yes	'initiate a dialogue on the possibilities of visa facilitation'	'Initiate a dialogue on readmission in the perspective of concluding a readmission agreement between Moldova and EU'
Morocco	Yes	'constructive dialogue … including examination of visa facilitation'	'conclusion and implementation of balanced readmission agreement with the EC'

Palestinian Authority	Yes	No specific action	No specific action
Syria	No		
Tunisia	Yes	'facilitating the movement of persons … by looking in particular at possibilities of relaxing short-stay visa formalities for certain categories of persons'	'initiate a dialogue on return and readmission with a view to concluding a readmission agreement with the EU'
Ukraine	Yes	'establish constructive dialogue on visa facilitation'	'need for progress on the ongoing negotiations for an EC–Ukraine readmission agreement'

Notes: The ENP Action Plans with Israel, Jordan, Moldova, Morocco, Palestinian Territory, Tunisia and Ukraine were adopted in 2005, with Armenia, Azerbaijan, Georgia in late 2006 and with Lebanon and Egypt in early 2007.

Source: ENP Action Plans and Country Reports, downloadable on the homepage of the European Commission: http://ec.europa.eu/world/enp/documents_en.htm (last accessed on 13 August 2009).

However, even if the EU's strategy for ENP participating states contains elements of the experiences acquired in the Western Balkans, it is not the same. According to a Commission official, the most important difference relates to a clearer distinction between the use of visa facilitation and the use of visa liberalisation as an incentive (interview EU21, 15 September 2009, Brussels). Despite the fact that the visa facilitation agreements that the EU signed with ENP participating states usually recognise the introduction of a visa-free regime 'as a long term perspective' (see e.g. the EC–Ukrainian visa facilitation agreement 2007c: 3), the complete abolishment of visa requirements is currently not envisaged for any ENP participating states. As the Commission official underlined, the decision to allow visa liberalisation for the Western Balkans was a difficult one to achieve in the EU and reflected these countries' particular standing as potential future EU member states (ibid). The previous section has demonstrated that the EU ministers of the interior were initially reluctant to employ the incentive of visa-free travel due to fear that a new window for irregular migration would be opened, whereas EU ministers of foreign affairs were more open to the Western Balkans' grievance that the EU visa regime has functioned as an obstacle in their transformation towards stable democracies and open, European-oriented societies. Similar struggles and divergent preferences between the more inward-looking actors, typically the ministers of the interior, and the more traditional EU foreign policy actors are present in relation to ENP participating states.

It is more likely for ENP participating states that the time-span between visa facilitation and visa liberalisation will be substantially prolonged compared to the Western Balkans, or that visa facilitation will even be the only reward the EU is willing to offer. A final point to which the Commission official drew attention related to the 'time- and human-resources consuming experience' of evaluating the implementation of Visa Liberalisation Roadmaps (ibid). In the Western Balkans, more than 1,000 pages of evaluation reports and a considerable number of expert missions were needed for each country to comprehensively assess the progress. So far, the EU lacks the political and financial commitment to reproduce a task comparable to that of the Western Balkans in the context of the European Neighbourhood Policy (ibid).

Notes

1 Following Kosovo's declaration of independence, the National Assembly of the Republika Srpska adopted a resolution which condemned the step and announced that the Republika Srpska may also seek a referendum on independence if Kosovo is recognised by a majority of EU and UN member states (Commission of the European Communities, 2008b: 7).

2 See Eurobarometer 71, June–July 2009, available at: http://ec.europa.eu /public_opinion/archives/eb/eb71/eb71_std_part1.pdf (accessed 10 September 2009); for a specific survey on the attitudes towards EU enlargement, see Special Eurobarometer 255/2006, available at: http://ec.europa.eu/public_opinion/archives /ebs/ebs_255_en.pdf (accessed 10 September 2009).

3 It needs mentioning that discussions on whether the EU would be able to work effectively post-accession have taken place, in varying intensity, in every enlargement round (Piedrafita, 2008: 1–2). The difference between the present and earlier enlargements has been that the EU's integration capacity was upgraded to a *de facto* new criterion for deciding upon the accession of an applicant country.

4 In Bulgaria and Romania's case, however, the early mentioning of the accession date was believed to have a detrimental effect on the EU's capacities to encourage pre-accession reforms and adaptation processes (Noutcheva and Bechev, 2008).

5 In November 2008, the Commission provided Croatia with a roadmap on how to reach the final stages of the accession negotiations with the EU (see Commission of the European Communities, 2008f: Annex 1).

6 As the two MEPs Jelko Kacin and Henrik Lax (2006) noted, the hope for an end to the international isolation was among the key reasons why Serbian citizens contested Slobodan Milosevic's regime. After the end of Milosevic's regime, however, the EU made its visa regime vis-à-vis Serbia even stricter, resulting in what has been described as a 'virtual imprisonment' of Serbs inside Serbia (ibid).

7 The goal of the ESI's Schengen White List Project was to contribute to the abolition of the visa requirements for the entire Western Balkans region; for more details, see: www.esiweb.org/index.php?lang=en&id=342 (accessed 4 October 2009).

8 In January 2008, Serbia was the first country which received a roadmap, followed by Macedonia, Albania and Montenegro. In May 2008, Bosnia and Herzegovina was the final country to open a dialogue on the abolition of the visa requirements. The dialogues have been based on the premise that if the Western Balkans met the relevant conditions and benchmarks, they would gradually advance towards visa liberalisation.

9 The Council official gave the example of establishing anti-corruption agencies, an issue area where the EU is believed to be stricter in the Visa Liberalisation Dialogue with the Western Balkans than in the accession negotiations with the Central and

Eastern European countries (interview EU12, 17 March 2009, Brussels).

10 'Without prejudice to Member States' positions on status' (footnote of the original text).

11 This section draws on Trauner and Kruse (2008).

12 In 2001, negotiations started with Hong Kong, Macao, Russia, Sri Lanka, Morocco, and Pakistan; in 2002, with Ukraine; in 2003 with Albania and Turkey; in 2004, with China; in 2005 with Algeria; in 2006 with Bosnia, Macedonia, Montenegro and Serbia; in 2007 with Moldova; and in 2008 with Georgia.

PART IV

Conclusions

7

Conclusions

This book has aimed at presenting a theoretically informed yet empirically thorough research on the Europeanisation of the Western Balkans by elaborating on Croatia's and Macedonia's adjustment to EU justice and home affairs. The guiding research interest was whether more uncertainty about the credibility of the membership prospects and a different, arguably less favourable, enlargement context have resulted in less external EU influence on domestic policy-making in the aspiring South-Eastern European candidates.

Recapitulating the analysis findings
The analysis has considered the EU's pre-accession strategy a chief mechanism for stimulating the Western Balkan states to come closer to EU standards. In exerting influence on the Western Balkan states' domestic policy-making, the EU has built upon 'mechanisms of Europeanisation' similar to those identified for the Eastern enlargement (Grabbe, 2001), even though the EU's pre-accession strategy contains some new features. With the exception of Croatia, the aspiring candidate countries of the Western Balkans have only a middle-range membership perspective without a clear timeframe for accession. Also, the political and economic conditions for entering the EU are more comprehensive, and new procedural safeguards are included to ensure compliance and reforms at an earlier stage of EU integration. A target country's progress in the rapprochement process depends on a sufficient degree of compliance with general and country-specific conditions, which may include cooperation with the International Criminal Tribunal for the former Yugoslavia, the return of refugees and the respecting of various peace agreements.

Cooperation in justice and home affairs matters has always been a priority for the EU, reflected in the fact that this policy field, together with economic development, were the most significant areas of the EU's pre-accession assistance. The upgrading and reform of border management in the Western Balkans were considered particularly important. When irregular migration from the region, measured through border apprehensions, saw a sharp rise in the year 2000, the EU started to view border security in the Balkans as a direct concern (see also Hills, 2004b). Owing to its self-interest in coping with the issue, the EU placed a strong, for some even a disproportionate, focus on the creation of efficient border security systems in South-Eastern Europe (Hänggi and Tanner, 2005: 51). The EU expected the Western Balkan states to reorganise their external border control systems in line with the EU's integrated border management (IBM) concept. In addition to border control, the IBM concept encompasses trade facilitation and border-region cooperation and should serve as the major means of tackling the interrelated issues of porous borders and cross-border problems. The overall aim was to facilitate legitimate cross-border activities such as tourism, trade and trans-border cooperation and, at the same time, to close the borders to criminal activities ('open but controlled and secure borders').

In its efforts to bring the states closer to EU standards in border control and management, the EU also relied on the Ohrid Border Process which was a joint effort of different international organisations to improve border security and management in the Balkans. In May 2003, representatives of the North Atlantic Treaty Organization, the Organization for Security and Co-operation in Europe, the EU and the Stability Pact for South-Eastern Europe met with specialists from the Western Balkan countries to address the sensitive issue of border security and management. The four organisations were assigned different tasks: NATO as the principal organisation to strengthen border control and to interdict smuggling in the crisis areas where NATO forces were dispatched; the EU, to support developing integrated border management systems in each country within the context of the Stabilisation and Association Process; the OSCE as a 'civilian actor' concentrating on training and know-how transfer; and the Stability Pact for South-Eastern Europe, to enhance the regional aspect of border cooperation and to offer a common roof for the activities of the four partner organisations (Common Platform, 2003). The Western Balkan countries, in turn, were expected to subscribe to the implementation of concrete measures aimed at developing and implementing an integrated border security approach on the basis of the EU border model.

The analysis has demonstrated that the EU's strategies have succeeded in making Croatia and Macedonia adjust to the EU and strengthen their external border control policies. Both countries showed strong compliance efforts in the field of justice and home affairs.

Regarding Croatia, the process of adjustment to the EU included the creation of new legislation and the reorganisation of the administrative structure and hierarchy of border policing. Also, the Croatian government promoted regionally coordinated management of the borders and developed a strategic approach to domestic implementation of the respective *acquis* (a Schengen Action Plan was approved in February 2007). The most problematic issue concerned Croatia's failure to achieve a major breakthrough in solving outstanding border disputes with Bosnia and Herzegovina, Serbia, Montenegro and Slovenia. The dispute between Slovenia and Croatia over the drawing of the maritime border in the Piran Bay has become a particularly salient issue. Croatia has eagerly sought to decouple this – according to Croatia 'bilateral' – issue from the EU accession process. An important result of Croatia's adjustment was that the country had to assume greater responsibility for curbing illegal transit migration flows to the EU. The number of illegal crossings at the Croatian state border has increased in recent years. In view of EU accession, the country signed a whole network of readmission agreements and strengthened the capacities of institutions dealing with irregular migration.

In Croatia's case, the prospect of an eventual EU membership proved to be the most powerful incentive for rule adoption. Contrary to the Eastern enlargement, 'where preparations for accession in the areas of justice and home affairs started relatively late' (Monar, 2001b: 6), the EU incorporated JHA policies at an early stage of the accession process and emphasised their link to the country's rapprochement process with the Union. The conditionality principle was provided by the title on justice and home affairs (Chapter VII) in the Stabilisation and Association Agreement, which demanded that Croatia gradually align its policies with the EU's *acquis* on border control, visa policy, migration and asylum. As part of the conditionality principles linked to an eventual EU integration, Croatian actors agreed to introduce reforms in the sensitive policy domain of justice and home affairs. The domestic adaptation costs of taking more responsibility in guarding the EU's external borders and preventing irregular migrants from entering the EU were accepted in view of the expected benefits of full membership. The value added by the Ohrid Border Process was openly questioned, however, because the initiative was counterproductive in terms of time and energy.

The second case study analysed was Macedonia – a country with a medium-term membership prospect, but where reforms in the Ministry of the Interior and in border policing were considered crucial after the near-civil war of 2001. The empirical findings suggest that Macedonia was highly ambitious to come closer to EU standards in justice and home affairs. Despite a rather remote membership prospect, the country placed priority on speedily developing a functioning border control service and improving its ability to fight illegal migration and human trafficking.

In certain issue areas, the country's adjustment efforts even got ahead of the EU's demands. For instance, even before the issue of readmission agreements could be raised at the first meeting of the EU–Macedonia Stabilisation and Association Council, the Macedonian government had installed an inter-ministerial working group responsible for intensifying and accelerating the process of concluding bilateral readmission agreements with EU member states. In September 2007, Macedonia endorsed an EC readmission agreement. Moreover, the country was the first in the region to complete the process of border demilitarisation by transferring the border guarding responsibility from the Ministry of Defence to the Ministry of the Interior.

The process of creating non-military border guarding structures involved establishing new institutions such as the Department of Border Police, re-drafting relevant legislation and training a considerable number of border crossing guards. At the regional level, Macedonia signed several bilateral agreements and protocols on enhancing border management cooperation and data sharing with neighbouring states.

Similar to the case of Croatia, Macedonia's choice of rule adoption was affected by the expected benefits of an eventual membership; however, even if the prospect of joining the EU gave Macedonian politicians a strong moti-vation to pursue reform policies, membership conditionality was not the sole stimulus for EU rule adoption. Macedonia's urge to rule alignment was not driven by the fear of being detached from EU integration, but by the earnest desire to get rid of the visa requirements for Macedonian citizens.

In Macedonia, the issue of visa liberalisation has ranked high on the political agenda, no matter which parties have held the power. Realising that its visa regime could function as an effective 'carrot', the EU allowed Macedonia to enter a visa liberalisation process and linked an improved visa regime to the fulfilment of a whole series of conditions. The strategy proved highly effective in terms of encouraging Macedonian actors to strengthen their domestic reform efforts. The prospect of a more relaxed visa regime was frequently named as the strongest single incentive to speed up reform efforts in domestic justice and home affairs. The Macedonian government felt the reform pressure not only from the EU but also from NGOs and other members of civil society from within the country, who demanded that their government enhance its efforts to quickly achieve visa-free travel. Against this background, the Macedonian authorities considered the Ohrid Border Process a useful additional project providing them with clear ideas on how and when they should reform their external border control system.

In search of theoretical explanations

By elaborating on the mechanisms of adjustment and the Europeanisation of justice and home affairs in Croatia and Macedonia, this analysis has disproved the assumption that the EU's external influence has decreased in the present enlargement round. In the aspiring South-Eastern European candidate countries, the EU has developed additional ways to render its conditionality approach credible (see also Trauner, 2009).

Although the hurdles for entering the EU have been raised, Croatia's compliance efforts can be considered similar to the logic observed in the Eastern enlargement. The key to understanding the compliance efforts of Macedonia, whose membership prospect is less certain, is to take into account policy conditionality in addition to membership conditionality. The EU ensured its leverage to shape domestic policy-making in the country by substantially increasing the value of the 'intermediary reward' (Vachudova, 2005: 251) of visa-free travel. The issue of facilitated travel opportunities has been of high political salience in Macedonia and the other Western Balkan countries located on the EU's negative visa list (Serbia, Kosovo, Montenegro, Bosnia and Herzegovina and Albania). The EU took advantage of the issue by inventing 'negotiations on visa liberalisation', meaning that in exchange for the fulfilment of a whole range of conditionality requirements, from signing an EC readmission agreement and improving border controls to reforming public administration and fighting organised crime, the EU would talk with the target Balkan countries about visa-free travel.

The use of visa liberalisation as an incentive is not new. It has already led to strenuous efforts in Bulgaria and Romania to implement the Schengen rules (Grabbe, 2005). The EU's approach in the Western Balkans was different, however. Here, the EU introduced the concept of a graduated approach towards lifting the visa requirements, developed a more sophisticated system of evaluating the implementation of the conditions set by the EU and linked an unusually broad range of conditionality requirements to the reward. The promise of visa-free travel turned into a moving target used by the EU to encourage compliance with an increasing list of conditions. In a situation where membership rewards were less tangible due to the uncertainties of the accession process, the key variable for successful *acquis* adoption became policy conditionality.

In theoretical terms, the analysis therefore supports the external incentives model of EU external governance (Schimmelfennig and Sedelmeier, 2004: 663f), yet suggests a stronger focus on material rewards that do not relate to EU accession. In proposing policy-related incentives in addition to the coveted prospect of membership, the EU managed to fill its conditionality approach with more substance and to establish a more tangible relationship between demand and reward. With this approach, the EU was able to counterbalance the possible weaknesses of the pre-accession strategy and divert the candidate countries' calculations of the non-adaptation costs.

Conclusions

This analysis does not claim that the effectiveness of EU *acquis* conditionality in the policy field of justice and home affairs allows for drawing conclusions about EU democratic and economic conditionality in the Western Balkans in general. Scholarly work has convincingly demonstrated that the EU's external power in areas of state sovereignty and political conditionality has remained weak in some Western Balkan states (Anastasakis, 2008, Noutcheva, 2009, Batt and Obradovic-Wochnik, 2009).

This book seeks to contribute to a more nuanced view of the dynamics of EU rule transfer to South-Eastern Europe in the present enlargement round. Even if the EU lacks effectiveness at the levels of political and democratic accession conditionality, it may nevertheless succeed at advancing integration at a more subordinated level by establishing favourable cost–benefit structures in the respective policy fields. A process similar to what has been analysed here in the field of justice and home affairs has been observed in the field of energy policy, where the success of EU rule transfer to Serbia was dependent on the EU's offer of additional short-term incentives, particularly extra financial incentives (Hofer, 2008, Renner, 2009). Because the Western Balkan states have come closer to the EU in a more open-ended and uncertain process, these states have had more room to manoeuvre when deciding which policy fields to integrate. The key to successful EU rule adoption in the Western Balkans has therefore been to provide clear short-term incentives in addition to the still powerful but less tangible incentive of membership. Rather than full membership, the result has been sectoral integration and a creeping process towards EU membership (Renner and Trauner, 2009).

With this strategy, the EU has been successful in creating an extended zone of governance in South-Eastern Europe and establishing 'fuzzy borders' (Christiansen et al., 2000) with these neighbours. In order for the EU's strategy to remain effective, however, the short-term incentives need to be supported by serious commitments concerning any prospects of full membership. The entering into force of the Treaty of Lisbon on 1 December 2009 has opened a window of opportunity in this respect, possibly establishing a renewed consensus on enlargement and bringing the current *fatigue de l'élargissement* to an end.

*B*IBLIOGRAPHY

Agence Europe, EU bulletin, 4 May 2006; 14 May 2008; 21 June 2008; 30 July 2008; 30 July 2008; 17 December 2008.

Ahlbrecht, K. (2004) 'Coherent European Foreign Policy in Macedonia: From Test Case to Prime Example?' in Mahncke, D., Ambos, A. and Reynolds, C. (eds), *European Foreign Policy. From Rhetoric to Reality?* (Brussels: P.I.E.-Peter Lang), pp. 255–77.

Ahtisaari, M. (2007) 'Report of the Special Envoy of the Secretary General on Kosovo's Future Status', *Südosteuropa Mitteilungen*, March 2007 (Munich: Südosteuropa-Gesellschaft).

Altmann, F.-L. (1998) 'Die Balkanpolitik der EU: Regionalansatz und Prinzip der Konditionalität', *Südosteuropa*, 47, 503–15.

Altmann, F.-L. (2004) 'Regional Economic Problems and Prospects', in Batt, J. (ed.), *The Western Balkans: Moving On*, Chaillot Paper No. 70 (Paris: Institute for Security Studies (ISS)), pp. 69–84.

Anastasakis, O. (2008) 'The EU's Political Conditionality in the Western Balkans: Towards a More Pragmatic Approach', *Journal of Southeast European and Black Sea Studies*, 8:4, 365–77.

Anastasakis, O. and Bechev, D. (2003) 'EU Conditionality in South East Europe: Bringing Commitment to the Process', *South East European Studies Programme* (Oxford: University of Oxford).

Andreev, S. A. (2004) 'The Borders in Southeast Europe: Democratic Legitimacy and Security Issues in an Enlarged European Union', *Southeast European and Black Sea Studies*, 4:3, 379–98.

Apap, J., Boratynski, J., Emerson, M., Gromadzki, G., Vahl, M. and Whyte, N. (2001) 'Friendly Schengen Borderland Policy on the New Borders of an Enlarged EU and its Neighbours', CEPS Policy Brief No. 7 (Brussels: Centre for European Policy Studies).

Apap, J., Carrera, S. and Kirisci, K. (2004) 'Turkey in the European Area of Freedom, Security and Justice', EU–Turkey Working Papers No. 3 (Brussels: Centre for European Policy Studies).

Avery, G. and Batt, J. (2007) 'Balkans in Europe: Why, When and How?', EPC Policy Brief (Brussels: European Policy Centre).

Baldwin-Edwards, M. (2006) 'Visa Policies in South Eastern Europe: A Hindrance or a Stepping Stone to European Integration?', EWI Policy Brief, November 2006 (Brussels, New York and Moscow: East-West Institute).

Balkan Commission (2004): 'The Balkans in Europe's Future', Sofia: International Commission on the Balkans, available at: www.balkan-commission.org/ (accessed 16 June 2007).

Balzacq, T. (2008) 'The Implications of European Neighbourhood Policy in the Context of Border Controls (Readmission Agreements, Visa Policy, Human Rights)', Ad-Hoc Briefing Paper for the European Parliament (Brussels: Directorate-General Internal Policies).

Balzacq, T. (ed.) (2009) *The External Dimension of EU Justice and Home Affairs: Governance, Neighours, Security* (Houndmills: Palgrave).

Barroso, J. M. (2008): 'Speaking Points of Commission President José Manuel Barroso

During the Press Point, Following his Meeting with Croatian Prime Minister Ivo Sanader', Brussels: European Commission, 13 March 2008, available at: http://ec.europa.eu/commission_barroso/president/pdf/speaking_points_20080313_en.pdf (accessed 14 September 2008).

Batory, A. (2008) *The Politics of EU Accession: Ideology, Party Strategy and the European Question in Hungary (Manchester and New York: Manchester University Press)*.

Batt, J. (2004a) 'Introduction: The Stabilisation/Integration Dilemma', in Batt, J. (ed.), *The Western Balkans: Moving On*, Chaillot Paper No. 70 (Paris: Institute for Security Studies), pp. 7–21.

Batt, J. (2004b) *The Western Balkans: Moving On*, Chaillot Paper No. 70 (Paris: Institute for Security Studies).

Batt, J. and Obradovic-Wochnik, J. (2009) *War Crimes, Conditionality and EU Integration in the Western Balkans*, Chaillot Paper No. 116 (Paris: Institute for Security Studies).

BBC (1999) 'Croatia in Border Dispute with Yugoslavia', BBC News, 21 April 1999, available at: http://news.bbc.co.uk/2/hi/europe/324999.stm (accessed 5 March 2006).

BBC (2001) 'EU Backs Balkan Borders Plan', *BBC News*, 15 March 2001, available at: http://news.bbc.co.uk/2/hi/europe/1222304.stm (accessed 4 February 2007).

BBC (2005) 'EU Stalls over Talks with Croatia', BBC News, 10 March 2005, available at: http://news.bbc.co.uk/2/hi/europe/4337777.stm (accessed 28 January 2007).

BBC (2008) 'Serbia's Neigbhours Accept Kosovo', *BBC News*, 9 March 2008, available at: http://news.bbc.co.uk/2/hi/europe/7304488.stm (accessed 4 February 2009).

Bennet, A. and George, A. (2005) *Case Studies and Theory Development in the Social Sciences* (Cambridge, MA: MIT Press).

Berg, E. and Ehin, P. (2006) 'What Kind of Border Regime in the Making?: Towards a Differentiated and Uneven Border Security', *Cooperation and Conflict*, 41:1, 53–71.

Bertozzi, S. (2008) 'Schengen: Achievements and Challenges in Managing an Area Encompassing 3.6 million km?', CEPS Working Document No. 284 (Brussels: Centre for European Policy Studies).

Beunderman, M. (2005) 'Macedonia Feels Enlargement Blues as Paris Blocks EU Status', *euobserver.com*, 13 December 2005, available at: http://euobserver.com/9/20529 (accessed 7 April 2008).

Bigo, D. (2001) 'The Möbius Ribbon of Internal and External Security(ies)', in Albert, M., Jacobson, D. and Lapid, Y. (eds), *Identities, Borders and Orders* (Minneapolis: Minnesota University Press), pp. 91–136.

Bigo, D. and Guild, E. (2005a) 'Introduction: Policing in the Name of Freedom', in Bigo, D. and Guild, E. (eds), *Controlling Frontiers: Free Movement Into and Within Europe* (Aldershot: Ashgate Publishing Limited), pp. 1–14.

Bigo, D. and Guild, E. (2005b) 'Policing at a Distance: Schengen Visa Policies', in Bigo, D. and Guild, E. (eds), *Controlling Frontiers: Free Movement Into and Within Europe* (Aldershot: Ashgate Publishing Company), pp. 233–64.

Biscevic, H. (2008): 'Transforming the Stability Pact: Regional Cooperation Council', Brussels: Stability Pact for South-Eastern Europe, available at: www.stabilitypact.org/about/SPownershipprocessPortal.asp (accessed 6 May 2009).

Blockmans, S. (2006) 'The Western Balkans (Albania, Bosnia-Herzegovina, Croatia, Macedonia and Serbia and Montenegro, including Kosovo)', in Blockmans, S. and Lazowski, A. (eds), *The European Union and Its Neighbours: A Legal Appraisal of the EU's Policies of Stabilisation, Partnership and Integration* (The Hague: TMC Asser Press), pp. 315–57.

Blockmans, S. (2007) *Tough Love: The European Union's Relations with the Western Balkans* (The Hague: TMC Asser Press).

Blockmans, S. and Lazowski, A. (eds) (2006) *The European Union and its Neighbours: A Legal Appraisal of the EU's Policies of Stabilisation, Partnership and Integration* (The

Hague: TMC Asser Press).

Bolton, H. (2005) 'Border Management in the Kosovo-Southern Serbia-FYR Macedonia Vortex', Policy Brief, February 2005 (Brussels, New York, Moscow: East-West Institute).

Borissova, L. (2003) 'The Adoption of the Schengen and the Justice and Home Affairs Acquis: The Case of Bulgaria and Romania', *European Foreign Affairs Review*, 8:1, 105–24.

Boromisa, A.-M., Cuckovic, N., Samardzija, V. and Stanicic, M. (2007) 'Croatia', in IEP (ed.), *EU-25/27 Watch. No. 5* (Berlin: Institute for European Politics).

Boromisa, A.-M., Cuckovic, N., Samarkzija, V., Stanicic, M. and Vidacak, I. (2006) 'Croatia', in IEP (ed.), *EU-25 Watch, No 2:3* (Berlin: Institute for European Politics).

Börzel, T. A. (1999) 'Towards Convergence in Europe? Institutional Adaptation to Europeanization in Germany and Spain', *Journal of Common Market Studies*, 39:4, 573–96.

Busek, E. (2007) *Remarks by Erhard Busek, Special Co-ordinator of the Stability Pact for South-Eastern Euorpe at the 10th Meeting of the Heads of State and Governments of the SEECP*, Zagreb: Stability Pact for South-Eastern Europe, 11 May 2007.

Butini, G. (2005): *The Role of the EUPOL-Proxima Mission in the Former Yugoslav Republic of Macedonia: Special Focus on the Support of the Implementation of the Integrated Border Management Strategy*, Ohrid: EAPC/SEEGROUP Workshop on Reflections on Border Management, 8–10 June 2005.

Cafruny, A. (1998) 'The European Union and the War in the Former Yugoslavia: The Failure of Collective Diplomacy', in Cafruny, A. and Peters, P. (eds), *The Union and the World: The Political Economy of a Common European Foreign Policy* (The Hague: Kluwer Law International), pp. 133–51.

Caparini, M. (2004) 'Security Sector Reform and Post-Conflict Stabilisation: The Case of the Western Balkans', in Bryden, A. and Hänggi, H. (eds), *Reform and Reconstruction of the Security Sector* (Berlin, Hamburg, Münster: LIT-Verlag).

CARDS Regional Programme (2005): *Establishment of EU Compatible Legal, Regulatory and Institutional Frameworks in the Field of Asylum, Migration and Visa Matters*, Zagreb: Migrationsverket, European Commission, International Organization for Migration.

Centre for Research and Policy Making (2008) 'Should Macedonia Recognize Kosovo as an Independent State?' 19 March 2008 (Skopje: CRPM Public Opinion Poll), available at: www.crpm.org.mk (accessed 22 January 2009).

Checkel, J. T. (2001) 'Why Comply? Social Learning and European Identity Change', *International Organization*, 55:3, 553–88.

Checkel, J. T. (2005) 'It's the Process Stupid! Process Tracing in the Study of European and International Politics', Arena Working Paper No. 26, October 2005 (Oslo: Arena Centre for European Studies).

Christiansen, T., Petito, F. and Tonra, B. (2000) 'Fuzzy Politics around Fuzzy Borders: The European Union's "Near Abroad"', *Cooperation and Conflict*, 35:4, 389–415.

Commission of the European Communities (1999) *Commission Report on the Feasibility of Negotiating a Stabilisation and Association Agreement with the Former Yugoslav Republic of Macedonia*, Brussels: COM (1999) 300.

Commission of the European Communities (2000) *Report from the Commission on the Feasibility of Negotiating a Stabilisation and Association Agreement with the Republic of Croatia*, Brussels: COM (2000) 311 final.

Commission of the European Communities (2001a) *CARDS Assistance Programme to the Western Balkans: Regional Strategy Paper 2002–2006*, Brussels: External Relations Directorate General.

Commission of the European Communities (2001b) *EU Justice and Home Affairs Policy and the Western Balkans*, Brussels: Conference paper from the European Commission for the Second Regional Conference for South-East Europe.

Commission of the European Communities (2001c): *Proposal for a Council Decision Concerning the Signature of the Stabilisation and Association Agreement between the European Communities and its Member States and the Republic of Croatia on Behalf of the European Community*, Brussels: COM (2001) 371.

Commission of the European Communities (2001d) *The Stabilisation and Association Process and CARDS Assistance 2000 to 2006*, Brussels: European Commission Paper for the Second Regional Conference for South-Eastern Europe.

Commission of the European Communities (2002a) *CARDS Country Strategy Paper for Croatia 2002–2006'*, Brussels, available at: http://ec.europa.eu/enlargement /pdf/financial_assistance/cards/publications/croatia_strategy_paper_en.pdf (accessed 6 September 2007).

Commission of the European Communities (2002b) *Communication from the Commission to the Council and the European Parliament towards Integrating Management of the External Borders of the Member States of the European Union*, Brussels: COM (2002) 233, 7 May 2002.

Commission of the European Communities (2002c) *Croatia: Stabilisation and Association Report*, Brussels: COM (2002) 163, 4 April 2002.

Commission of the European Communities (2003a) *Boost for Border Policing*, Zagreb: Delegation of the European Commission to the Republic of Croatia.

Commission of the European Communities (2003b) *CARDS Twinning Project Fiche: Capacity Building in the Area of Illegal Migration*, Zagreb: Delegation of the European Commission to the Republic of Croatia.

Commission of the European Communities (2003c) *Croatia: Stabilisation and Association Report 2003*, Brussels: COM (2003) 139, 26 March 2003.

Commission of the European Communities (2003d): *Former Yugoslav Republic of Macedonia: Stabilisation and Association Report 2003*, Brussels: SEC (2003) 342, 26 March 2003.

Commission of the European Communities (2003e) *Rapid Reaction Mechanisms End of Programme Report Former Yugoslav Republic of Macedonia*, Brussels: European Commission Conflict Prevention and Crisis Management Unit.

Commission of the European Communities (2004a) *Council Decision on the Principles, Priorities and Conditions Contained in the European Partnership with Croatia*, Brussels: COM (2004) 275, 20 April 2004.

Commission of the European Communities (2004b) *Former Yugoslav Republic of Macedonia: Stabilisation and Association Report 2004*, Brussels: SEC (2004) 373.

Commission of the European Communities (2004c) *Opinion on the Application of Croatia for Membership of the European Union*, Brussels: COM (2004) 257, 20 April 2004.

Commission of the European Communities (2005a) *Assessment Mission (peer based) under Chapter 23 (Judiciary and Fundamental Rights and Chapter 24 (Justice, Freedom and Security) in the Republic of Macedonia, 4–8 July 2005*, Brussels.

Commission of the European Communities (2005b) *Communication from the Commission. Commission Opinion on the Application from the Former Yugoslav Republic of Macedonia for Membership of the European Union*, Brussels: COM (2005) 562, 9 November 2005.

Commission of the European Communities (2005c) *Communication from the Commission: 2005 Enlargement Strategy Paper*, Brussels: COM (2005) 561, 9 November 2005.

Commission of the European Communities (2005d) *Regional Workshop on Cross-Border Co-operation between Border Police and Customs*, Tirana, 14–16 November 2005: The European Commission Delegation to Bosnia and Herzegovina.

Commission of the European Communities (2006a) *Communication from the Commission to the Council and the European Parliament of 8 November 2006: Instrument for Pre-*

Accession Assistance. Multi-Annual Indicative Financial Framework for 2008–2010, Brussels: COM (2006) 672 final, 5 March 2008.

Commission of the European Communities (2006b) *Communication from the Commission to the Council and the European Parliament on Strengthening the European Neighbourhood Policy*, Brussels: COM (2006) 726 final, 4 December 2006.

Commission of the European Communities (2006c) *Communication from the Commission to the European Parliament and the Council. Enlargement Strategy and Main Challenges 2006–2007. Including Annexed Special Report on the EU's Capacity to Integrate New Members*, Brussels: COM (2006) 649, 8 November 2006.

Commission of the European Communities (2006d) *Communication from the Commission: The Western Balkans on the Road to the EU: Consolidating Stability and Raising Prosperity*, Brussels: COM (2006) 27, 27 January 2006.

Commission of the European Communities (2006e) *Croatia 2006 Progress Report*, Brussels: SEC (2006) 1385, 8 November 2006.

Commission of the European Communities (2006f) *The Former Yugoslav Republic of Macedonia 2006 Progress Report*, Brussels: SEC (2006) 1387, 8 November 2006.

Commission of the European Communities (2006g) *Screening Report: Croatia. Chapter 24 – Justice, Freedom and Security*, Brussels, 2 June 2006.

Commission of the European Communities (2007a) *Commission Decision on a Multi-annual Indicative Planning Document (MIDP) 2007–2009 for Albania*, COM (2007) 2245, 31 May 2007.

Commission of the European Communities (2007b) *Croatia 2007 Progress Report*, Brussels: SEC (2007) 1431, 6 November 2007.

Commission of the European Communities (2007c) *The Former Yugoslav Republic of Macedonia 2007 Progress Report*, Brussels: SEC (2007) 1432, 6 November 2007.

Commission of the European Communities (2008a) *Adopting a National Programme for the Former Yugoslav Republic of Macedonia under the IPA: Transition Assistance and Institution Building Component for the year 2008*, December 2008, available at: http://ec.europa.eu/enlargement/pdf/the_former_yugoslav_republic_of_macedonia/ipa/2008/com_dec_ipa_2008_comp_i_tc_en.pdf (accessed 6 June 2009).

Commission of the European Communities (2008b) *Bosnia and Herzegovina 2008 Progress Report*, Brussels: SEC (2008) 2693 final, 5 November 2008.

Commission of the European Communities (2008c) *Commission Communication: Preparing the Next Steps in Border Management in the European Union*, Brussels: COM (2008) 69 final, 13 February 2008.

Commission of the European Communities (2008d) *Commission Communication. Report on the Evaluation and Future Development of the FRONTEX Agency*, Brussels: COM (2008) 67 final, 13 February 2008.

Commission of the European Communities (2008e) *Croatia 2008 Progress Report*, Brussels: SEC (2008) 2694, 5 November 2008.

Commission of the European Communities (2008f) *Enlargement Strategy and Main Challenges 2008–2009*, Brussels: COM (2008) 674 final, 5 November 2008.

Commission of the European Communities (2008g) *The Former Yugoslav Republic of Macedonia 2008 Progress Report*, Brussels: SEC (2008) 2695, 5 November 2008.

Commission of the European Communities (2008h) *Non-Paper Expanding on the Proposals Contained in the Communication to the European Parliament and the Council on 'Strengthening the ENP' - COM (2006) 726 Final of 4 December: ENP – Visa facilitation*, Brussels, January 2008.

Commission of the European Communities (2009a) *The Former Yugoslav Republic of Macedonia 2009 Progress Report*, Brussels: SEC (2009) 1335, 14 October 2009.

Commission of the European Communities (2009b) *Proposal for a Council Regulation Amending Regulation (EC) No 539/2001 Listing the Third Countries Whose Nationals*

Must be in Possession of Visas when Crossing the External Borders and Those Whose Nationals are Exempt from that Requirement, Brussels: COM (2009) 366 final, 15 July 2009.

Commission of the European Communities (2009c) *Updated Assessment of the Implementation by the Former Yugoslav Republic of Macedonia of the Roadmap for Visa Liberalisation*, Brussels, 18 May 2009.

Common Platform (2003) *Common Platform of the Ohrid Regional Conference on Border Security and Management*, Ohrid, 22/23 May 2003.

Consortium Implementing the CARDS Regional Programme (2005) *Information Note: CARDS Regional Programme 2002/2003 (Contract Nr 81242). Support to and Coordination of Integrated Border Management Strategies*, Zagreb.

Council of the European Union (1999a): *Recommendation for a Council Decision Authorising the Commission to Negotiate a Stabilisation and Association Agreement with the Former Yugoslav Republic of Macedonia*, Brussels: SEC (1999) 1279 final, 8 September 1999.

Council of the European Union (1999b) *The Schengen Acquis Integrated into the European Union*, Brussels: Official Journal, L 176/1, 10 July 1999.

Council of the European Union (2000) *Council Regulation (EC) No 2666/2000 of 5 December 2000 on Assistance for Albania, Bosnia and Herzegovina, Croatia, the Federal Republic of Yugoslavia and the Former Yugoslav Republic of Macedonia, Repealing Regulation (EC) No 1628/96 and Amending Regulations (EEC) No 3906/89 and (EEC) No 1360/90 and Decision 97/256/EC and 1999/311 EC*, Brussels: Official Journal L 306, 07/12/2000.

Council of the European Union (2001a) *Annex Council Report – Review of the Stabilisation and Association Process*, Luxembourg: General Affairs Council.

Council of the European Union (2001b) *Council Regulation (EC) No 539/2001 of 15 March 2001 Listing the Third Countries Whose Nationals Must be in Possession of Visas when Crossing the External Borders and Those Whose Nationals are Exempt from that Requirement'*, Brussels: Official Journal, L 81, 21 March 2001.

Council of the European Union (2001c) *Press Release, 2356th Council Meeting*, Luxembourg: General Affairs, PRES/O1/226, 11–12 June 2001.

Council of the European Union (2001d) *Stabilisation and Association Agreement between the European Communities and their Member States, of the One Part, and the Former Yugoslav Republic of Macedonia, of the Other Part*, Brussels: 6726/01.

Council of the European Union (2002a) *EU Schengen Catalogue: External Borders Control, Removal and Readmission: Recommendations and Best Practices*, Brussels: General Secretariat, DG H.

Council of the European Union (2002b): *Plan for the Management of the External Borders of the Member States of the European Union*, Brussels: 10019/02, 14 June 2002.

Council of the European Union (2003a) *EU-Western Balkans Forum: Joint Conclusions*, Brussels: 15578/03, 28 November 2003.

Council of the European Union (2003b) *EU Action against Organised Crime in the Western Balkans*, Brussels: 14810/03, 2 December 2003.

Council of the European Union (2003c) *Press Briefing: Termination of the EU-led Military Operation Concordia. Launch of the EU Police Mission Proxima*, Brussels, 08/12/2003.

Council of the European Union (2003d) *The Thessaloniki Agenda for the Western Balkans: Moving Towards European Integration*, Thessaloniki: Western Balkans – General Affairs and External Relations Council (GAERC) Conclusions, 16 June 2003.

Council of the European Union (2004a) *Council Regulation (EC) No 377/2004 of 19 February 2004 on the Creation of an Immigration Liaison Officers Network*, Brussels: Official Journal L 64, 2 March 2004.

Council of the European Union (2004b) *'Council Regulation (EC) No 2007/2004*

Establishing a European Agency for the Management of Operational Cooperation at the External Borders of the Member States of the European Union, Brussels: 10827/04, 26 October 2004.

Council of the European Union (2004c) *The Hague Programme: Strengthening Freedom, Security and Justice in the European Union*, Brussels: 16054/04, 13 December 2004.

Council of the European Union (2005a) *EU Police Advisory Team (EUPAT) in the Former Yugoslav Republic of Macedonia: Factsheet*, Brussels: EUPAT/00, December 2005.

Council of the European Union (2005b) *Negotiating Framework, Croatia*, Luxembourg, 3 October 2005.

Council of the European Union (2005c) *Stabilisation and Association Agreement between the European Communities and their Member States, of the One Part, and the Republic of Croatia, of the Other Part*, Brussels: Official Journal L 26/3, 28 January 2007.

Council of the European Union (2005d) *A Strategy for the External Action of JHA: Global Freedom, Security and Justice*, Brussels: 15446/05, 6 December 2005.

Council of the European Union (2006a) *2006/145/EC: Council Decision of 20 February 2006 on the Principles, Priorities and Conditions Contained in the Accession Partnership with Croatia and Repealing Decision 2004/648/EC*, Brussels: Official Journal L 55, 25 February 2006.

Council of the European Union (2006b) *Action Oriented Paper on Improving Cooperation, on organised Crime, Corruption, Illegal Immigration and Counter-terrorism, Between the EU, Western Balkans and Relevant ENP countries*, Brussels: 9272/06, 12 May 2006.

Council of the European Union (2006c) *Council Decision of 30 January 2006 on the Principles, Priorities and Conditions contained in the European Partnership with the former Yugoslav Republic of Macedonia and Repealing Decision 2004/518/EC*, Brussels: 2006/57/EC.

Council of the European Union (2006d) *Council Regulation (EC) No 1085/2006 of 17 July 2006 Establishing an Instrument for Pre-Accession Assistance (IPA)*, Brussels: Official Journal L 210, 31 July 2006.

Council of the European Union (2006e) *Police Cooperation Convention for South East Europe*, Vienna: Press Release of the Presidency of the European Union, 3–4 May 2006.

Council of the European Union (2006f) *Presidency Statement on the EU-Western Balkan Forum on Justice and Home Affairs*, Tirana, 16 and 17 November 2006.

Council of the European Union (2006g) *Regulation (EC) No 526/2006 of the European Parliament and of the Council establishing a Community Code on the Rules Governing the Movement of Persons Across Borders*, Brussels: OJ L 105, 13 April 2006.

Council of the European Union (2006h) *Report on the State of Implementation by Member States and EU bodies of Action-Oriented Paper on Improving Cooperation on Organised Crime, Corruption, Illegal Immigration and Counter-terrorism, between the EU, the Western Balkans and Relevant ENP Countries*, Brussels: 15013/1/06, 21 November 2006.

Council of the European Union (2007a) *Agreement Between the European Community and the Former Yugoslav Republic of Macedonia on the Facilitation of the Issuance of Visas*, Brussels: Official Journal L 334/125, 19 December 2007.

Council of the European Union (2007b) *Council Decision Concerning the Signing of the Agreement between the European Community and the Former Yugoslav Republic of Macedonia on Readmission of Persons Residing without Authorisation*, Brussels: 12199/07, 7 September 2007.

Council of the European Union (2007c) *Council Decision on the Signing of the Agreement Between the European Community and Ukraine on the Facilitation of the Issuance of Visas*, Brussels 9323/07, 29 May 2007.

Council of the European Union (2008a) *2008/212/EC: Council Decision of 18 February 2008 on the Principles, Priorities and Conditions Contained in the Accession Partnership with the Former Yugoslav Republic of Macedonia and Repealing Decision 2006/57/EC*, Official

Journal L 080, 19 March 2008.

Council of the European Union (2008b) *Press Release. 2850th Council Meeting: General Affairs and External Relations*, Brussels, 18 February 2008.

Council of the European Union (2008c) *Second Report on the State of Implementation by Member States and EU Bodies of Action-Oriented Paper on Improving Cooperation on Organised Crime, Corruption, Illegal Immigration and Counter-terrorism, Between the EU, the Western Balkans and Relevant ENP countries*, Brussels: 8827/1/08, 8 May 2008.

Council of the European Union (2009a) *Council Regulation Amending Regulation (EC) No 539/2001 Listing the Third Countries whose Nationals must be in Possession of Visas when Crossing the External Borders and Those Whose Nationals are Exempt from that Requirement*, Brussels: 2009/0104(CNS), 24 November 2009.

Council of the European Union (2009b) *Press Release. 2979th Council Meeting: Justice and Home Affairs*, Brussels: 16883/1/09 REV 1, 30 November and 1 December 2009.

Council of the European Union (2009c) *Press Release. 2984th Council Meeting: General Affairs*, Brussels: 17217/09, 7 December 2009.

Cowles, M. G., Caporaso, J. A. and Risse, T. (eds) (2001) *Transforming Europe: Europeanization and Domestic Change* (Ithaca and London: Cornell University Press).

Dalem, A. (2006) 'France', in IEP (ed.), *EU-25 Watch. No 2* (Berlin: Institute for European Politics).

Damjanovski, I. and Vurmo, G. (2004) 'Support to Promoting Reciprocal Under-standing and Dialogue between the EU and Western Balkan Countries: Research on the Progress of Republic of Macedonia in the Area of Justice and Home Affairs' (Sofia: European Institute), available at: www.westernbalkans.info/htmls/page.php?category =339&id=539 (accessed 5 July 2007).

DCAF (2007) *DCAF's Border Security Programme. Lessons Learned from the Establishment of Border Security Systems: Executive Summary Fact Sheet*, Geneva: Geneva Centre for the Democratic Control of Armed Forces (DCAF).

DeBardeleben, J. (ed.) (2008) *The Boundaries of EU Enlargement: Finding a Place for Neighbours* (Basingstoke: Palgrave Macmillan).

Delevic, M. (2007) *Regional Cooperation in the Western Balkans*, Chaillot Paper No. 104 (Paris: Institute for Security Studies).

Dimitrova, A. (ed.) (2004a) *Driven to Change: The European Union's Enlargement Viewed from the East* (Manchester and New York: Manchester University Press).

Dimitrova, K. R. (2004b) 'Municipal Decisions on the Border of Collapse: Macedonian Decentralisation and the Challenge of Post-Ohrid Democracy', *Southeast European Politics*, V:2–3, 172–86.

Dittrich, M. (2005) 'Facing the Global Terrorist Threat: a European Response', EPC Working Paper No. 14 (Brussels: European Policy Centre).

Donev, J. (2003) 'Macedonia: A Promising Journey Interrupted?' in van Meurs, W. (ed.), *Prospects and Risks Beyond EU Enlargement. Southeastern Europe: Weak States and Strong International Support* (Opladen: Leske & Budrich), pp. 227–37.

EAR (2002) *Annual Programme 2002: Immigration and Asylum*, Skopje: European Agency for Reconstruction.

EAR (2005a) *EU gives Macedonian Border Police Euro 2,8 million of Equipment*, Thessaloniki: European Agency for Reconstruction, 14 June 2005.

EAR (2005b) *Former Yugoslav Republic of Macedonia. Justice and Home Affairs: Agency's Activities 1998–2005*, Skopje: European Agency for Reconstruction.

EAR (2006) *Better Border Management: EU Funds New National Coordination Centre*, Thessaloniki: European Agency for Reconstruction, 10 April 2006.

Eising, R. and Kohler-Koch, B. (1999) 'Governance in the European-Union: A Comparative Assessment', *The Transformation of Governance in the European Union* (London: Routledge), pp. 267–85.

Elbasani, A. (2008) 'The Stabilisation and Association Process in the Balkans: Overloaded Agenda and Weak Incentives?', EUI Working Paper SPS 2008/03 (Florence: European University Institute).

ESI (2005) *Moment of Truth. Macedonia, the EU Budget and the Destabilisation of the Balkans*, Berlin, Brussels, Istanbul: European Stability Initiative, 15 December 2005.

ESI (2008a) *Strict but Fair – the Declaration*, Berlin, Brussels, Istanbul: European Stability Initiative, 19 March 2008.

ESI (2008b) *The White List Project. EU Policies on Visa-Free Travel for the Western Balkans*, Berlin, Brussels, Istanbul: European Stability Initiative, 1 November 2008.

EurActiv (2009a) 'Balkan EU Visa Deal Hailed as "Giant Step for Macedonia"', *EurActiv.com*, 16 July 2009, available at: www.euractiv.com/en/enlargement/balkan-eu-visa-deal-hailed-giant-step-macedonia/article-184185 (accessed 23 July 2009).

EurActiv (2009b) 'Macedonia EU Talks Decision Postponed until 2010', *EurActiv.com*, 8 December 2009, available at: www.euractiv.com/en/enlargement/macedonia-eu-talks-decision-postponed-2010/article-188120 (accessed 15 December 2009).

EurActiv (2009c) 'Slovenia Waves Referendum Card at Croatia', *EurActiv.com*, 8 January 2009, available at: www.euractiv.com/en/enlargement/slovenia-waves-referendum-card-croatia/article-178349 (accessed 20 February 2009).

European Council (2000) *Presidency Conclusions*, Santa Maria da Feira, 19 and 20 June 2000.

European Council (2001) *Presidency Conclusions*, Laeken, 14 and 15 December 2001.

European Council (2002) *Presidency Conclusions*, Copenhagen, 12 and 13 December 2002.

European Council (2003) *Presidency Conclusions*, Thessaloniki, 19 and 20 June 2003.

European Council (2004) *Presidency Conclusions*, Brussels, 17 and 18 June 2004.

European Council (2005) *Presidency Conclusions*, Brussels, 15 and 16 December 2005.

European Council (2006) *Presidency Conclusions*, Brussels, 14 and 15 December 2006.

European Council (2007) *Presidency Conclusions*, Brussels, 14 December 2007.

European Parliament (2009) *Report on the Proposal for a Council Regulation Amending Regulation (EC) No 539/2001 Listing the Third Countries Whose Nationals Must Be in Possession of Visas when Crossing the External Borders and Those Whose Nationals are Exempt from That Requirement*, Committee on Civil Liberties, Justice and Home Affairs (A7–0042/2009), 27 October 2009.

FAZ (2005) 'EU beginnt Verhandlungen mit Türkei und Kroatien', *Frankfurter Allgemeine Zeitung*, 4 October 2005.

Framework Agreement (2001), Ohrid, 13 August 2001, available at: http://faq .macedonia.org/politics/framework_agreement.pdf (accessed 5 November 2008).

Friis, L. and Murphy, A. (2000) '"Turbo-charged negotiations": The EU and the Stability Pact for South-Eastern Europe', *Journal of European Public Policy*, 7:5, 767–86.

Frontex (2009) *Press Release. Working Agreement with the fYR of Macedonia Concluded*, Warsaw, 3 February 2009.

Futo, P. and Jandl, M. (eds) (2004) *2003 Year Book on Illegal Migration, Human Smuggling and Trafficking in Central and Eastern Europe: A Survey and Analysis of Border Management and Border Apprehension Data from 19 States* (Vienna: International Centre for Migration Policy Development).

Gagnon, V. P. (2004) *The Myth of Ethnic War: Serbia and Croatia in the 1990s* (Ithaca: Cornell University Press).

Glenny, M. (2004a) 'The Kosovo Question and Regional Stability', in Batt, J. (ed.), *The Western Balkans: Moving On*, Chaillot Paper No. 70 (Paris: Institute for Security Studies (ISS)), pp. 87–99.

Glenny, M. (2004b) 'Migration Policies of Western European Governments and the Fight Against Organised Crime in SEE', *Southeast European and Black Sea Studies*, 4:2, 240–56.

Goetz, K. H. and Meyer-Sahling, J.-H. (2008) 'The Europeanisation of National Political Systems: Parliaments and Executives', *Living Reviews in European Governance*, 3:2, available at: http://europeangovernance.livingreviews.org/Articles/lreg-2008–2/ (accessed 23 January 2009).

Government of the Republic of Croatia (2003a) *The Programm of the Government of the Republic of Croatia for the 2003-2007 Mandate*, Zagreb, 23 December 2003.

Government of the Republic of Croatia (2003b) *Questionnaire of the European Commission*, Zagreb, available at: www.vlada.hr/default.asp?ru=278&sid=&jezik=2 (accessed 5 February 2007).

Government of the Republic of Croatia (2005) *National Programme for the Integration of the Republic of Croatia into the European Union – 2005*, Zagreb: Ministry for Foreign Affairs and European Integration, available at: www.mvpei.hr/ei/download /2005/06/27/NPIEU_2005_en1.pdf (accessed 12 March 2007).

Government of the Republic of Croatia (2006a) *Croatia to draw up Schengen Action Plan by Year's End*, Press Release, Zagreb, available at: www.vlada.hr/default .asp?gl=200602230000021 (accessed 18 February 2007).

Government of the Republic of Croatia (2006b) *National Programme for the Integration of the Republic of Croatia into the European Union – 2006*, Zagreb: Ministry of Foreign Affairs and European Integration.

Government of the Republic of Croatia (2006c) *Overview of Activities on the State Border of the Republic of Croatia in 2005*, Zagreb: Ministry of the Interior.

Government of the Republic of Croatia (2006d) *Return of Displaced Persons and Refugees to Croatia*, Zagreb.

Government of the Republic of Croatia (2007a) *National Programme for the Integration of the Republic of Croatia into the EU – 2007*, Zagreb: Ministry of Foreign Affairs and European Integration.

Government of the Republic of Croatia (2007b) *Sanader Comments on Open Issues in Croatian–Bosnian Relations*, Zagreb: Press Release, 3 May 2007.

Government of the Republic of Croatia (2008a) *Croatia to Follow EU on Kosovo's Independence*, Zagreb: Press Release, 18 February 2008.

Government of the Republic of Croatia (2008b) *National Programme for the Integration of the Republic of Croatia into the European Union – 2008*, Zagreb: Ministry of Foreign Affairs and European Integration.

Government of the Republic of Croatia (2009) *Croatia, Slovenia Open New Chapter in Their Relations, PMs Say*, Zagreb: Press Release, 4 November 2009.

Government of the Republic of Macedonia (2004) *National Strategy for European Integration of the Republic of Macedonia*, Skopje, September 2004.

Government of the Republic of Macedonia (2005) *Questionnaire for the Preparation of the European Commission's Opinion on the Application of the Republic of Macedonia for Membership of the European Union*, Skopje, available at: www.sei.gov.mk/questionnaire/ (accessed 8 April 2008).

Government of the Republic of Macedonia (2006a) *Draft National Programme for Adoption of the Acquis Communautaire*, Skopje: Secretariat for European Affairs, available at: www.sei.gov.mk/portal/eng/npaa/01%20NPAA.pdf (accessed 19 December 2007).

Government of the Republic of Macedonia (2006b) *Justice and Home Affairs Subcommitee: European Community – Republic of Macedonia*, Brussels: Internal Compendium, 30 November–1 December 2006.

Government of the Republic of Macedonia (2006c) *Law on Foreigners*, Skopje: The Ministry of Internal Affairs, available at: http://www.iomskopje.org.mk/Legal /Law_on_Foreigners_ENG.pdf (accessed 5 April 2009).

Government of the Republic of Macedonia (2007) *National Programme for Adoption of the*

Acquis Communautaire, Skopje, April 2007.

Government of the Republic of Slovenia (2005) *Speech of Minister Dragutin Mate on the 5th Regional Ministerial Conference on Illegal Migration, Organised Crime, Corruption and Terrorism*, Brdo: Ministry of the Interior.

Government of the Republic of Slovenia (2008) *Reactions to Croatia's Declaration of Ecological-Fisheries Zone*, Ljubljana: Slovene Press Agency, Public Relations and Media Office, 10 April 2003.

Grabbe, H. (2000) *The Sharp Edges of Europe: Security Implications of Extending EU Border Policies Eastwards*, Occasional Paper 13, March 2000 (Paris: Institute for Security Studies).

Grabbe, H. (2001) 'How Does Europeanization Affect CEE Governance? Conditionality, Diffusion and Diversity', *Journal of European Public Policy*, 8:6, 1013–31.

Grabbe, H. (2002) 'Stabilising the East While Keeping Out the Easterners: Internal and External Security Logics in Conflict', in Lavenex, S. and Ucarer, E. M. (eds), *Migration and the Externalities of European Integration* (Lanham, MD: Lexington Books), pp. 91–104.

Grabbe, H. (2003) 'Europeanization Goes East: Power and Uncertainty in the EU Accession Process', in Featherstone, K. and Radaelli, C. M. (eds), *The Politics of Europeanization* (Oxford: Oxford University Press), pp. 303–31.

Grabbe, H. (2005) 'Regulating the Flow of People across Europe', in Schimmelfennig, F. and Sedelmeier, U. (eds), *The Europeanization of Central and Eastern Europe* (Ithaca and London: Cornell University Press), pp. 112–35.

Grabbe, H. (2006) *The EU's Transformative Power: Europeanization through Conditionality in Central and Eastern Europe* (New York: Palgrave Macmillan).

Graziano, P. and Vink, M. P. (eds) (2007) *Europeanization: New Research Agendas* (Basingstoke: Palgrave Macmillan).

Guild, E., Carrera, S. and Geyer, F. (2008) 'The Commission's New Border Package: Does it Take Us One Step Closer to a "Cyber-fortress Europe"?' CEPS Policy Brief No. 154, March 2008 (Brussels: Centre for European Policy Studies).

Hänggi, H. and Tanner, F. (2005) *Promoting Security Sector Governance in the EU's Neighbourhood*, Chaillot Paper No. 80, July 2005 (Paris: Institute for Security Studies).

Hills, A. (2004a) 'Assumptions, Principles and Strategy', *Adelphi Papers*, 44:371, 11–40.

Hills, A. (2004b) *Border Security in the Balkans: Europe's Gatekeepers*, Adelphi Paper 371 (New York: Oxford University Press).

Hills, A. (2004c) 'Macedonia and Albania', *Adelphi Papers*, 44:371, 59–76.

Hix, S. and Goetz, K. H. (2000) *Europeanised Politics? European Integration and National Political Systems* (London: Frank Cass Publishers).

Hobbing, P. (2005) 'Integrated Border Management at the EU Level', CEPS Working Paper No. 227/August 2005 (Brussels: Centre for European Policy Studies).

Hofer, S. (2008) *Die Europäische Union als Regelexporteur: Die Europäisierung der Energiepolitik in Bulgarien, Serbien und der Ukraine* (Baden-Baden: Nomos).

House of Lords (2000) *Enlargement and EU External Frontier Controls, Seventeenth Report, 24 October 2000*, London: Select Committee on European Union.

House of Lords (2003) *Proposal for a European Border Guard*, London: Session 2002–2003, available at: www.publications.parliament.uk/pa/ld200203/ldselect/ldeucom/133 /13301.htm (accessed 4 January 2007).

House of Lords (2006) *'further Enlargement of the EU: Corrected Oral Evidence Given By Mr Vladmir Drobnjak and Mr Josip Paro*, London.

Huysmans, J. (2000) 'The European Union and the Securitization of Migration', *Journal of Common Market Studies*, 38:5, 751–77.

IBM Guidelines (2004) *Guidelines for Integrated Border Management in the Western Balkans*, Brussels, available at: http://ec.europa.ehu/enlargement/key_documents

/cards_reports_and_publications_en.htm#13 (accessed 26 April 2007).

IBM Guidelines (2007) *Guidelines for Integrated Border Management in the Western Balkans: Updated Version*', available at: www.icmpd.org/840.html?&F =hbjpdkoevpf&tx_icmpd_pi2[document]=584&cHash=4d9b94add0 (accessed 11 June 2009).

ICG (2003) 'Macedonia: No Room for Complacency', Europe Report No. 149, 23 October 2003 (Skopje/Brussels: International Crisis Group).

ICG (2004) 'Macedonia: Make or Break', ICG Europe Briefing, 3 August 2004 (Skopje/ Brussels: International Crisis Group).

ICG (2005a) 'EU Visas and the Western Balkans', Europe Report No. 168 – 29 November 2005 (Brussels: International Crisis Group).

ICG (2005b) 'Macedonia: Not out of the Woods Yet', Europe Briefing No. 37, 25 February 2005 (Skopje/ Brussels: International Crisis Group).

ICG (2006) *Country Profile. Macedonia,* London: International Crisis Group, available at: www.crisisgroup.org/home/index.cfm?id=1244&l=1 (accessed 5 December 2006).

ICG (2009) 'Macedonia's Name: Breaking the Deadlock', Europe Briefing No. 52: International Crisis Group, January 2009.

ICMPD (1999a) *The Border Control System in the Republic of Macedonia. Internal Compendium on Border Management in South Eastern Europe. Albania, Bosnia and Herzegovina, Croatia, Macedonia (FYR), Serbia and Montenegro. Compiled in the Framework of the Budapest Process/Stability Pact Border Guard Task Force. Financed by the Government of Norway,* (Vienna: International Centre for Migration Policy Development).

ICMPD (1999b) *South East Europe as a Key Area for Illegal Migration. Statement by Mr. Jonas Wildgren, Director of ICMPD in Vienna at the Symposium Organised by Bundesnachrichtendienst (BNP) in Pullach (Germany) on 28 October 1999,* (Pullach: International Centre for Migration Policy Development).

ICMPD (2000) *How to Halt Illegal Migration to, from and through South East Europe: A report on the activities of the Working Group on South East Europe of the Budapest Group, with proposals on further action in the overall framework of the Stability Pact. Prepared by the Secretariat of the Budapest Group for the Meeting of the Working Group in Skopje on 27–28 November 2000* (Vienna: International Centre for Migration Policy Development).

ICMPD (2003) *Internal Compendium on Border Management in South Eastern Europe. Albania, Bosnia and Herzegovina, Croatia, Macedonia (FYR), Serbia and Montenegro. Compiled in the framework of the Budapest Process/Stability Pact Border Guard Task Force. Financed by the Government of Norway* (Vienna: International Centre for Migration Policy Development).

ICMPD (2005) *ICMPD Activities in the Field of Integrated Border Management* (Vienna: International Centre for Migration Policy Development).

IHT (2008) 'EU says Croatia on Course to Join the Bloc in 2010', *International Herald Tribune,* 13 March 2008.

Ioannides, I. (2006) 'EU Police Mission Proxima: Testing the "European" Approach to Building Peace', in Nowak, A. (ed.), *Civilian Crisis Management: The EU Way,* Chaillot Paper No. 90 (Paris: Institute for Security Studies), pp. 62–87.

IOM (2006) *Legal Resources,* Skopje: International Organization for Migration, available at: www.iomskopje.org.mk (accessed 4 November 2008).

Javno (2009) 'PM Kosor: 3 Billion Kuna Budget Amendment', *Javno.com,* 11 July 2009, available at: www.javno.com/en-croatia/pm-kosor—3–billion-kuna-budget-amendment_269761 (accessed 2 August 2009).

Johansson-Nogués, E. (2007) 'The EU and its Neighbourhood: An Overview', in Weber, K., Smith, M. and Baun, M. (eds), *Governing Europe's Neighbourhood. Partners or*

Periphery? (Manchester and New York: Manchester University Press), pp. 21–39.

Jovic, D. (2006) 'Croatia and the European Union: A Long Delayed Journey', *Journal of Southern Europe and the Balkans*, 8:1, 85–103.

Kacin, J. and Lax, H. (2006) 'A Visa Policy that Crushes Balkan Hopes', *International Herald Tribune*, 27 September 2006.

Karpat, C. (2006) 'Euro-Atlantic Axis in the Balkans: Macedonia-Kosovo-Albania', *Axis: Information and Analysis. Global Challenge Research*, 2 May 2006.

Kelley, J. G. (2004) *Ethnic Politics in Europe: The Power of Norms and Incentives* (Princeton, NJ: Princeton University Press).

Kelley, J. G. (2006) 'New Wine in Old Wineskins: Promoting Political Reforms through the New European Neighbourhood Policy', *Journal of Common Market Studies*, 44:1, 29–55.

Kennard, A. (2002) 'The Changing Role of Border Regions in Central and Eastern Europe', in Ingham, M. and Ingham, H. (eds), *EU Expansion to the East: Prospects and Problems* (Northampton: Edward Elgar Publishing), pp. 189–204.

Kirchner, E. and Sperling, J. (2007) *EU Security Governance* (Manchester: Manchester University Press).

Kochenov, D. (2005) 'EU Enlargement Law: History and Recent Developements: Treaty – Custom Concubinage?' *European Integration Online Papers*, 9:6.

Kolakovic, P., Martens, J. and Long, L. (2002) 'Irregular Migration through Bosnia and Herzegovina', in Laczko, F., Stacher, I. and Klekowski von Koppenfels, A. (eds), *New Challenges for Migration Policy in Central and Eastern Europe* (The Hague: TMC Asser Press, IOM and ICMPD), pp. 119–50.

Koveca, M. (2004) 'Preventing Conflict in Macedonia: The Role of the International Community – OSCE, UN, EU and NATO', Master Thesis, Diplomatic Academy Vienna.

Kruse, I. (2006) 'EU Readmission Policy and Its Effects on Transit Countries – The Case of Albania', *European Journal of Migration and Law*, 8:2, 115–42.

Kurowska, X. and Pawlak, P. (2009) 'The Politics of European Security Policies: Actors, Dynamics and Contentious Outcomes', *Perspectives on European Politics and Society*, 10:4, Special Issue.

Kušić, S. (2005) 'Kroatien', in Weidenfeld, W. and Wessels, W. (eds), *Jahrbuch der Europäischen Integration 2005* (Baden-Baden: Nomos), pp. 439–41.

Ladrech, R. (1994) 'Europeanization of Domestic Politics and Institutions: The case of France', *Journal of Common Market Studies*, 32:1, 69–99.

Ladrech, R. (2009) 'Europeanization and Political Parties', *Living Reviews in European Governance*, 4:1, available at: europeangovernance.livingreviews.org/Articles/lreg-2009–1/ (accessed 5 November 2009).

Lavenex, S. (2004) 'EU External Governance in "Wider Europe"', *Journal of European Public Policy*, 11:4, 680–700.

Lavenex, S. (2005) 'The Politics of Exclusion and Inclusion in "Wider Europe"', in DeBardeleben, J. (ed.), *Soft or Hard Borders? Managing the Divide in an Enlarged Europe* (Cornwall: MPG Books Ltd), pp. 123–45.

Lavenex, S. (2008) 'A Governance Perspective on the European Neighbourhood: Integration beyond Conditionality?', *Journal of European Public Policy*, 15:6, 938–55.

Lavenex, S. (2009) 'Transgovernmentalism in the European Area of Freedom, Security and Justice', in Verdun, A. and Tömmel, I. (eds), *Innovative Governance in the European Union: The Politics of Multilevel Policymaking* (Boulder: Lynne Rienner), pp. 255–72.

Lavenex, S. and Uçarer, E. M. (2002) *Migration and the Externalities of European Integration* (Lanham/Boulder/New York/Oxford: Lexington Books).

Lavenex, S. and Uçarer, E. M. (2004) 'The External Dimension of Europeanization: The Case of Immigration Policies', *Cooperation and Conflict: Journal of the Nordic*

International Studies Association, 39:4, 417–43.

Lavenex, S. and Wallace, W. (2005) 'Justice and Home Affairs', in Wallace, H., Wallace, W. and Pollack, M. A. (eds), *Policy-Making in the European Union. Fifth Edition* (Oxford: Oxford University Press).

Lavenex, S. and Wichmann, N. (2009) 'The External Governance of EU Internal Security', *Journal of European Integration*, 31:1, 83–102.

London Statement (2002) *Defeating Organised Crime in South Eastern Europe*, 25 November 2002 (London: Lancaster House Ministerial Conference).

Lucarelli, S. (2000) *Europe and the Breakup of Yugoslavia: A Political Failure in Search of a Scholarly Explanation* (The Hague: Kluwer Law International).

Luif, P. and Riegler, H. (2006) 'The External Dimension of the EU's Area of Freedom, Security and Justice in Relation to the Western Balkan Countries', Briefing Paper for the European Parliament (Strasbourg: Directorate-General for External Policies of the European Union.).

Lynch, T. and Samardzija, V. (2008) 'Analysis of the 2007 Annual Action Programme for Croatia under the Pre-Accession Instrument in Preparation of the Review of the Relevant Mulit-Annual Indicative Programme', Briefing for the Foreign Affairs Committee of the European Parliament under the framework contract with the Trans European Policy Studies Association (TEPSA) (Brussels).

MacDonald, N. (2007) 'Kosovo Prime Minister Plays Down Border Dispute', *Financial Times*, 27 April 2007, available at: www.ft.com/cms/s/0/4304a52e-d5fb-11da-8b3a-0000779e2340.html?nclick_check=1 (accessed 6 September 2008).

Magas, B. and Zanic, I. (eds) (2001) *The War in Croatia and Bosnia-Herzegovina 1991-1995* (Oxon: Frank Cass Publishers).

Mak Fax (2007) *Press Release*, Skopje, 25 January 2007.

March, J. G. and Olsen, J. P. (1998) 'The Institutional Dynamics of International Political Orders', *International Organisation*, 52:4, 943–69.

MARRI (2006) *Questionnaire: Republic of Macedonia*, Skopje: Migration, Asylum, Refugee Regional Initiative.

Massari, M. (2005) 'Do All Roads Lead to Brussels? Analysis of the Different Trajectories of Croatia, Serbia-Montenegro and Bosnia-Herzegovina', *Cambridge Review of International Affairs*, 18:2, 259–73.

Matovski, A. (2008) 'Macedonia after Bucharest: Avoiding Another European Failure in the Balkans', *Opinion*, 13 June 2008 (Paris: Institute for Security Studies).

Miošić-Lisjak, N. (2006) 'Croatia and the European Union: A Social Constructivist Perspective', *Policy Studies*, 27:2, 101–14.

Mitreva, I. (2006) *Minister Mitreva Sends Letter to EC Vice-President Frattini*, Skopje: Government of the Republic of Macedonia, 16 January 2006, available at: www.vlada.mk/english/News/January2006/ei16–1–2006.htm (accessed 6 March 2007).

Mitsilegas, V. (2007) 'The External Dimension of EU Action in Criminal Matters', *European Foreign Affairs Review*, 12, 457–97.

Mitsilegas, V., Monar, J. and Rees, W. (2003) *The European Union and Internal Security: Guardian of the People?* (Basingstoke: Palgrave Macmillan).

Monar, J. (2000) 'Justice and Home Affairs in a Wider Europe: The Dynamics of Inclusion and Exclusion', ESRC 'One Europe or Several?' Programme Working Paper 07/00 (Leicester: Centre for European Politics and Institutions, Department of Politics, University of Leicester).

Monar, J. (2001a) 'The Dynamics of Justice and Home Affairs: Laboratories, Driving Factors and Costs', *Journal of Common Market Studies*, 39:4, 747–64.

Monar, J. (2001b) 'EU Justice and Home Affairs and the Eastward Enlargement: The Challenge of Diversity and EU Instruments and Strategies', Discussion Paper C 91 (Bonn: Zentrum für Europäische Integrationsforschung).

Monar, J. (2004a) 'The EU as an International Actor in the Domain of Justice and Home Affairs', *European Foreign Affairs Review*, 9, 395–415.

Monar, J. (2004b) 'Justice and Home Affairs', *Journal of Common Market Studies*, 42 (Annual Review), 117–33.

Monar, J. (2005) 'The European Union's "Integrated Management" of External Borders', in DeBardeleben, J. (ed.), *Soft or Hard Borders? Managing the Divide in an Enlarged Europe* (Aldershot: Ashgate Publishing Company), pp. 145–65.

Monar, J. (2006) 'Cooperation in the Justice and Home Affairs Domain: Characteristics, Constraints and Progress', *European Integration*, 28:5, 495–509.

Montanaro-Jankovski, L. (2005) 'Good Cops, Bad Mobs? EU Policies to Fight Trans-national Organised Crime in the Western Balkans', EPC Issue Paper No. 40 (Brussels: European Policy Centre).

National IBM Strategy (2003) *Republic of Macedonia. Government of the Republic of Macedonia: National Integrated Border Management Strategy*, Skopje: Project realized by the Inter-ministerial Working Group on Integrated Border Management Project. (Financed by the EU, managed by the European Agency for Reconstruction.)

Nelkovski, F. (2006) 'Access Denied! The EU's Visa Policy as Presented by the Macedonian Media', *deScripto* 03/2006 (Vienna: South East Europe Media Organisation – SEEMO).

Niemenkari, A. (2002) 'EU/Schengen Requirements for National Border Security Systems', DCAF Working Paper Series No. 8 (Geneva: Geneva Centre for the Democratic Control of Armed Forces).

Noutcheva, G. (2009) 'Fake, Partial and Imposed Compliance: The Limits of the EU's Normative Power in the Western Balkans', *Journal of European Public Policy*, 16:7, 1065-84.

Noutcheva, G. and Bechev, D. (2008) 'The Successful Laggards: Bulgaria and Romania's Accession to the EU', *East European Politics and Societies*, 22:1, 114–44.

Observer (2003) 'Secret Balkan Camp Built to Hold UK Asylum Seekers', 15 June 2003.

Ordanovski, S. and Matovski, A. (2008) 'Serbian Presidential Elections: The View From Macedonia', *Opinion*, February 2008 (Paris: Institute for Security Studies).

Papadimitriou, D. (2003) 'Exporting Europeanization: The Twinning Exercise and Administrative Reform in the Candidate Countries and Beyond', *Journal of South East European and Black Sea Studies*, 3:2, 1–22.

Paradzik, J. (2005): *Minutes of the CARDS Regional Programme. Seminar on 'Expulsion, Voluntary Return and Readmission'*, Zagreb: International Organization for Migration.

Pastore, F. (2001) 'Reconciling the Prince's Two "Arms": Internal-external Security Policy Coordination in the European Union', Occasional Papers 30 (Paris: The Institute for Security Studies).

Patten, C. (2002): *Speech at the Western Balkans Democracy Forum*, Thessaloniki, 11 April 2002, available at: http://ec.europa.eu/enlargement/archives/ear/publications/main/pub-speech_thessaloniki_20020411.htm (accessed 24 March 2008).

Peers, S. (2006) *EU Justice and Home Affairs Law* (Oxford: Oxford University Press).

Petrenko, A. (2006) 'Cross-border Co-operation. South-eastern Europe Shows the Way Forward', in Magazine, O. (ed.), *Open, Safe and Secure: Managing Borders in the OSCE Area* (Vienna: Organization for Security and Cooperation in Europe), pp. 10–11.

Pettifer, J. (ed.) (2001) *The New Macedonian Question* (New York: Palgrave).

Phuong, C. (2003) 'Enlarging "Fortress Europe": EU Accession, Asylum and Immigration in Candidate Countries', *International and Comparative Law Quaterly*, 52:3, 641–64.

Piedrafita, S. (2008) 'The Treaty of Lisbon: New Signals for Future Enlargement?' *EIPASCOPE*, 2008/1, 33–38.

Pippan, C. (2004) 'The Rocky Road to Europe: The EU's Stabilisation and Association Process for the Western Balkans and the Principle of Conditionality', *European Foreign Affairs Review*, 9, 219–45.

Pirker, H. (2006) 'Panel Intervention at the confererence "Eine Strategie der Stärkung der Freiheit, der Sicherheit und des Rechts für die Menschen in der EU"', 13 October 2006 (Vienna: Renner Institute and Institute for the Danube Region and Central Europe).

Pop, A. (2003) 'Security: From Powder Keg to Cooperation', in von Meurs, W. (ed.), *Prospects and Risks Beyond EU Enlargement. Southeastern Europe: Weak States and Strong International Support* (Opladen: Leske & Budrich), pp. 117–51.

Pridham, G. (2005) *Designing Democracy: EU Enlargement and Regime Change in Post-Communist Europe* (New York: Palgrave Macmillan).

Pridham, G. and Ágh, A. (eds.) (2001) *Prospects for Democratic Consolidation in East Central Europe* (Manchester and New York: Manchester University Press).

Prodi, R. (2002) *A Wider Europe: A Proximity Policy as the Key to Stability*, Brussels, 5–6 December 2002: SPEECH/02/619.

Radaelli, C. (2000) 'Whither Europeanization? Concept Stretching and Substantive Change', *European Integration Online Papers*, 4:8, available at: http://eiop.or .at/eiop/texte/2000–008.htm (accessed 5 April 2007).

Radonjic, B. (2003) *Croatia: Rapprochement with Serbia Harms the Ruling SDP*, (Cyprus: Civilitas Research Network).

Ragaru, N. (2008) 'The Former Yugoslav Republic of Macedonia: Between Ohrid and Brussels', in Batt, J. (ed.), *Is There an Albanian question?*, Chaillot Paper No 107 (Paris: Institute for Security Studies), pp. 41-61.

Rees, W. (2008) 'Inside Out: The External Face of EU Internal Security Policy', *Journal of European Integration*, 30:1, 97–111.

Renner, S. (2009) 'The Energy Community of Southeast Europe: A Neo-functionalist Project of Regional Integration', *European Integration Online Papers*, 13:1, available at: http://eiop.or.at/eiop/index.php/eiop/article/view/2009_001a/88 (accessed 4 October 2009).

Renner, S. and Trauner, F. (2009) 'Creeping EU-membership in Southeast Europe: The Dynamics of EU Rule Rransfer to the Western Balkans', *Journal of European Integration*, 31:4, 449–65.

Samardzija, V. and Stanicic, M. (2005) 'Croatia on the Path Towards the EU: Conditionality and Challenge of Negotiations', *Croatian International Relations Review*, 10:36/37, 97–103.

Schelter, K. (2003) 'Challenges for Non (and Not-Yet) Schengen Countries', Paper presented at the Workshop 'Managing International and Inter-Agency Cooperation at the Border', organised by the Working Group on the Democratic Control of Internal Security Services of the Geneva Centre (Geneva: Geneva Centre for the Democratic Control of Armed Forces (DCAF)).

Schimmelfennig, F. (2001) 'The Community Trap: Liberal Norms, Rhetorical Action, and the Eastern Enlargement of the European Union', *International Organization*, 55:1, 47–80.

Schimmelfennig, F. (2002) 'Introduction: The Impact of International Organizations on the Central and Eastern European States – Conceptual and Theoretical Issues', in Linden, R. H. (ed.), *Norms and Nannies: The Impact of International Organizations on the Central and East European States* (Lanham/Boulder/New York/Oxford: Rowman & Littlefield Publishers, Inc.), pp. 1–33.

Schimmelfennig, F. (2006) 'Prozessanalyse', in Behnke, J., Gschwend, T., Schindler, D. and Schnapp, K.-U. (eds), *Methoden der Politikwissenschaft: Neuere Qualitative und Quantitative Analyseverfahren* (Baden-Baden: Nomos), pp. 263–71.

Schimmelfennig, F. (2009) 'Europeanization Beyond Europe', *Living Reviews in European Governance*, 4:3, available at: http://europeangovernance.livingreviews.org/Articles /lreg-2009–3/ (accessed 24 September 2009).

Schimmelfennig, F., Engert, S. and Knobel, H. (2003) 'Costs, Commitment and

Compliance: The Impact of EU Democratic Conditionality on Latvia, Slovakia and Turkey', *Journal of Common Market Studies*, 41:3, 495–518.

Schimmelfennig, F. and Sedelmeier, U. (2002) 'Theorizing EU Enlargement: Research Focus, Hypotheses, and the State of Research', *Journal of European Public Policy*, 9:4, 500–28.

Schimmelfennig, F. and Sedelmeier, U. (2004) 'Governance by Conditionality: EU Rule Transfer to the Candidate Countries of Central and Eastern Europe', *Journal of European Public Policy*, 11:4, 661–79.

Schimmelfennig, F. and Sedelmeier, U. (eds) (2005a) *The Europeanization of Central and Eastern Europe* (Ithaca and London: Cornell University Press).

Schimmelfennig, F. and Sedelmeier, U. (2005b) 'Introduction: Conceptualizing the Europeanization of Central and Eastern Europe', in Schimmelfennig, F. and Sedelmeier, U. (eds), *The Europeanization of Central and Eastern Europe* (Ithaca and London: Cornell University Press), pp. 1–29.

Schmidt, F. (2008) 'Kosovo – Post-status Challenges to Governability', in Batt, J. (ed.), *Is There an Albanian question?*, Chaillot Paper No. 107 (Paris: Institute for Security Studies), pp. 27–41.

Sedelmeier, U. (2002) 'Sectoral Dynamics of EU Enlargement: Advocacy, Access and Alliances in a Composite Policy', *Journal of European Public Policy*, 9:4, 627–49.

Sedelmeier, U. (2005) *Constructing the Path to Eastern Enlargement: The Uneven Policy Impact of EU Identity* (Manchester and New York: Manchester University Press).

Sedelmeier, U. (2006) 'Europeanisation in New Member and Candidate States', *Living Reviews in European Governance*, 1:3, available at: http://europeangovernance.livingreviews.org/Articles/lreg-2006–3/ (accessed 2 February 2008).

Setimes (2006a) 'Croatia, Slovenia Spar over Unresolved Issues', *Southeast European Times – SETimes.com*, 19 September 2006.

Setimes (2006b) 'Macedonia Hopes for Liberalisation of the Visa Regime', *Southeast European Times – SETimes.com*, 13 April 2006.

Setimes (2006c) 'Visa Issue Makes for Common Cause in the Western Balkans', *Southeast European Times – SETimes.com*, 5 June 2006.

Setimes (2007a) 'Croatia's Fishermen want Ecological Zone Implemented, Despite EU Warnings', *Southeast European Times – SETimes.com*, 11 December 2007.

Setimes (2007b) 'Macedonian Citizens get Biometric Passports', *Southeast European Times – SETimes.com*, 7 May 2007.

Setimes (2008a) 'Co-operation Council Replaces Stability Pact', *Southeast European Times – SETimes.com*, 28 February 2008.

Setimes (2008b) 'Police Break Up Human-trafficking Ring Operating at Skopje's Airport', *Southeast European Times – SETimes.com*, 15 May 2008.

Setimes (2009) 'Survey Suggests Croats Growing Less Enamoured with EU', *Southeast European Times – SETimes.com*, 11 February 2009.

Sopf, D. (2002) *Asylum and Illegal Migration in the Republic of Croatia* (Zagreb: UNHCR Branch Office).

Sotnichenko, D. (2003) 'TOPA (Temporary Operating Procedures Agreement)', *KFOR Chronicle of 3 June 2003*, available at: http://www.nato.int/kfor/chronicle/2003/chronicle_05/09.htm (accessed 21 December 2007).

Spongenberg, H. (2007) 'Balkan Travellers to Get Cheaper EU Visas', *euobserver.com*, 16 April 2007, available at: http://euobserver.com/?aid=23875 (accessed 5 July 2008).

Stabilisation and Association Council (2006) *Minutes of the Second Meeting of the EU–the Former Yugolsav Republic of Macedonia Stabilisation and Association Council, Brussels, 18 July 2005*, Brussels: UE-FM 3952/06, 7 November 2006.

Stability Pact (1999) *SCSP Constituent Document*, Cologne: Stability Pact for South-Eastern Europe, 10 June 1999.

Stability Pact (2008) *Eight Years of the Stability Pact for South-Eastern Europe – From Stabilisation to Integration*, Brussels: Stability Pact for South-Eastern Europe.

Stability Pact for South-Eastern Europe (2001) *National and Regional Management and Development of Border Control*, Regional Conference Bucharest: Working Table III, Institution Building.

Stability Pact for South-Eastern Europe (2003) *MARRI – Programme of Action*, Vienna: MARRI – Migration, Asylum, Refugees Regional Initiative, Secretariat.

Stability Pact for South-Eastern Europe (2005) *First Report for Discussion at the Regional Table in Prague*, Brussels: Senior Review Group on the Stability Pact for South-Eastern Europe, 16 November 2005.

Stability Pact for South Eastern-Europe (2006) *Chairman's Conclusions, Regional Table of the Stability Pact*, Belgrade Regional Table, 30 May 2006.

Stability Pact for South-Eastern Europe (2007) *Briefing on the Ohrid Process on Border Security and Management to the COWEB – Mr. Pieter Verbeek, Director of the Stability Pact Working Table III*, Brussels: Stability Pact Working Table III, 18 January 2007.

Stability Pact for South-Eastern Europe (2008) *About the Stability Pact*, Brussels, available at: www.stabilitypact.org/about/default.asp (accessed 26 November 2008).

Tonra, B. and Christiansen, T. (eds) (2004) *Rethinking European Union Foreign Policy* (Manchester and New York: Manchester University Press).

Trauner, F. (2009) 'From Membership Conditionality to Policy Conditionality: EU External Governance in South Eastern Europe', *Journal of European Public Policy*, 16:5, 774–90.

Trauner, F. and Kruse, I. (2008) 'EC Visa Facilitation and Readmission Agreements: A New Standard EU Foreign Policy Tool?', *European Journal of Migration and Law*, 10:4, 411–38.

Treaty of Accession (2003) *Treaty Concerning the Accession of the Czech Republic, the Republic of Estonia, the Republic of Cyprus, the Republic of Latvia, the Republic of Lithuania, the Republic of Hungary, the Republic of Malta, the Republic of Poland, the Republic of Slovenia and the Slovak Republic to the European Union*, Brussels, 16 April 2003.

Tulmets, E. (2005) 'The Management of New Forms of Governance by Former Accession Countries of the European Union: Institutional Twinning in Estonia and Hungary', *European Law Journal*, 11:5, 657–74.

Tziampiris, A. (2000) *Greece, European Political Cooperation and the Macedonian Question* (Aldershot: Ashgate Publishing Company).

UNHCR (2003) *The EU Enlargement Process and the External Dimension of the EU JHA Policy*, Geneva: United Nations High Commissioner for Refugees.

UNHCR (2006) *2004 UNHCR Statistical Yearbook Country Data Sheet – Croatia*, Geneva: United Nations High Commissioner for Refugees, 21 August 2006.

Vachudova, M. A. (2005) *Europe Undivided: Democracy, Leverage and Integration after Communism* (Oxford: Oxford University Press).

van Meurs, W. (ed.) (2003) *Prospects and Risks beyond EU Enlargement. Southeastern Europe: Weak States and Strong International Support* (Opladen: Leske & Budrich).

VC Experts Group Research (2004) 'Liberalisation of Visa Regime in the Region of South Eastern Europe. Obstacles and Possible Solutions', Belgrade: Citizens Pact for South East Europe, available at: www.citizenspact.org/docs /VC%20Experts%20Group%20Research.doc (accessed 23 January 2007).

Visa Liberalisation Roadmap (2008) *Visa Liberalisation with the Republic of Macedonia. Roadmap*, the Ministry of Foreign Affairs of the Republic of Macedonia, available at: www.mfa.gov.mk/default1.aspx?ItemID=387 (4 September 2009).

Vlahutin, R. (2004) 'The Croatian Exception', in Batt, J. (ed.), *The Western Balkans: Moving On*, Chaillot Paper No. 70 (Paris: Institute for Security Studies (ISS)), pp. 21–34.

Wallace, H. (2000) 'The Policy Process. A Moving Pendulum', in Wallace, H. and Wallace, W. (eds), *Policy-making in the European Union* (Oxford: Oxford University Press), pp. 39–64.

Way Forward Document (2003) *Ohrid Regional Conference on Border Security and Management*, Ohrid, 22/23 May 2003.

Weber, K., Smith, M. E. and Baun, M. (eds) (2007) *Governing Europe's Neigbhourhood* (Manchester and New York: Manchester University Press).

Wichmann, N. (2006) 'The Participation of the Schengen Associates: Inside or Outside?', *European Foreign Affairs Review*, 11:1, 87–109.

Wolff, S., Wichmann, N. and Mournier, G. (2009) 'Special Issue: The External Dimension of Justice and Home Affairs? A Different Security Agenda for the EU', *Journal of European Integration*, 31:1.

World Bank (2009) *EU 10 Regular Economic Report: Croatia Supplement*, Washington, May 2009.